PRENUPTIAL AGREEMENTS AND THE PRESUMPTION OF FREE CHOICE

This book provides an alternative perspective on an issue fraught with difficulty—the enforcement of prenuptial agreements. Such agreements are enforced because the law acknowledges the rights of spouses to make autonomous decisions about the division of their property on divorce. Yet this book demonstrates that, in the attempt to promote autonomy, other issues, such as imbalance of power between the parties, become obscured.

This book offers an academic and practical analysis of the real impact of prenuptial agreements on the relationships of those involved. Using a feminist and contractual theoretical framework, it attempts to produce a more nuanced understanding of the autonomy exercised by parties entering into prenuptial agreements. This book also draws on an empirical study of the experiences and views of practitioners skilled in the formation and litigation of prenuptial agreements in New York. Lastly, it explores how the court might address concerns regarding power and autonomy during the drafting and enforcement processes of prenuptial agreements, which in turn may enhance the role that 'prenups' can play in the judicial allocation of spousal property on the breakdown of marriage.

Prenuptial Agreements and the Presumption of Free Choice

Issues of Power in Theory and Practice

Sharon Thompson

• HART •
PUBLISHING
OXFORD AND PORTLAND, OREGON
2017

Hart Publishing
An imprint of Bloomsbury Publishing Plc

Hart Publishing Ltd
Kemp House
Chawley Park
Cumnor Hill
Oxford OX2 9PH
UK

Bloomsbury Publishing Plc
50 Bedford Square
London
WC1B 3DP
UK

www.hartpub.co.uk
www.bloomsbury.com

Published in North America (US and Canada) by
Hart Publishing
c/o International Specialized Book Services
920 NE 58th Avenue, Suite 300
Portland, OR 97213-3786
USA

www.isbs.com

First published in hardback, 2015
Paperback edition, 2017

British Library Cataloguing-in-Publication Data
A catalogue record for this book is available from the British Library.

ISBN: PB: 978-1-50991-774-7
HB: 978-1-84946-598-4

Typeset by Compuscript Ltd, Shannon
Printed and bound in Great Britain by
Lightning Source UK Ltd

To Chris, with love.

PREFACE

A short time ago, in England, Wales or Northern Ireland a spouse could never be certain that a prenuptial agreement would have any influence on divorce. Nowadays, provided it is not unfair, a prenuptial agreement carries decisive weight when divorcing spouses' assets are divided. Furthermore, recent reform proposals have advocated legislative change that would enable prenuptial agreements to oust the court's discretionary power to determine financial provision on divorce. Thus unsurprisingly, much of the debate surrounding prenuptial agreements has been confined to their status in the event of relationship breakdown.

In this book, the enforceability of prenuptial agreements is not the focus; it is the relationships underpinning them. This is because an examination of the ways in which power is exercised by parties to prenuptial agreements reveals significant inequalities when the agreement is created and given effect. When speaking with expert divorce attorneys in New York City, it became clear how entrenched these inequalities are, as I was told that every prenuptial agreement is affected by issues of power. This book examines the findings of this research, and the relationship between the parties involved in a prenuptial agreement is theorised in light of feminist and relational contract perspectives. I hope that this analysis will encourage prenuptial agreements to be thought about differently, so that the power inequalities affecting these agreements are brought into focus.

I have recently learned that one of the attorneys interviewed for the study on which this book is based has passed away. I hope that he would have enjoyed reading the extracts from my interview with him in this book, and in particular, his illuminating anecdote at the very beginning.

Sharon Thompson

ACKNOWLEDGEMENTS

When writing this book I have received help and support from many friends and colleagues. First, I would like to thank my PhD supervisors, Sara Ramshaw and Norma Dawson, for their continuous intellectual support, inspiration and generosity. I am also very grateful to the staff in the School of Law at Queen's University Belfast, for creating a stimulating and welcoming environment for PhD students.

I am indebted to Rosemary Auchmuty and David Capper for their valuable guidance and direction, and for taking the time to read and comment on my work. Many thanks also to Rob George and Anne Barlow for their advice and detailed feedback on individual chapters.

I would like to give special thanks to my colleagues at Keele University for their engagement with my research and for their wonderful support of early career scholars. In particular I would like to thank Katie Cruz, for her probing questions, and for our many conversations about prenups in the last two years. Thank you also to Tsachi Keren-Paz and Michael Haley for reading my work, and for helping me to develop my research.

The empirical study on which this book is based would not have been possible without funding from the County Antrim Grand Jury Bursary. I would like to thank the 20 interviewees who kindly agreed to take part in the study, and Marsha Garrison, for her help in New York.

My thanks also go to the editors at Hart Publishing, for their patience and help when developing this book.

Finally, I would like to thank my family and friends, especially Chris Mercer, Marion Thompson, Pat Cowan, Linda Black and Paul Thompson, for reading my work, patiently listening to me talk about my research and most importantly, for making the years spent writing this book bearable.

CONTENTS

LIST OF ABBREVIATIONS

AAML	American Academy of Matrimonial Lawyers
ALI	American Law Institute
FRCT	feminist relational contract theory
MCA	Matrimonial Causes Act
MWPA	Married Women's Property Act
para/paras	paragraph/paragraphs
prenup	prenuptial agreement
s/ss	section/sections
UK	United Kingdom
UPAA	Uniform Premarital Agreement Act
UPMAA	Uniform Premarital and Marital Agreements Act
US	United States

TABLE OF CASES

United Kingdom

United States

TABLE OF LEGISLATION

United Kingdom

United States

NOTE ON TERMINOLOGY

The term 'prenuptial agreement' (or 'prenup') is employed throughout the book, but these agreements are also referred to by the Supreme Court and Law Commission of England and Wales as 'ante-nuptial agreements'. Distinguishing between other types of marital property agreement is also important. Prenuptial agreements are made before marriage, but postnuptial agreements are made after the wedding and during the marriage, to provide for economic distribution on divorce. Separation agreements are made at the time of separation and, like prenuptial and postnuptial agreements, they control the division of parties' assets on divorce. Prenuptial, postnuptial and separation agreements are also categorised as marital property or nuptial agreements. Lastly, the phrase 'qualifying nuptial agreement' is a marital property agreement that would meet the procedural requirements proposed by the Law Commission in its report on this matter.[1] At the time of writing, Parliament has not indicated whether or not it intends to implement the Law Commission's recommendations.

[1] Law Commission, Matrimonial Property, Needs and Agreements (Law Com No 343, 2014).

Introduction

> I represented a woman who was marrying a doctor. And the doctor was giving her nothing in the prenup ... I said to ... the doctor ... 'What's she getting under this agreement?' ... And he looks at me and says, 'Marrying a doctor!' ... That happens frequently, and many people will take less ... because they love the person and they don't think the agreement will ever come into effect.[1]

For many wealthy individuals, marriage is inconceivable without a prenuptial agreement (prenup), because they need to be satisfied that divorce will not cost them half of their wealth. For many others, signing an agreement that waives the entitlement they would otherwise have to their partner's assets on divorce is a powerful statement that they are not marrying for money. Yet as the above example demonstrates, this dynamic can mean that one party financially benefits much more under the prenup than the other. Put another way, one party may get 'nothing in the prenup'—apart from marrying a doctor of course.

The demand for prenups is increasing,[2] because entering into a contract that states what both spouses get on divorce is often perceived to be a favourable alternative to the uncertainty and expense of leaving financial provision to be decided by a judge. From the perspective of Baroness Deech, a prenup can prevent the moneyed spouse from being deprived of all he or she has worked for, as without an agreement:

> The wife who is least likely ever to have put her hand in cold water during the marriage is the one most likely to walk off with millions, regardless of her contributions or conduct. Hence we find that ... the phrases 'gold digger' or 'alimony drone' have been coined.[3]

This vision of the wife who contributes little but takes almost everything has led to calls for reform to make prenups binding. On the contrary, this book demonstrates that the stereotype of the covetous spouse is inconsistent with the reality for most couples getting married and entering into prenups. Rather than focusing on the perceived dangers of 'gold diggers', this book is concerned with the problematic aspects of such agreements, in particular issues of power. It aims to

[1] Practitioner 20, interviewed by the author in New York City, September 2010.

[2] See research findings in E Hitchings, *Law Commission Report: A study of the views and approaches of family practitioners concerning marital property agreements* (2011), which indicate that practitioners have seen an increase in work concerned with prenups. See also A Barlow and J Smithson, 'Is modern marriage a bargain? Exploring perceptions of pre-nuptial agreements in England and Wales' (2012) 24(3) *Child and Family Law Quarterly* 304, which found that the public is generally in favour of couples being able to make binding prenups.

[3] HL Deb 27 June 2014, vol 754, col 1491.

expose these issues by presenting an empirically-based study of the occurrences and consequences of power inequalities between parties to prenups.

Background

Prenuptial agreements are not binding in English law. On divorce, the Matrimonial Causes Act (MCA) 1973[4] provides the court with discretion to make financial provision orders (also known as ancillary relief) in respect of spousal property. For example, the court can make orders that adjust the ownership of spousal property,[5] or it can divide the parties' pensions,[6] or order one spouse to pay the other either a lump sum or money in instalments (known as periodical payments).[7] When exercising its discretion, the only statutory guide is section 25 of the 1973 Act, which provides a list of factors for the court to take into account when making a financial order. However, it is for the judiciary to decide how these factors should be applied, and so its power to award financial provision is broad and virtually unlimited by statute. It is also this discretionary power[8] that has prevented the court from giving effect to prenups, because it is against public policy for the court to enable such an agreement, rather than the judiciary's assessment of the case, to govern the financial consequences of divorce. This public policy objection is the reason prenups are still not binding,[9] and the only way these agreements can oust the jurisdiction of the court is if Parliament introduces legislation to that effect.

In the 1990s and early 2000s, if a spouse sought to rely on a prenup during financial relief proceedings, it would have little, if any, effect on the court's decision. But gradually prenups became more influential as regards the financial outcome on divorce, as the court considered that nuptial agreements could be included within the scope of factors for consideration under section 25 of the MCA 1973.[10] From being a factor to consider, the position of prenups has developed case by case, to the point where the court can now decide to attribute decisive weight to an agreement. In fact, as a result of precedent set by the Supreme Court in *Radmacher v Granatino*, the judiciary *must* now attribute decisive weight to a prenup if it is not unfair.[11] In short, the court can no longer ignore an agreement in the way it would have

[4] In Northern Ireland, the corresponding statute is the Matrimonial Causes Order 1978.

[5] MCA 1973, s 21(2).

[6] For example, a judge can make a pension-sharing order pursuant to MCA 1973, s 21A, which permits a spouse to share his or her former partner's pension rights. Alternatively, pursuant to s 21B, the judge can award a pension compensation-sharing order, which permits a spouse to share in his or her former partner's Pension Protection Fund (PPF) compensation.

[7] MCA 1973, s 21(1).

[8] Conferred by Parliament under MCA 1973, s 23.

[9] Other public policy objections have historically prevented the enforcement of prenups but, as ch 1 will explain, changing attitudes towards financial provision on divorce have rendered these other objections obsolete.

[10] Specifically as part of s 25(1), which directs the court to consider 'all the circumstances of the case'.

[11] *Radmacher v Granatino* [2010] UKSC 42.

20 years ago.[12] As a result, if the judge decides that it is appropriate to give effect to a prenup on divorce, the parties' decision replaces the court's evaluation as to which financial orders to make in that case. This means that individuals who either have or are anticipating accruing significant wealth can agree with their partners before marriage how these assets will be divided in the event of divorce. Moneyed spouses can even decide to use an agreement to ring-fence their assets completely.

The effect of prenups is also to contract out of the default system of financial provision on divorce. A desire to contract out of this discretionary procedure in the United Kingdom (UK) has highlighted the problems couples face when resolving financial issues in court. On divorce, the valuation of parties' assets can be a lengthy and costly process, and as financial orders depend on the facts in individual cases, parties often have no way of knowing how their assets will be split, particularly when there is a surplus once their needs have been met. These issues have led Sir James Munby to say:

> I should be very surprised if our law of ancillary relief does not undergo more or less radical reform over the coming years … We need to reconsider practice and procedure so as to facilitate the use of out-of-court methods of resolving financial disputes …[13]

These out-of-court methods include mediation for individuals who can no longer access legal representation, since legal aid has been cut for family law in England and Wales.[14] But prenups are another a form of private ordering which can, in theory, circumvent many of the current uncertainties produced by the law applicable to financial orders on divorce. Before marriage, couples are able to determine their financial interests, discuss their expectations in the event of divorce, and can avoid complicated valuations and costly litigation on divorce having resolved these matters outside the courtroom.

Although there are potential benefits to entering into prenups, there are equally as many potential problems. The purpose of the court's discretion to make financial orders on divorce is to achieve a fair outcome which is tailor-made to that particular couple's circumstances.[15] However, a prenup cannot account for a family's situation on relationship breakdown, as it is created before the marriage, at a time when the couple's circumstances might be very different. Furthermore, as prenups are scrutinised less and given more weight by the court, issues of power between the parties are potentially hidden or not addressed.

When exploring these issues further, the UK is not necessarily the best place on which to focus, because although prenups are arguably increasing in popularity,[16] legally, weight has not been attached to such agreements for nearly as long as in other jurisdictions. For example, in New York prenups have been binding for

[12] *F v F (Ancillary Relief: Substantial Assets)* [1995] 2 FLR 45.

[13] J Munby, 'The Family Justice Reforms' (29 April 2014), available at <http://www.judiciary.gov.uk/wp-content/uploads/2014/05/family-justice-reforms-29042014.pdf>.

[14] Pursuant to the Legal Aid, Sentencing and Punishment of Offenders Act 2012.

[15] *White v White* [2000] UKHL 54.

[16] One indication of this is the increased number of reported judgments where there was a relevant prenup.

almost 35 years.[17] The default system of financial provision in New York is equitable distribution, which provides the court with extensive discretion to make financial orders in a very similar way as applies in the UK.[18] And so it is conceivable that information on the experiences of expert attorneys in this field would enable a detailed assessment as to how prenups operate in practice. In 2010 I interviewed 20 practitioners in Manhattan, New York City, on this subject, some of whom had over 30 years' experience of prenups. The clients of these attorneys were exceptionally wealthy, and included world-famous actors, businessmen and musicians. But when speaking to these attorneys, it did not seem to matter who they were representing, the response was the same—there is always inequality of bargaining power between parties entering prenups. As one attorney put it, 'I have always defined prenups as agreements by which one party, usually the party with the wealth, wants to cheat the other one.'[19] The views of these individuals provide a very interesting insight into the practical issues with prenups, and so extracts from their interviews appear throughout this book.

Although the research carried out in New York adds a comparative and empirical basis, this book presents an analysis of the position of prenups in the UK. There will be a focus on England, Wales and Northern Ireland, as the status of prenups in these countries is the same. In England and Wales, agreements are enforced as part of the process of financial redistribution on divorce under the MCA 1973. In Northern Ireland, this procedure is mirrored in the Matrimonial Causes (Northern Ireland) Order 1978, which contains the same provisions as the 1973 Act. In Scotland, however, the approach to family law is very different from the rest of the UK. Scotland is a mixed jurisdiction where prenups (referred to as 'marriage contracts') are enforced in the same way as other contracts.[20] As there is a distinct difference between Scots law and the law in England, Wales and Northern Ireland, Scotland is not considered in this book. Thus, hereafter, reference to the UK position includes England, Wales and Northern Ireland, but excludes Scotland.

Power

The theme of this book is power, specifically *expressions* of power between parties to prenups.[21] Power is a crucial aspect of prenups, as the terms of these agreements

[17] Pursuant to NY Domestic Relations Law § 236(B)(3) (McKinney 1986), which was introduced in 1980.

[18] NY Domestic Relations Law, § 236(B) (McKinney 1986).

[19] Practitioner 14.

[20] K Norrie, 'Marital Agreements and Private Autonomy in Scotland' in J Scherpe (ed), *Marital Agreements and Private Autonomy in Comparative Perspective* (Hart Publishing 2012) 293.

[21] The analysis of power in this book focuses on the relationships between engaged heterosexual couples and between husbands and wives. There is less information on prenups entered into by same sex couples, because at the time of writing, same sex couples have been only able to legally marry less than a year (pursuant to the Marriage (Same Sex Couples Act) 2013).

could ultimately benefit one party much more than the other, or the outcome of an agreement tainted by power disparity could be especially detrimental to one party in the light of changed circumstances. As Barlow and Smithson's research has found, issues of power related to prenups are a 'perceived problem' by members of the public.[22] However, recognising power in practice is a familiar problem for the court when giving effect to prenups, as there is a tension, first, between promoting one person's power to control his or her property in the event of relationship breakdown and, secondly, protecting the other person who may be powerless within this arrangement. Since the Supreme Court decided that prenups are to have decisive weight, the court's approach has been to recognise the importance of giving effect to a couple's agreement out of respect for their autonomy. This has also meant limiting the court's evaluation of power imbalance in less extreme cases, because addressing issues of power could lead to a restriction of the original agreement's enforcement. But exposing power and the associative difficulties with it is important in the context of prenups, because if power is obscured by respect for autonomy it is likely to be overlooked completely. Of course we should have the ability to protect our property interests, but a blinkered view which focuses only on the individual property rights of spouses assimilates prenups with agreements made in the normal course of business. Yet a prenup is not the same as a standard insurance contract, and saying it is, is particularly problematic, as Cotterrell describes:

> Through the use of the concept of property, it becomes possible to banish almost entirely from the discourse of private law recognition of one of the most dominant features of life in a society of material inequalities—that of *private power*.[23]

Indeed, limiting our view of prenups to a discrete contract ignores the 'society of material inequalities' to which Cotterrell refers. If these inequalities are missing from the court's assessment of prenups, they become a private and accepted feature of the marriage and family.

In the context of prenups, one of the most prevalent manifestations of this is the gendered power dimension. As Lady Hale explains:

> Above all, perhaps, the court hearing a particular case can all too easily lose sight of the fact that, unlike a separation agreement, the object of an ante-nuptial agreement is to deny the economically weaker spouse the provision to which she—it is usually although by no means invariably she—would otherwise be entitled ... In short, there is a gender dimension to the issue which some may think ill-suited to decision by a court consisting of eight men and one woman.[24]

The force of Lady Hale's assertion indicates the importance of gender in the prenuptial context, but as this book will demonstrate, the law does not always recognise it. One

[22] Barlow and Smithson, above n 2.

[23] R Cotterrell, 'Power, Property and the Law of Trusts: A Partial Agenda for Critical Legal Scholarship' (1987) 14 *Journal of Law and Society* 77.

[24] *Radmacher* above n 11, [137].

possible explanation for this, which this book will develop further, is that the contractual view of autonomy often followed by the court is associated with the perception that prenups are entered into by two independent, gender-neutral individuals, both seeking to safeguard their property and finances. But adding a gender dimension to this context demands a different view of these agreements. For example, in the UK the moneyed spouse with the wealth to protect through a prenup is statistically more likely to be the husband.[25] Furthermore, even if men and women enter into prenups as financially independent individuals, dependency can develop during marriage which changes their positions. These dependencies are often gendered, as the division of labour within the family means that most non-financial contributions are made by women.[26] At the same time, this analysis also applies to a smaller number of husbands taking on these gendered roles, and so recognising a gendered power dimension does not, as Mr Justice Holman insinuated, lead to gender bias, or to a 'stereo–typical view that a wife may be dependent upon her husband but not vice versa'.[27]

In any case, even if couples enter a prenup with a clear vision of their intended future in their minds, this vision is susceptible to change, not least from an economic point of view. This long-term view of prenups is one of the most powerful illustrations of how a contractual relationship between spouses is *different*, as Regan puts it:

> While it is plausible to say that members of an economic partnership may regard themselves as strangers in the market after the partnership ends, it is far less reasonable to characterize ex-spouses solely in this way. Ex-spouses are not simply individuals who revert to the status of detached individuals. They have shared an experience that has affected them deeply, so much that in a sense they are not the same persons they were when they entered the marriage.[28]

Put simply, prenups are not only different in nature from agreements made in business, but they are also particularly problematic in their nature and effect compared with other types of intimate agreements. Separation agreements, which couples use to divide their assets on divorce, are made at a time when both parties know how the marriage has changed them. But for couples entering into prenups (which, as their name implies, are entered into before marriage), these circumstances are not known.[29] All of this makes it very difficult to create a prenup that will adequately reflect the intentions of spouses on divorce. From this perspective,

[25] Office of National Statistics, 'Women in the labour market' (2013), available at <http://www.ons.gov.uk/ons/dcp171776_328352.pdf> states not only that more men than women tend to work in professional occupations that are associated with higher levels of pay, but also that men outnumber women in the top 10% of earners.

[26] See ibid. This is highlighted by statistics, which show rising employment for women in general, but also that women with children are less likely to work than those without, whilst the opposite is true for men. See also S Duncan *et al*, 'Motherhood, paid work and partnering: values and theories' (2003) 17(2) *Work, Employment and Society* 309.

[27] *Luckwell v Limata* [2014] EWHC 502 (Fam) [132].

[28] M Regan, *Alone Together: Law and the Meanings of Marriage* (OUP 1999) 189–90.

[29] See *Radmacher*, above n 11 [175] (Lady Hale).

the notion of contractual autonomy is even more flawed, because the spouse with less bargaining power and who is on the short end of the agreement, cannot predict what the effect of contracting out of his or her entitlement on divorce will be.

As a result, this book provides a critique of prenups, both in the way in which they are given effect in *Radmacher v Granatino* and in general (that is, for jurisdictions that do not have matrimonial legislation that reserves discretion to the court to decide the financial outcome of divorce). By examining how the court's concept of autonomy is affected by power, and how both contract law and the law applicable to prenups does not address these issues of power, this book seeks to find a different way of viewing the context in which prenups are made. Addressing these issues is particularly important at a time when the status of such agreements is under review by the Government, since the Law Commission published its recommendations for legislative reform of nuptial agreements at the beginning of 2014.[30]

Theoretical Perspectives Employed in this Book

Contract Theory

Contract theory is an important tool when exploring the nature of prenups because these agreements must have contractual validity to be enforced.[31] However, it is emphasised that the use of contractual perspectives does not mean that prenups are viewed as ordinary business contracts in this book, though later chapters consider whether this is the case in practice.[32] Rather, the idea that such agreements should be freely entered (without duress) emerges from contract law, thus it is inextricably linked to the enforcement of prenups.

When evaluating how power and autonomy are conceptualised in relation to prenups, contract theory is extremely useful, particularly due to its influence on the creation and enforcement of these agreements. Moreover, autonomy is fundamental to the enforcement of contracts, as von Mehren explains:

> Contract … implies autonomous ordering. The ordering should, therefore, be done by parties who act with a degree of awareness, independence and responsibility. Where these qualities are not present in requisite measure, the requirements of procedural justice immanent in the concept of contract are not met.[33]

[30] Law Commission, *Matrimonial Property, Needs and Agreements* (Law Com No 343, 2014).

[31] See *Radmacher* above n 11, [71] (Lord Phillips). Note, however, that in *Radmacher* the relevance of contract law to the weight to be attributed to prenups is distinguished from the question of whether or not prenups have binding contractual status ([62]).

[32] In particular ch 3, which examines empirical evidence of prenups in practice.

[33] A von Mehren, 'A General View of Contracts' in *International Encyclopedia of Comparative Law* vol 7 (Tübingen 1982), 64.

This emphasis on contractual autonomy goes to the heart of why prenups are enforced. From a contractual perspective, the point of prenups is to enable people to be autonomous without state intervention. A number of commentators claim that 'autonomy is good for you', because people can avoid the imposition of what some believe to be oppressive paternalistic values.[34] Within the boundaries of reasonableness and conscience, couples can tailor their own financial consequences to divorce.[35] This perspective undoubtedly influenced the majority in *Radmacher v Granatino*,[36] but whilst it is of course important for parties to control what happens to their own property, there are still significant concerns, expressed by commentators like Bix, that unequal bargaining power could affect the operation of autonomy:

> [F]or every person who makes choices ... fully aware of what he or she is giving up and freely choosing to do so for whatever benefits may seem to come from the choice, there will be many others who act in ways that are less free, knowing, or autonomous.[37]

On a broader theoretical level, McLean suggests that an 'individualistic model of autonomy is largely unconcerned with what the decision is; rather, it is interested in the right to make it'.[38] This could explain why autonomy in the prenuptial context is presumed, as the judiciary in the UK appears to focus on parties' right to enter into prenups, and on whether this right is repressed by public policy issues.

Contract theory is used here in two ways. First, it is a lens through which power and autonomy are considered in the context of prenups. To understand this perspective, the law of contract relevant to prenups is examined, in particular the effect of vitiating factors on the enforcement of these agreements.

Secondly, alternative contractual perspectives are used to conceptualise autonomy in a way different from the judiciary's approach to autonomy in cases such as *Radmacher v Granatino*, which is examined in chapter one. A particularly helpful perspective when exploring the variety of pressures affecting autonomy in practice is the relational contract school of thought. Relational contract theory was established primarily by Ian Macneil, and posits that contracts should not be confined to the point at which an agreement is signed: the focus should instead be directed to the wider context in which contracts operate.[39] This is one layer of analysis which will be employed in later chapters to re-evaluate how issues of power can be made more visible in the case of prenups.

[34] M Ertman, 'Commercializing Marriage: A Proposal for Valuing Women's Work through Premarital Security Agreements' (1998) 77 *Texas Law Review* 17.

[35] See S Cretney, 'The Family and the Law—Status or Contract?' (2003) 15 *Child and Family Law Quarterly* 403.

[36] See *Radmacher*, above n 11, [78] (Lord Phillips).

[37] B Bix, 'Bargaining in the Shadow of Love: The Enforcement of Premarital Agreements and How We Think About Marriage' (1998) 40 *William and Mary Law Review* 145, 171.

[38] S McLean, Autonomy, Consent and the Law (Routledge 2010) 20.

[39] I Macneil, *Contract: Exchange Transactions and Relations* (2nd edn, Foundation Press 1978).

Feminist Critiques of Contract

Another way of recognising issues of power in a way that is different from current practice is to employ feminist theory to criticise contract law. A feminist perspective is useful because it does not aim to present men as *necessarily* having an oppressive role in a prenup, but it recognises that there *is* a power dimension between men and women when prenups are being entered into. As Brod puts it, the gendered power dimension of prenups is severe because it means that '[p]remarital agreements adversely affect the economic and social wellbeing of many women, they contribute to the financial vulnerability of women as a class, and they magnify society's unequal distribution of resources along gender lines'.[40] This, she says, can be explained by the fact that prenups are used to protect the wealth and income of the prospective spouse, who is commonly male. It is this connection rather than any 'intent to disadvantage or discriminate against women as a group'[41] which creates a gendered power dimension.

Atwood corroborates this view on prenups with evidence that the wife challenges the agreement in 85 per cent of cases.[42] Identifying the same gender dimension as Brod, she asserts that '[s]ince men generally occupy a position of economic superiority, strict enforcement of premarital agreements may work to the ultimate economic disadvantage of women'.[43] Lady Hale's view in *Radmacher v Granatino* supports this argument. In the sole dissent to the all-male majority judgment in this case, Lady Hale employs a feminist perspective to expose the complexities of prenups:

> Would any self-respecting young woman sign up to an agreement which assumed that she would be the only one who might otherwise have a claim, thus placing no limit on the claims that might be made against her, and then limited her claim to a pre-determined sum for each year of marriage regardless of the circumstances, as if her wifely services were being bought by the year? … [T]hat is what these precedents do.[44]

Thus, as Lady Hale suggests, prenups are not only gendered in the way they are negotiated, but are also gendered in their effect. For example, it is not uncommon for the female spouse to undertake unpaid labour in the home, such as childcare. But a prenup can potentially contract out of the economic entitlement generated by this non-financial contribution, or, as Lady Hale puts it, could buy these services by the year.

Nevertheless, the purpose of feminist perspectives in this book is not *only* to expose prenups as being gendered. Rather, this particular lens allows autonomy

[40] G Brod, 'Premarital Agreements and Gender Justice' (1994) 6 *Yale Journal of Law and Feminism* 229.

[41] Ibid.

[42] B Atwood, 'Ten Years Later: Lingering Concerns about the Uniform Premarital Agreement Act' (1993) 19 *Journal of Legislation* 127. See also Barlow and Smithson, above n 2, who, in an empirical study of views of members of the public, found that women perceive prenups differently from men.

[43] Ibid, 129.

[44] See *Radmacher*, above n 11, [137].

and power issues to be viewed differently by criticising orthodox ideas of contract. Atwood, for example, believes that an emphasis on contractual autonomy overshadows the 'empirical reality of unequal bargaining positions [, which] for most women will result in unequal bargains'.[45] With feminist theory, however, these inequalities can be recognised.

As a result, alternative perceptions of autonomy are explored, which have the potential to empower women to counteract power issues connected to prenups. By criticising and moving away from the traditional constraints of contract, feminist theory does not portray women as disadvantaged simply because they are women, but *does* recognise that power imbalances within prenups disadvantage women. By identifying these situations of power imbalance, a feminist critique of contract can ensure that the voices of both parties to a prenup are heard.

Chapter Outline

Chapter one of this book reveals how prenups are given effect in the UK by presenting a full exposition of *Radmacher v Granatino*[46] and the impact this case has had. *Radmacher* is significant because it was the first time the Supreme Court had the opportunity to decide the weight a prenup should have when financial provision orders are made. In this case, the justification of the majority of the Court for holding that the weight of a prenup should be decisive was that the autonomy of the parties should be respected. In the leading judgment, Lord Phillips said that respect for autonomy was important even if there are power imbalances between the parties, because adults can work these things out for themselves.[47] But leaving the couple to resolve issues of power could be difficult when one party is in a stronger bargaining position. The Court's approach is also problematic because it avoids a detailed assessment of the context of the agreement, as the parties are assumed to have freely chosen the terms (even when one party is clearly on the short end of the agreement). Lady Hale adopted a different approach in *Radmacher*, and provided a dissenting judgment. She recognised the importance of context, and how the relationship of the parties is an important consideration when evaluating a prenup. However, the precedent created by the majority in this case is adopted in later cases, and autonomy is now the basis on which prenups are given effect, unless this would produce an unfair outcome. Chapter one concludes with an examination of why the *Radmacher* interpretation of autonomy is problematic.

Chapter two extends the analysis of prenups in chapter one by examining how financial provision on relationship breakdown has evolved. The development of

[45] See Atwood, above n 42, 130.
[46] See *Radmacher*, above n 11.
[47] Unless the circumstances explicitly show there has been unfair exploitation: ibid, [71].

judicial attitudes towards financial provision on divorce correlates with how attitudes towards prenups have changed, and tracing the history of financial provision on divorce also reveals the traditional structural inequalities between spouses which created a foundation of gendered power imbalance. These issues are now addressed by the courts, which have said that financial contributions should not be valued more than non-financial contributions, as both are vital to the marital partnership.[48] However, as chapter two explains, prenups can contract out of this ethos of sharing the fruits of the marriage,[49] and so the default system of financial provision on divorce is examined so that it is clear what this means. In addition, prenups are given effect as part of the court's discretion to make financial provision orders on divorce, and so it is important to examine the way in which this discretion is exercised.

Chapter three shows that the power inequalities explored in chapters one and two have empirical basis in a study drawn on by this book. Using the accounts of practitioners specialising in the area of prenups in New York, chapter three outlines what independent and competent legal advice should entail, the consequences of prenups being difficult to challenge and the problems contingent on legislative regulation of prenups. Practitioners identified the ways in which power imbalances affect prenups and suggested various ways of addressing these issues, from 'sunset clauses', which place an expiry date on the agreement, to the integration of a 'wedding present', whereby the non-moneyed spouse receives a sum of money in exchange for giving up her right to court-awarded financial provision on divorce. In spite of this, the courts in New York still have limited scope to ameliorate power inequalities that have ultimately resulted in unfairness at the time of divorce. Furthermore, not everyone entering prenups has access to the expertise of the practitioners interviewed: non-expert legal advice could be particularly detrimental for the spouse with less power if it means that his or her lawyer is unaware of potential ways to counteract power inequalities. Chapter three concludes with a comparison of the empirical findings in New York with Emma Hitchings' study on practitioners' approaches to prenups in the UK.[50] Though it is not assumed that the context of prenups in the UK and in New York is the same, the experiences of the practitioners interviewed in New York provide valuable insight into the potential consequences of binding prenups in the UK.

Chapter four examines contract doctrines to see if they can address the problems with making prenups binding identified in earlier chapters. As prenups must have contractual validity in order to be valid, these doctrines are relevant to parties' ability to challenge an agreement on divorce. In particular, the doctrines of duress, undue influence and unconscionable bargaining will be even more important if the Law Commission's recommendations are introduced,[51] because the courts' discretion to

[48] See *White*, above n 15.

[49] *Miller v Miller; McFarlane v McFarlane* [2006] UKHL 24, [141] (Baroness Hale of Richmond).

[50] See Hitchings, above n 2.

[51] The Law Commission has recommended that prenups will be binding, provided a number of procedural requirements are met: see Law Commission, above n 30.

address power imbalance will be limited by legislation and so must be examined further in the context of prenups. However, examining the inadequacies of current legal doctrines highlights why issues of power between parties to prenups are often not addressed: it is because contract doctrines do not deal with the frequent and subtle imbalances of power existing within the prenuptial relationship.

Chapter five explores this further, by presenting a feminist and relational critique of contractual approaches to prenups. In particular, the orthodox contractual view of autonomy is criticised, as it influences how prenups are given effect by the court. First, relational contract theory challenges the orthodox view by highlighting the *relationship* between the parties, which in the context of prenups recognises that the parties are not always rational, unemotional or in many cases even bargaining for individual gain. Relational contract also criticises the established traditional approach for focusing on the time the agreement is made instead of the duration of the contractual relationship. By viewing autonomy as something which is exercised throughout the relationship, the intentions of the parties can be appreciated as they evolve during the marriage.

Secondly, classical perceptions of autonomy are challenged by feminist perspectives on contract law. A feminist approach is particularly useful when thinking about power because, as Conaghan has said, women-centred strategies typically rely on power, or lack of it.[52] The 'particular and contextual accounts'[53] proffered by feminist perspectives also makes the gender dimension of prenups visible, which Lady Hale noted was rendered invisible by the all-male majority in *Radmacher*.[54]

In the penultimate section of chapter five, these theories are combined to produce a perspective named 'feminist relational contract theory', which provides a lens through which existing concepts of autonomy and power are criticised, whilst making it possible for alternative approaches to autonomy within the context of prenups to be discovered.

Chapter six outlines various ways in which legislative and judicial approaches to prenups could manage issues of power. By taking the context of the spouses' relationship into account, power imbalances can be recognised, and so when the court has respect for party autonomy (as Lord Phillips said it should in *Radmacher*), this respect will be informed by the parties' relational circumstances and expectations instead of compliance with prescribed contractual formalities. To show how this approach would work in practice, *Radmacher v Granatino* is revisited in light of feminist relational contract theory, which underlines the importance and significance of Lady Hale's perspective in this case. However, Lady Hale's contextual view is not held by many, as the debate surrounding prenups tends to focus on the right to make binding agreements rather than on underlying issues of power. This book aims to bring these underlying issues to the fore.

[52] J Conaghan, 'Reassessing the Feminist Theoretical Project in Law' (2000) 27(3) *Journal of Law and Society* 351, 364.

[53] Ibid.

[54] See *Radmacher*, above n 11, [137].

1

Radmacher v Granatino and the 'New Respect'[1] for Autonomy

There has undoubtedly been growing public awareness of prenups following their emergence in media and pop culture. In particular, the culture of celebrity in our society means there is interest in what happens to the fortunes of the famous, from discussions in the press of golfer Tiger Wood's prenup,[2] to speculation that Beatle Paul McCartney could have saved millions in his infamous divorce from Heather Mills had he entered into such an agreement.[3]

As well as being associated with celebrities, pop culture also portrays prenups as an essential antidote to the stereotypical 'gold-digging' wife. In the Coen Brothers' film *Intolerable Cruelty*, Catherine Zeta Jones plays a character who marries in an attempt to secure a lucrative divorce settlement, whilst scheming to evade an iron-clad prenup. Kayne West's hit *Gold Digger* makes a similar connection, with the lyrics, 'if you ain't no punk holla we want prenup … It's something that you need to have, 'cause when she leaves yo ass she gonna leave with half'.

Unfortunately this misogynistic portrayal of gold-digging women marrying wealthy men is also evident in tabloid coverage of English cases like *Crossley v Crossley*,[4] which became a millionaires' parable after Mr Crossley described ex-wife Mrs Sangster as a 'career divorcée',[5] who had allegedly made her millions from her ex-husbands. The prenup in this case was the first of its time to be considered by the court as having 'magnetic importance',[6] which suddenly made prenups a serious form of asset protection in the UK. One of the prevalent concerns to emerge from the debate surrounding prenups is summarised by Lord Davies of Stamford, who said:

> People have been deeply offended by some of the gold-digging—that is the word one must use—that has had a lot of publicity recently … That offends the public's sense of

[1] *V v V* [2011] EWHC 3230 (Fam) [36] (Charles J).

[2] N Allen, 'Tiger Woods' wife will get $100 million in divorce', *Telegraph* (London, 2 July 2010), available at <http://www.telegraph.co.uk/sport/golf/tigerwoods/7869437/Tiger-Woods-wife-will-get-100-million-in-divorce.html>.

[3] C Gentry, 'Why prenuptial agreements may be a smart option for women', *Guardian* (London, 1 September 2009), available at <http://www.theguardian.com/lifeandstyle/2009/sep/01/prenuptial-agreements-women>.

[4] *Crossley v Crossley* [2007] EWCA Civ 1491.

[5] A Gillan, 'Divorcee gets day in court to claim share of £45 million fortune', *Guardian* (London, 20 December 2007), available at <http://www.theguardian.com/uk/2007/dec/20/uknews4.mainsection1>.

[6] See *Crossley*, above n 4, [15] (Thorpe LJ).

> justice … prenuptial agreements would tend to address that issue and make the law more obviously fair and just.[7]

This portrayal of prenups worryingly obscures issues of power affecting these agreements. Skewed depictions of women as financial predators present a particularly dangerous view when, as this book will argue, the non-moneyed spouse does not have the same autonomy or power as his or her partner, and these inequalities are often also gendered.

Notwithstanding these difficulties, in the UK the court has a 'new respect' for autonomy when evaluating prenups,[8] which has been shaped by the seminal Supreme Court decision in *Radmacher v Granatino*.[9] This judgment provides the most comprehensive evaluation of prenups in England and Wales, and is used as a starting point when uncovering the court's approach to autonomy and how this relates to prenuptial power. This chapter is centred on a detailed analysis of *Radmacher* and the cases which have applied it. The context in which the position of prenups has been debated is also explored, with a particular focus on the recommended legislative reform of these agreements before and after *Radmacher*. Prior to *Radmacher*, numerous proposals for reform of prenups were made, but the nature of the debate surrounding the legislative position of such agreements changed after *Radmacher* was decided. Clear examples of this are the Law Commission's report on marital property agreements and Baroness Deech's Private Members Bill, both of which build on the approach set out in *Radmacher*. In the penultimate section of this chapter, the concept of autonomy which was posited in *Radmacher* is critically examined, to expose the potential problems and limitations of the approach established by the majority of the Supreme Court in this case.

Background

To understand the complexities encountered when prenups are given effect in the UK, the context in which these agreements are made must be examined. This context contrasts with that in most civil law jurisdictions, where spouses can elect a marital property regime to determine the allocation of property during the marriage and in the event of divorce. Couples adopt their chosen regime by entering into an agreement before marriage, which is commonly referred to as a 'prenuptial agreement'. Put simply, the prenup is used to select a template of property rights and interests, and if there is no prenup, a default regime applies instead. For example, in France, couples can choose to apply one of several regimes, such as separate property, instead of the default community property regime, the latter triggering

[7] HL Deb 27 June 2014, vol 754, cols 1496–1497.

[8] See *V v V*, above n 1.

[9] *Radmacher v Granatino* [2010] UKSC 42.

automatic joint ownership from the marriage onwards. The default regimes and options for couples differ from country to country,[10] but in the UK prenups operate in a very different context.[11]

There is no marital property regime in the UK. The court does not apply a formula on divorce when making financial provision orders, and each spouse does not automatically get a 50:50 share of the total pool of assets on relationship breakdown. Instead, the judge has a wide discretion to redistribute the parties' assets as he or she sees fit. Therefore, unlike many European jurisdictions, a prenup applicable to matrimonial law in the UK does not adopt a marital property regime in order to avoid the default regime; instead, it purports to override the judge's decision regarding financial provision on divorce by stipulating how assets will be distributed. Herein lies the complication with prenups. The applicable legislation, which is the MCA 1973, says that the court decides what spouses get on divorce. If the parties can make a binding agreement before marriage, the court is not determining what they get. The court's discretion to make financial provision on divorce is prescribed by Parliament,[12] and so prenups do not have the power to supersede this discretion unless Parliament introduces legislation to that effect. A binding prenup is contrary to public policy for this reason.[13]

It has also been argued that prenups are not in the public interest because they specifically contemplate divorce,[14] and therefore are considered to be inimical to the institution of marriage. This policy objection is rooted in *Cartwright v Cartwright*,[15] a nineteenth-century case that said agreements made by spouses that provide for future separation are void.[16] Denning LJ reiterated these concerns in *Bennett v Bennett*, but he also said that contracts between spouses *can* be 'perfectly lawful, so long as the agreement is made *because of* the separation and not *with a view* to divorce'.[17] Thus it is the concept of future separation as opposed to impending separation that has offended public policy, as Wall J said in 1999 that

[10] Community property can be immediate, deferred or universal. An immediate community property regime is when joint ownership of property is triggered by the marriage. Deferred community means that property remains separate during marriage, but on divorce the property accrued during the marriage is divided equally. Universal community means that all property and debt owned by each spouse is subject to equal division.

[11] See N Lowe, 'Marital Property Agreements' in K Boele-Woelki *et al* (eds), *Principles of European Family Law Regarding Property Relations Between Spouses* (Intersentia 2013) 99–138.

[12] Specifically, the court's jurisdiction is the discretionary power granted by MCA 1973, s 23 to grant ancillary relief on divorce.

[13] Before *Radmacher*, however, the idea that prenups were unenforceable on this basis was confusing when other nuptial agreements, like separation agreements, were not. This is because separation agreements are validated by consent order, which does not affect the court's jurisdiction because, instead of the parties to the separation agreement, it is the court which authorises a consent order in ancillary relief proceedings.

[14] See *B v S (Financial Remedy: Marital Property Regime)* [2012] EWHC 265 (Fam) [5].

[15] *Cartwright v Cartwright* (1853) 3 de GM & G 982.

[16] The principle in this case, that the father of the wife could not arrange her finances in the event of future separation, was regarded as being applicable to prenups. It should also be noted that marriage settlements providing for death rather than separation were enforceable.

[17] *Bennett v Bennett* [1952] 1 KB 249, [261] (emphasis added).

prenups undermine marriage as a lifelong union.[18] By making provision for the end of marriage, the couple is perceived to precipitate it.

Not only is this argument undermined by a lack of evidence showing that the creation of a prenup makes divorce more likely; the policy rule is based on the outdated nineteenth-century notion that husband and wife had an enforceable duty to live together,[19] and that agreements that anticipated breach of this duty would be immoral and contrary to public policy.[20] One of the reasons *Radmacher v Granatino* is so significant to the position of prenups in the UK is that it declared this public policy objection to be obsolete.[21] However, the Supreme Court in *Radmacher* could not do anything to change the fact that judicial power is derived from legislation, and only Parliament can reverse the public policy rule preventing prenups from ousting the court's jurisdiction. Shortly before hearing the *Radmacher* case, Lady Hale confirmed this in the Privy Council decision *Macleod v Macleod*[22] and also concluded that 'the validity and effect of ante-nuptial agreements is more appropriate to legislative rather than judicial development'.[23]

However, in the absence of legislation, there has been significant confusion regarding the extent to which public policy precluded the enforcement of prenups. As Rix LJ explained,

> pre-nuptial agreements are at one and the same time both unenforceable and invalid as being against public policy and matters which the court is prepared to take into account (and possibly decisively) for the purposes of its [statutory] jurisdiction. That is a situation which has been criticised as 'the worst of both worlds' … and … strikes me as anomalous, albeit plainly the present state of the law. On the one hand the pre-nuptial agreement is invalid as being contrary to public policy, and on the other hand it may be and is taken into account by the court.[24]

In other words, before *Radmacher* the court could give effect to an agreement, but it was not clear how much weight the court could attribute to a prenup before the agreement would limit its discretionary power. As a result, the Supreme Court's assessment of prenups in *Radmacher* was hugely significant, because it reconciled

[18] *N v N* [1999] 2 FLR 745.

[19] This duty was important in the 19th century because the only option available to a deserted spouse in the Ecclesiastical Courts was to secure a decree of restitution of conjugal rights. Pursuant to the MCA 1884, a spouse could rely on his or her partner's failure to comply with this decree in order to prove desertion and obtain judicial separation: Law Commission, *Proposal for the Abolition of the Matrimonial Remedy of Restitution* (Law Com No 23, 1969), para 3; *Cocksedge v Cocksedge* (1844) 14 Sim 244. As there was no need to apply for a decree of restitution of conjugal rights once the grounds for divorce were extended by the MCA 1923, the duty for husband and wife to live together was no longer necessary either. The Matrimonial Proceedings and Property Act 1970, s 20 abolished this duty, but the public policy rule relevant to prenups remained.

[20] Law Commission, *Marital Property Agreements* (Law Com No 198, 2011), para 1.6.

[21] This public policy objection was swept away for postnuptial agreements in *Macleod v Macleod* [2008] UKPC 64, and *Radmacher v Granatino*, above n 9 clarified that the objection would be swept away for prenups too.

[22] See *Macleod*, above n 21.

[23] Ibid, [35].

[24] *Radmacher v Granatino* [2009] EWCA Civ 649, [64] (Rix LJ).

the need for greater certainty with the bottom line that the court must decide financial provision for divorcing spouses. Moreover, the impact *Radmacher* has had is striking when case law and legislative recommendations concerning prenups before and after *Radmacher* was decided are juxtaposed.

Cases Before *Radmacher*

When deciding the effect a prenup would have, the court's approach over the last 20 years has changed significantly, and agreements that would previously have been considered irrelevant are now decisive when financial provision orders are being made. The 1990s saw the emergence of mediation and private ordering among couples, but prenups were not encouraged by the courts as part of this general trend. In *F v F*,[25] Thorpe J (as he then was) was influenced by public policy, and held that prenups were of very limited significance because 'the rights and responsibilities of those whose financial affairs are regulated by statute cannot be much influenced by contractual terms'.[26] However, attitudes towards agreements soon developed, as Wilson J held in *S v S (Divorce: Staying Proceedings)*[27] that a prenup could be relevant to the court's assessment of financial provision without the judiciary's discretionary power being interfered with.[28] Taking prenups into account, he said, did not contravene statute because the MCA 1973 provides the court with considerable discretionary power to examine a wide range of matters when making a financial provision order on divorce. Specifically, section 25 of the Act states that the court has a duty to consider all the circumstances of the case,[29] and this could be interpreted to include a prenup.[30]

Extra-judicially, however, Wilson J expressed serious reservations about prenups and said the majority of the judiciary felt that they should be permitted 'slightly, but only slightly, greater prominence'[31] because of the concern that such agreements precondition couples for separation and potentially leave spouses dependent on the state. It was also feared that agreements making insufficient provision for a primary parent would be detrimental to a child of the family. In spite of this, the move towards much greater prominence for prenups was gaining momentum. For example, Connell J in *M v M* reasoned that 'it would be as unjust to the husband to ignore the existence of the agreement and its terms as it would

[25] *F v F (Ancillary Relief: Substantial Assets)* [1995] 2 FLR 45.

[26] Ibid, 66. Thorpe J's attitude prevailed in *Dart v Dart* [1996] 2 FLR 286 when he reiterated his position that ancillary relief is dictated by statute and not by prenup, even if the agreement had been entered into in a jurisdiction where prenups are enforced.

[27] *S v S (Divorce: Staying Proceedings)* [1997] 2 FLR 100.

[28] MCA 1973, s 25(1).

[29] Ibid.

[30] See *S v S*, above n 27, 103.

[31] N Wilson, 'Ancillary Relief Reform: Response of the Judges of the Family Division to the Government Proposals (made by way of submission to the Lord Chancellor's Ancillary Relief Advisory Group)' (1999) 29(3) *Family Law* 159.

be to the wife to hold her strictly to those terms'.[32] Though there was an acute awareness of the potential injustice to the non-moneyed spouse (who was usually, though not always, the wife), the judiciary could not just pretend that no agreement had been made by the couple either. And so the importance of the intentions expressed in a prenup was emphasised more than ever before.

One year after *M v M*, the outcome in *K v K*[33] was almost completely determined by the prenup in question. This decision represents the first in a series of cases where the agreement was viewed not simply as relevant, but as *significant* to the court's assessment of financial provision. The court decided that even though there had not been full disclosure of assets, the agreement should not be disregarded. This is because the husband had not endeavoured to conceal his assets, the wife had simply not pressed for values. The court held that ignoring the agreement would cause more injustice than adhering to it, because the marriage had been short and the wife contributed nothing to the husband's wealth.[34] The significance of this reasoning is better understood when compared to the situation of the Miller couple in *Miller; McFarlane*.[35] In both cases, the husband was very wealthy (with fortunes of £32 million and £25 million respectively) and each marriage lasted less than three years. Despite these similarities, the wife in *K v K* received a capital sum of £120,000, yet Mrs Miller, who did not sign a prenup, was awarded £5 million. This is even more surprising given that the Millers had no children, unlike the parties in *K v K*. Therefore, even though *K v K* was not viewed as a 'blanket endorsement'[36] of prenups, Freeman said that an agreement which fitted with the requirements set out in this case[37] would ultimately be 'a heavyweight and hard to knock out'.[38]

This was even more apparent in *Crossley v Crossley*, where Thorpe LJ, the same judge who had decided that prenups were of little relevance in *F v F*, held instead that the prenup in question was a 'factor of magnetic importance'.[39] Undoubtedly, *Crossley* was a 'paradigm'[40] case, in that the marriage had been short, childless and therefore relatively uncomplicated. Yet it was still significant that Thorpe LJ upheld every term of the contract. Regrettably, Mrs Crossley withdrew her claim against the agreement, so that a judgment on substantive application of the law in this case was prevented. Nevertheless, the attitude towards prenups had changed. This was certainly apparent when *Radmacher v Granatino* was decided.

[32] *M v M* [2002] 1 FLR 654 [20].

[33] *K v K (Ancillary Relief: Prenuptial Agreement)* [2003] 1 FLR 120. The wife was held to the capital provision of the agreement, and only slight amendments were made regarding provision for the child.

[34] Ibid, 131.

[35] *Miller v Miller; McFarlane v McFarlane* [2006] UKHL 24.

[36] J Freeman *et al*, 'Guarding the Triple Crown: Pre-Nuptial Agreements in Three Jurisdictions' (2008) 38 *Family Law* 239.

[37] See *K v K*, above n 33, 131 (Rodger Hayward Smith QC).

[38] See Freeman, above n 36.

[39] See *Crossley*, above n 4, [15] (Thorpe LJ).

[40] Ibid.

Proposed Reform Before *Radmacher*

Proposals to reform the position of prenups indicated a cautious approach to the introduction of legislation which would make these agreements binding, with enforcement qualified by prescribed safeguards allowing such agreements to be set aside in some situations. The perceived need for and emphasis on safeguards was influenced by the judiciary's suspicion of prenups, and by clear discomfort with the idea that such agreements could take away the court's ability to produce the outcome they thought the law demanded. Like any contract there are always exceptions to prenups being absolutely binding;[41] but before *Radmacher*, recommendations for legislative reform focused more on safeguards than on enforcement. For example, in 1998 the Home Office attempted to reform the position of prenups in the Green Paper *Supporting Families*, but the proposals were tentative and were unimplemented.[42] The Paper recommended that the enforcement of prenups should be subject to six safeguards. An agreement would be set aside if:

(a) there was a child;
(b) either party did not receive independent legal advice;
(c) there was not full disclosure of assets when the agreement was made;
(d) it was signed fewer than 21 days prior to the marriage;
(e) enforcement would cause significant injustice; and
(f) it did not adhere to the general rules of contract.

These safeguards would mean many agreements would be not enforced, and so the proposed reform would not really strengthen the position of prenups. As Milligan explained at the time of these proposals, entering into a prenup would be futile if statutory safeguards allowed it to be set aside too easily.[43] But at this time these proposals were quite progressive given that the judiciary was unwilling to recognise prenups in the courtroom. Indeed, *Supporting Families* received a cautious and non-committal response from the judiciary, with Wilson J (as he then was) reluctant to support legislative reform before research had established whether prenups conditioned couples for divorce or made marriage a more attractive concept.[44] Although concerns remain that prenups could somehow psychologically prepare couples for divorce before they are even married,[45] it is difficult to imagine how research could definitively confirm this.

[41] A contract can be vitiated for a number of reasons, such as duress and undue influence, which are considered in ch 4. In most common law jurisdictions the enforcement of prenups is based on safeguards such as independent legal representation and adequate financial disclosure (see uniform laws in the US, specifically the Uniform Premarital and Marital Agreements Act 2012, s 9).

[42] Home Office, *Supporting Families: A Consultation Document* (1998).

[43] P Milligan, 'Pre-Nuptials Beware' (1999) 29 *Family Law* 483.

[44] See Wilson, above n 31.

[45] Particularly among those who view marriage as a sacramental vow: J Bingham, 'Prenup plans could empty "till death do us part" vow of all meaning, Bishop', *Telegraph* (London, 17 February 2014), available at <http://www.telegraph.co.uk/news/religion/10642082/Prenup-plans-could-empty-till-death-do-us-part-vow-of-all-meaning-Bishop.html>.

The National Organisation of Family Lawyers, Resolution, completed two reports containing recommendations for reform in 2005[46] and 2009.[47] In 2005, Resolution suggested that prenups should be binding, but that the judiciary would have a discretionary power to overturn agreements that produced significant injustice. This would arguably have been problematic and arbitrary, as it could mean that an unjust prenup would be acceptable so long as the relevant injustice was not *significant*. In 2009, therefore, Resolution instead proposed that agreements should meet a threshold of 'substantial hardship' in order to be overturned. In addition, safeguards were set out, which included requirements such as independent legal advice, an absence of unfair pressure, full disclosure and that agreements must be signed at least 42 days before the marriage.

The Centre for Social Justice also published recommendations in 2009.[48] Its proposed safeguards were similar to those set out by Resolution in 2009, though it was suggested that agreements should be signed 28 days before the wedding. 'Significant injustice' was again proposed as the standard for setting aside agreements.

Although none of these reform proposals was implemented, the safeguards proposed by the Home Office in 1998 did influence the courts when considering whether an agreement should be enforced.[49] But all of this changed when *Radmacher* reached the Supreme Court.

Since *Radmacher*, the conversation surrounding appropriate safeguards and how to *protect* the interests of the non-moneyed spouse has now been replaced by a concern for the *promotion* of party autonomy. When examining *Radmacher* it is important to note that many of the elements considered to be so crucial previously (such as independent legal advice and complete disclosure) are missing. This move away from a protective or 'paternalistic' approach[50] arguably has significant ramifications for how power issues are recognised and addressed. Indeed, as the following sections will discuss, the judiciary's position in *Radmacher* and the cases that have followed is increasingly fixed on autonomy.

Radmacher v Granatino

Radmacher v Granatino has been the most eagerly awaited English case on prenups. Before this decision, numerous reports recommending legislative reform had been

[46] Resolution, *A more certain future—Recognition of pre-marital agreements in England and Wales* (2005).

[47] Resolution, *Family Agreements—Seeking certainty to reduce disputes: the recognition and enforcement of pre-nuptial and post-nuptial agreements in England and Wales* (2009).

[48] The Centre for Social Justice, *Every Family Matters: An in-depth review of family law in Britain* (2009).

[49] For example, in *K v K*, above n 34, 131, Rodger Hayward Smith QC suggested that if there was a lack of provision made for children, incomplete disclosure of assets and no independent legal advice, the agreement could not stand.

[50] See *Radmacher*, above n 9, [78] (Lord Phillips).

shelved, and a prenup was 'simply one of the peripheral factors in the case'[51] unless it had been created in optimum circumstances like those in *Crossley v Crossley*. To reiterate, the court in *Crossley* said it was a paradigm case because the parties were both independently wealthy, had not made a significant amount of money during the marriage, and the marriage was short and childless.[52] The circumstances in *Radmacher* were quite different: the parties had been married for eight years and they had two children. During the marriage, the husband, Mr Granatino, left his career as a merchant banker and began a PhD in biotechnology at Oxford University. The wife, Ms Radmacher, had a much larger fortune than her husband: she was from an exceptionally wealthy family, and was in possession of a portion of the family wealth at the time of the marriage. However, Ms Radmacher's family told her that she would not receive any further share in this wealth if she did not enter into a prenup. And so she did.

The general effect of the prenup was that the parties could not claim any interest or benefit in each other's property, both during the marriage and on divorce. In particular, the agreement declared that Ms Radmacher and Mr Granatino would each manage their own assets independently. They could not share in each other's pension rights, or claim any maintenance to which they would be entitled in the absence of a prenup.

On divorce, the husband made an application for financial provision contrary to the terms of the prenup; thus the principal issue was whether the court should set aside the agreement and make an award which was inconsistent with what the parties had agreed. However, *Radmacher v Granatino* was not a 'paradigm' case like *Crossley* because it had many more complexities, such as the couple's change in circumstances during the marriage. Therefore, it was not clear what the court's conclusion would be when deciding the influence the agreement would have on divorce. In fact, the *Radmacher* prenup arguably might not have had much clout for a number of reasons. When it was signed, procedural safeguards which had been considered fundamental in earlier cases were not complied with. For example, the agreement did not make provision for any children of the marriage. Furthermore, the husband did not receive independent legal advice, although he had been offered it. He read only the substance of the agreement, which had been translated into English because he is French and the agreement was in German, which language he was not fluent in (the wife is German and the agreement was drawn up by a notary in Germany). Lastly, the wife had not disclosed all of her assets at the time the agreement was entered into.

The Supreme Court's determination of the effect these procedural flaws would have on the agreement's validity was keenly anticipated. But the main reason *Radmacher* attracted such high levels of publicity was the fact that the Supreme Court Justices, for the first time, would be able to evaluate in full the position of prenups in England and Wales.

[51] See *Crossley*, above n 4, [8].
[52] Ibid, [15] (Thorpe LJ).

Radmacher in the Lower Courts

Following the established judicial approach to the enforcement of prenups, at first instance[53] Baron J reasoned that the agreement was tainted by lack of disclosure of the wife's assets and absence of independent legal advice about the consequences of the agreement.[54] On this basis, she considered that Mr Granatino's award 'should be circumscribed to a degree to reflect the fact that at the outset he agreed to sign the [prenuptial agreement]',[55] but that only modest weight should be attached to the agreement. Therefore, contrary to the prenup's terms, Baron J awarded Mr Granatino a £5.5 million lump sum, an income of £100,000 per year for life and £700,000 to pay off debt.

On appeal, however, it was held that this decision represented a 'sufficiently erroneous exercise of … judicial discretion',[56] because although the prenup was alluded to, the court did not give it sufficient weight. In light of the parties' agreement, the amount awarded to Mr Granatino should have been reduced considerably. Though the facts appeared to indicate that Mr Granatino was swept into an agreement under pressure from his fiancée and her father, the Court of Appeal looked past the flaws of the prenup and concluded that the husband *should* be bound by it because he understood the most important aspects of the agreement and had ample opportunity to seek independent legal advice if he had wished to do so. Importantly, the husband's experience in business matters also suggested that he appreciated the implications of the agreement (even if he was unaware of the particulars of it). Furthermore, lack of disclosure did not vitiate the agreement, as the court was not persuaded that Mr Granatino would have refused to sign the prenup if he had been aware of Ms Radmacher's true wealth.

As a result, the Court of Appeal overturned the decision at first instance and made an award which closely reflected the agreement that had been made. Mr Granatino was only awarded provision to allow him to continue his role as 'carer and home-maker for the children'.[57] His ownership of the family home would continue only until his younger daughter reached 22 years of age, and he would receive a much smaller Duxbury capital lump sum,[58] which would supplement his income until his parenting role ended. The Court of Appeal emphasised that the award made to Mr Granatino was 'as father rather than former husband'.[59] Mr Granatino appealed the decision to the Supreme Court.

[53] *NG v KR (Pre-Nuptial Contract)* [2008] EWHC 1532 (Fam).

[54] Extracts from S Thompson, '*Radmacher v Granatino* [2010] UKSC 42' (2011) 33(1) *Journal of Social Welfare and Family Law* 61 appear in this section of the chapter.

[55] See *NG v KR*, above n 53, [139].

[56] See *Radmacher*, above n 9, [44] (Thorpe LJ).

[57] Ibid, [81].

[58] A Duxbury lump sum is calculated so that investment of the sum will produce enough income to meet the needs of the recipient (usually for the rest of his or her life).

[59] See *Radmacher*, above n 24, [50].

Supreme Court

The principal question asked by the Supreme Court was whether the Court of Appeal was justified in finding that decisive weight should be accorded to the agreement in question. Eight of the nine Justices dismissed the appeal and decided that the Court of Appeal was right to give effect to the agreement in question. In addition, the majority introduced a presumption in favour of giving effect to prenups according to the following test:

> The court should give effect to a nuptial agreement that is freely entered into by each party with a full appreciation of its implications unless in the circumstances prevailing it would not be fair to hold the parties to their agreement.[60]

It appears that 'respect for individual autonomy' largely influenced this decision, as Lord Phillips argued that '[i]t would be paternalistic and patronising to override [an] agreement simply on the basis that the court knows best'.[61] However, he said the Court *would* override an agreement if giving effect to it would produce an unfair outcome. Yet unfairness is conceptually very difficult to define. Lord Phillips provided some guidance as to what could constitute unfairness, although he accepted that this would also 'necessarily depend upon the facts of the particular case'.[62] For instance, he highlighted that the reasonable requirements of any children of the family could not be prejudiced by an agreement, and that a prenup would also be unfair if it left one party 'in a predicament of real need, while the other enjoys a sufficiency or more'.[63] Aside from these specific instances, the Court said that an agreement could be rendered unfair if there were unforeseeable change during the marriage, and such change might be more likely the longer the marriage lasted.[64]

Applying this reasoning to the particular facts of the case, the Court held that decisive weight should be accorded to the agreement in question. In addition, it decided that enforcing the agreement would not cause unfairness. The fact that the parties were foreign did not influence the decision,[65] it simply provided additional evidence that the parties intended to be bound by their agreement (as it would have been binding in France or Germany).[66] Furthermore, it was held that even though the husband did not see the agreement until one week before the wedding, he did not receive a translation of the agreement itself and there was neither independent legal advice nor full disclosure of assets, the agreement was fair.

[60] *Radmacher*, above n 9, [78].
[61] Ibid.
[62] Ibid, [76].
[63] Ibid, [81].
[64] Ibid, [80].
[65] Ibid, [108].
[66] It remains unclear whether or not parties to a prenup formed 20 years ago in the UK (when such agreements were not enforced) would have been intended to be bound by it. However, in future, it will be inferred that parties to a prenup formed in the UK intended to be bound by it.

This can be contrasted with Baron J's approach, which drew heavily on the specific safeguards contained in the *Supporting Families* report outlined in the previous section. The Supreme Court thought that these safeguards were relevant, but that failing one or more of them would not necessarily invalidate an agreement.

Lady Hale's opinion as to how the prenup in *Radmacher* should be given effect also differed from the majority view. Though she agreed with the majority that Baron J had not attributed enough weight to the agreement, Lady Hale would have varied the Court of Appeal decision to allow the husband to remain in the English home for life, instead of until the younger daughter reached the age of 22. Her reasoning for this goes to the heart of why prenups are complex, particularly when they are given effect after a lengthy marriage, during which life can change in many unpredictable ways. As Lady Hale put it,

> [a] couple may think that their futures are all mapped out ahead of them when they get married but many things may happen to push them off course—misfortunes such as redundancy, bankruptcy, illness, disability, obligations to other family members and especially to children, but also unexpected opportunities and unexplored avenues.[67]

For this reason, she said, it is 'difficult, if not impossible'[68] to know how what the couples' financial relationship will be like on separation, and even parties with the best intentions to manage their assets independently of one another might not be able to do so if circumstances change, especially if they have children. This analysis reveals some of the problems with binding separating couples to their prenup. In particular, it demonstrates that couples do not enter such agreements in the same way business people enter commercial contracts, and couples are not mindful of the terms of the prenup during the relationship in the way that business partners are either. As a result, with new and unpredictable events during the marriage, Lady Hale said the parties 'often compromise their individual best interests to accommodate' these changes, and 'may have no choice if their marriage is to survive'.[69] She also explained that this intimate context creates a special power dynamic that can lead to problems at the time the prenup is entered into,[70] especially for parties who believe the marriage will endure and that the agreement will never take effect.[71] Therefore, Lady Hale suggested an outcome for Mr Granatino that was not limited to his role as parent, because Mr Granatino's decision to leave a lucrative career was made in the context of marriage and so might not have been self-interested (as the majority suggested it was).

This approach highlighted an important difference between the majority and Lady Hale's perspective regarding prenups. The majority did recognise that such agreements could be affected by power imbalances, but implied that these imbalances may differ depending on one's perspective, as the 'husband may be in the

[67] See *Radmacher*, above n 9, [175].
[68] Ibid, [176].
[69] Ibid, [175].
[70] Ibid, [137].
[71] Ibid, [175].

stronger position financially but the wife may be in the stronger position in relation to the children'.[72] As a result, Lord Phillips said that in most cases 'we must assume that each party … is able to look after him- or herself'.[73] On this assessment, prenups and parties' autonomy to enter into them are not *fundamentally* tainted by power imbalance, and so giving effect to an agreement is a sign that the autonomy of both parties is being respected.[74] Lady Hale's assessment, however, is based on a less individualised, case-by-case idea of power imbalance. She recognises that there are economic, social and gendered dimensions to power in the context of prenups, which make these agreements collectively problematic, and the court should not lose sight of this.

Public Policy

Radmacher v Granatino is also significant because it clarified the position of prenups in light of public policy. Of all the public policy obstacles, the one that continues to prohibit binding enforcement in spite of *Radmacher* is the policy that the jurisdiction of the court cannot be ousted by such an agreement. The Supreme Court in *Radmacher* could not have attached more weight than it did to prenups without conflicting with this rule by determining that such agreements could have decisive weight. In fact, Lady Hale thought the majority had gone too far by enabling prenups effectively to be enforced presumptively unless unfair, because, she argued, this is not compatible with the MCA 1973. She pointed out that this test constituted an 'impermissible gloss upon the courts' statutory duties',[75] as the presumption imposed by the majority could be interpreted as creating a starting point whereby financial provision orders would more often than not be dictated by the terms of the agreement instead of at the discretion of the judge. Instead, Lady Hale preferred an alternative formulation of the test put forward by the majority, which would enforce prenups if they were fair, which is the reverse of the presumption the majority favoured. She explicitly stated that prenups are not legally enforceable contracts, and reiterated her assertion in *Macleod v Macleod*[76] that it is open only to Parliament, and not the court, to hold that they are.[77]

The approach taken by Lady Hale is more compatible with the current law (prior to any amendments made by Parliament in accordance with the Law Commission's recommendations). The court can assess the fairness of an agreement in light of the probable outcome of exercising its statutory discretion. On the other hand, the approach of the majority is arguably consistent with statute, as the requisite assessment of unfairness preserves the court's discretion. Thus, the Supreme Court's gloss on the statute is perhaps not 'impermissible' if the jurisdiction of the

[72] Ibid, [42].
[73] Ibid, [51].
[74] Ibid, [78].
[75] Ibid, [138].
[76] See *Macleod*, above n 21.
[77] See *Radmacher*, above n 9, [138].

court is not ousted by the terms of an agreement. Furthermore, the test does not appear to 'fetter the flexibility that the court requires to reach a fair result'.[78] Whilst it is an uncertain concept, 'unfairness' allows the judiciary to exercise its discretion to consider all the circumstances of the case pursuant to section 25 of the MCA 1973. The difference since *Radmacher*, however, is that first consideration will be given to a prenup, and an agreement will not be set aside without good reason.[79]

Although the Supreme Court could not change the public policy rule that contracts purporting to oust the jurisdiction of the court are unenforceable, it did declare the rule that prenups are unenforceable because they provide for future separation to be obsolete. Lord Phillips applied the Privy Council case *MacLeod v MacLeod*,[80] where Lady Hale asserted that for postnuptial agreements, this policy objection is an 'old rule' because the duty of husband and wife to live together was abolished by the Matrimonial Proceedings and Property Act 1970.[81] On this basis, she concluded that postnuptial agreements could be enforced, as it was 'time for the [policy] rule … to disappear'.[82] In *Radmacher*, Lord Phillips agreed that this rule 'is obsolete and should be swept away',[83] not only for postnuptial agreements but also for prenups.

Since *Radmacher* was decided, it can no longer be said that giving effect to prenups is contrary to public policy for inducing couples to separate. However, unless Parliament makes such agreements legislatively binding, couples cannot oust the jurisdiction of the court to award financial provision under the MCA 1973. Furthermore, although the majority in *Radmacher* made it clear that decisive weight will be attached to a prenup unless it would lead to an unfair outcome, the judgment left many issues unresolved, most patently, the issue of what would constitute unfairness in order for the court to disregard an agreement. Indeed, Lord Phillips did not give details about when an agreement would be unfair. Whilst he said that 'sound legal advice is obviously desirable',[84] an absence of such advice (as in the particular facts of this case) will not necessarily render an agreement unfair. It appears, rather, that the circumstances as a whole are to be taken into account, meaning that factors such as 'a party's emotional state' and 'whether the marriage would have gone ahead without an agreement'[85] could be taken into account, but only as part of a general assessment as to whether or not the parties fully understood the terms and consequences of the agreement they were entering. This holistic approach also includes an examination of whether the parties' needs have been compromised by an agreement. Whilst this guide has some value, it does not explain *how* genuine need should be assessed. Lord Phillips used the

[78] Ibid, [76].
[79] See Thompson, above n 54.
[80] See *Macleod*, above n 21.
[81] Ibid, [38].
[82] Ibid, [39].
[83] See *Radmacher*, above n 9, [52].
[84] Ibid, [69].
[85] Ibid, [72].

example that the agreement in question would have been unfair if 'the husband had been incapacitated in the course of the marriage',[86] yet it is not clear whether a party will be in a situation of need in less extreme circumstances. The lack of predictability which remains with regard to the fairness assessment is illustrated by the divergence of opinion between Baron J at first instance and Lord Phillips, the former judge calling the agreement 'manifestly unfair',[87] the latter enforcing it and viewing it as fair. An absence of negotiations was also considered to be irrelevant by Lord Phillips, as he viewed this absence as merely further evidence that prenups were 'commonplace' to the parties involved.[88] An alternative view of this lack of negotiation, however, could be that one party's lack of participation in the agreement is indicative of power imbalance. Either way, there is no way of *knowing* how autonomy is exercised, unless the context in which the agreement is signed is probed further.

As a result, it is clear that the enforceability of prenups was not a closed matter after *Radmacher*. The Supreme Court could only decide whether and to what extent such agreements are valid within the existing statutory framework, as laying down detailed conditions for a prenup would have been incompatible with the judicial process. The Supreme Court Justices also emphasised the continued need for reform, which they said was a matter for consideration by the Law Commission of England and Wales. In particular, Lady Hale said the law applicable to prenups 'is a mess … ripe for systematic review and reform'.[89] However, before considering the outcome of the Law Commission's review and proposed reform of the law in this area, the judicial application of *Radmacher* in other cases is explored in order to determine the impact of this case.

Cases after *Radmacher*

Radmacher was not the first time the courts attributed considerable weight to a prenup in the UK. Before this decision, prenups had gradually become more prominent within the judiciary's discretionary redistribution of property on divorce, and so the Supreme Court's decision to give effect to the agreement in *Radmacher* was not revolutionary. Yet the effect of *Radmacher* on *how* prenups were to be enforced *was* new, because it created a presumption in favour of enforcement by reasoning that the agreements should be upheld unless unfair. As Moor J said in the first case to apply *Radmacher*, the Supreme Court decision led to a 'seismic shift' that 'changed the position fundamentally'[90] for prenups: although fairness is still part of the court's assessment, it must now be balanced against a need to respect the autonomy of the parties. The effect of this change,

86 Ibid, [119].
87 Ibid, [137].
88 Ibid, [116].
89 Ibid, [133].
90 *Z v Z (No 2)* [2011] EWHC 2878 (Fam) [33]–[34].

and what it means for power discourses between parties entering prenups, can be understood through an analysis of the court's approach following *Radmacher*.

One of the significant side-effects of the Supreme Court's focus on autonomy was that less emphasis was placed on safeguards like disclosure and independent legal advice, which had been considered to be of high importance previously. Though these elements are still relevant, they are regarded as part of a more general assessment of what the parties understood, or should have understood, in light of the information available to them at the time the agreement was signed. In other words:

> What is important is that each party should have all the information that is material to his or her decision, and that each party should intend that the agreement should govern the financial consequences of the marriage coming to an end.[91]

Thus, as long as the substance of the agreement is understood, a lack of specific information, disclosure or independent advice will not necessarily mean the parties did not freely enter into the agreement. The problem with this is that if a couple's general appreciation of the consequences of their agreement is sufficient, it is conceivable that power inequalities will not be addressed. But this will depend on how *Radmacher* is interpreted, and the advantage of not adopting a prescriptive approach is that the court is flexible to recognise that a party's understanding of the agreement depends on contextual factors other than uniform considerations like financial disclosure and independent legal advice.

An example of this is the approach in *GS v L*, where Eleanor King J did not uphold the agreement because she found that the parties did not share a common intention as to its purpose.[92] She said that it was inconceivable that the wife would knowingly have entered into an agreement which severely limited her entitlement to her husband's assets,[93] since the wife had suggested the agreement solely to ensure her own financial security in the event of her husband's death. As in *Radmacher*, there was an absence of independent legal advice and full disclosure; but unlike *Radmacher*, the wider context of the agreement did not suggest that the substance of the prenup was adequately understood by the parties involved. Similarly, in *Kremen v Agrest*[94] (which concerned a postnuptial agreement), Mostyn J emphasised the importance of nuptial agreement 'safeguards':

> [I]t will only be in an unusual case where it can be said that absent independent legal advice and full disclosure, a party can be taken to have freely entered into a marital agreement with a full appreciation of its implications. After all, almost every common law country that has legislated in this field has as a key pre-condition these requirements … It would surely have to be shown that the spouse, like Mr Granatino, had a high degree

[91] See *Radmacher*, above n 9, [69].

[92] *GS v L* [2011] EWHC 1759. See also *Y v Y (Financial Remedy—Marriage Contract)* [2014] EWHC 2920 (Fam).

[93] *GS v L*, above n 92, [63].

[94] *Kremen v Agrest (Financial Remedy: Non-Disclosure: Post-Nuptial Agreement)* [2012] 2 FLR 414.

> of financial and legal sophistication in order to have a full appreciation of what legal rights he or she is signing away. Equally, it seems to me that there would have to be clear evidence of significant economic capacity on the part of the claimant spouse before the assessment of needs was suppressed to that minimal level imposed on Mr Granatino.[95]

Thus, *Kremen v Agrest* suggests that it would be unusual for a prenup to be enforced in circumstances similar to those of Mr Granatino (where the agreement was not in his own language, he did not obtain independent advice and he did not receive full disclosure of Ms Radmacher's assets), unless the non-moneyed spouse was sophisticated in legal and financial matters. However, the approach adopted by Charles J in *V v V*[96] would suggest otherwise. The facts of this case suggest numerous power imbalances: the parties did not receive independent legal advice, the wife was not provided with detailed disclosure of the husband's assets and the agreement made no provision for future children. The husband clearly had the power: knowing his wife's desire to marry, he would only marry on condition that a prenup was signed.[97] In spite of this, the prenup was upheld. Charles J found that the parties were aware of the general purpose and effect of the agreement, and that there was no evidence to suggest that detailed financial disclosure would have changed the wife's decision. In particular, Charles J reasoned that the power imbalances in this case did not have any effect on the enforcement of the agreement, because

> such inequality of bargaining position, or the pressures on the wife … do not found a conclusion that the agreement was not one that was not willingly and honestly entered into by both parties to achieve the purpose identified by the judge (namely to protect the husband's separate and existing assets).[98]

This approach suggests that a court could be satisfied that the parties have been autonomous even if there have been bargaining inequalities and other pressures. The allowances made by the court in situations where full financial disclosure has not been forthcoming is also problematic, as the non-moneyed party's lack of specific information about his or her partner's finances also inevitably places that party in a weaker bargaining position. In *AH v PH*, for example, Moor J said that the 'millionaire's defence', which permits the moneyed spouse to provide a broad (rather than specific) outline of his or her wealth, is 'perfectly acceptable' in the prenuptial context.[99]

Thus, power inequalities, unless fairly extreme, do not appear to weigh heavily with the courts when considering whether a prenup should be considered unfair. In *V v V*, Charles J explained this change as a move away from the previous position, which was 'paternalistic and protective of the payee'.[100] But by rejecting an

95 Ibid, [73].
96 See *V v V*, above n 1.
97 Ibid, [61].
98 Ibid, [64].
99 *AH v PH* [2013] EWHC 3873 (Fam) [30].
100 See *V v V*, above n 1, [38].

approach based on protecting the interests of the non-moneyed spouse, it could be argued that the current autonomy-based stance might consequentially favour the party with greater bargaining power.

Proposed Reform after *Radmacher*

The Law Commission's Report, *Matrimonial Property, Needs and Agreements*

In addition to *Radmacher v Granatino*, the other most important development in the law applicable to prenups has been the Law Commission's project on marital property agreements. The report resulting from this project was published in February 2014 and recommended the introduction of a Nuptial Agreements Bill, which would add another schedule to the MCA 1973 and the Civil Partnership Act 2004 to make 'qualifying nuptial agreements' binding in England and Wales, provided the needs of the parties are met. Pursuant to the Law Commission's recommendations, a prenup is a qualifying nuptial agreement, provided several procedural requirements are satisfied: both parties must have provided material disclosure of their assets, signed the agreement at least 28 days before the wedding and obtained legal advice. The precise nature of the legal advice provided to couples entering prenups is not prescribed. However, each party must be advised independently (ie by different lawyers). Parties must also sign a statement confirming that they have been informed that their prenup will prevent financial provision different from that specified in the agreement (unless needs are not provided for), and that they are aware of the effect their agreement will have on divorce.

The most important effect of the proposed legislation, if implemented, would be that the court would no longer have the power to set aside an agreement at the time of divorce for being 'unfair'. Instead of carrying out a fairness assessment, the court would only consider whether the needs of the parties would be provided for if the qualifying nuptial agreement in question were enforced. However, as the Law Commission has acknowledged, assessing needs is a complex and subjective exercise, and so it has proposed that the Family Justice Council should prepare guidance on what it means for the parties' needs to be met.[101]

Professor Cooke, the Law Commissioner in charge of the project on marital property agreements, has said that the report 'does not recommend revolution, but builds on existing law and practice'.[102] This is clear when considering the

[101] Law Commission, *Matrimonial Property, Needs and Agreements* (Law Com No 343, 2014), para 9.1. The concept of needs will be discussed further in ch 2.

[102] E Cooke, 'The Law Commission's report on matrimonial property, needs and agreements' (2014) 44(3) *Family Law* 304, 308.

proposed procedural requirements, which, like *Radmacher*, recommend material but not *full* disclosure, and independent but not *competent* legal advice. Prescriptive statutory provisions governing the nature and content of legal advice would not ameliorate individual power imbalances, which is why the Law Commission has said it should be up to the lawyer to determine the detail of the advice.[103] However, the Law Commission did provide guidelines as to what legal advice might cover for parties entering into prenups,[104] though it was also noted that advice should be specific to the client's situation.[105] Indeed, in its consultation paper on marital property agreements,[106] the Law Commission highlighted the problems with enforcing prenups, and argued that the concept of autonomy should be considered with caution:

> [A]utonomy may be illusory, or at least vitiated. Those who marry or form civil partnerships are adults and can take their own decisions, but it is a matter of experience that most people are willing to agree, when they are in love, to things that they would not otherwise contemplate.[107]

Thus, although the Law Commission recommends reform, it also warns that the judiciary's emphasis on autonomy is potentially problematic.

Divorce (Financial Provision) Bill

In the same month that saw the publication of the Law Commission report, a Private Member's Bill was introduced into the House of Lords by Baroness Deech. In addition to reforming financial provision on divorce more generally, the proposed legislation aims to reform the status of prenups. At the time of writing, the committee stage of the Bill has taken place in the House of Lords and it is not apparent how far the Bill will proceed. However, the Bill has been met favourably in the House of Lords, and its progress adds further context to the way in which prenups are being debated in the UK. The proposed provisions are similar to the Law Commission's recommendations, and include procedural requirements for an agreement to be treated as binding, such as: contractual validity; legal advice; that the agreement must be signed at least 21 days before the marriage; full disclosure; and no imposition of any obligation on a third party without that party's permission. A significant difference between the recommendations suggested by the Law Commission and those put forward by Baroness Deech is that the latter did not include a provision that would enable a prenup to be set aside on the basis

103 See Law Commission, above n 101, para 6.143.
104 Ibid, para 7.59.
105 Ibid, para 7.60.
106 See Law Commission, above n 20.
107 Ibid, para 5.26.

of need. Baroness Deech's reason for this is that the fewer exceptions when making prenups binding, the less cost and litigation:

> The Supreme Court recently said that prenuptial agreements may be binding in principle, with a number of qualifications, and so has the Law Commission recommended. However, with all the exceptions, this invites litigation to challenge every prenuptial agreement, if they were to catch on. One couple recently spent £600,000 litigating over whether or not the prenup was binding. Another spent £2 million. In the most recent issue of *Family Law Reports*, one prenup was upheld, one was overwritten—even though the husband had signed it three times—and another half a dozen conditions were added for determining whether they should be binding. My Bill will make prenup and post-nup agreements binding, with very few exceptions.[108]

Of course, the mitigation of litigation costs must be balanced against the price paid by the spouse who might be detrimentally affected by a prenup but has no way of challenging it. The case to which Baroness Deech refers, in which an agreement had been signed by the husband three times, is *Luckwell v Limata*,[109] which was widely reported in the media because the wife, who was the moneyed spouse, was the daughter of the company director of children's television programme *Bob the Builder*. The court did not give effect to the prenup in this case, because with no home, no income, no capital and considerable debts, the husband was considered to be in a situation of real need.[110] In these circumstances, the prenup would have led to considerable hardship for the non-moneyed spouse, and so litigation was justifiable in spite of Baroness Deech's assertions to the contrary.

Nevertheless, it is more likely than not that a prenup will now be given effect on divorce. Whether the recommendations made by the Law Commission or Baroness Deech become law or not, Charles J has made the importance of autonomy post-*Radmacher* particularly clear:

> At the heart of that significant change, is the need to recognise the weight that should now be given to autonomy, and thus to the choices made by the parties to a marriage … The new respect to be given to individual autonomy means that the fact of an agreement can alter what is a fair result and so found a different award to the one that would otherwise have been made.[111]

Examining the implications of this 'new respect' for autonomy is important when considering how issues of power between parties entering prenups are perceived by the court. This is outlined in further detail in the next section.

Re-evaluating the *Radmacher* View of Autonomy

The emergence of autonomy as *the* reason to give effect to nuptial agreements in the UK since *Radmacher v Granatino* diverts attention from the problematic aspects

[108] HL Deb 27 June 2014, vol 754, col 1492.
[109] *Luckwell v Limata* [2014] EWHC 502.
[110] Ibid, [143].
[111] See *V v V*, above n 1, [36].

of these agreements—namely, issues of power between the parties. Recognising that a prenup can circumvent the state's control over the financial consequences of divorce does not necessarily mean that both parties have autonomy to set the terms of the agreement, particularly if it is made on an uneven playing field.[112] The case law discussed in this chapter suggests that evidence such as independent legal advice is sufficient to prove that both parties have been autonomous. But as prenups are now given effect on the basis of autonomy, it is imperative to explore whether autonomy is more nuanced than the law recognises.

McLean's perspective on autonomy in the area of biomedical law and ethics is especially useful, even though her analysis is rooted in a different context. She believes that the 'true' operation of autonomy should be recognised consistently in all legal spheres,[113] and that autonomy should be distinguished from legal autonomy. McLean criticises the law because it accepts that parties have been autonomous when their consent is valid. In other words, the meanings of consent and autonomy are assimilated. But McLean explains that it is too simplistic to assume that the rules of consent truly protect an individual's autonomy.[114] First, consent in law depends on parties' decision-making capacity. It does not depend on the quality of the decision, or on the impact of the decision on others. Furthermore, consent is connected to the concept of voluntariness in law,[115] whereby the court is satisfied that a voluntary choice has been made when the parties have capacity, are in receipt of adequate information and have not been subjected to unfair pressure. This approach, McLean says, demonstrates that the court perceives voluntariness and choice in an abstract way. This is because viewing the way in which choices are made as something that occurs in a vacuum, once certain procedures are followed, fails to recognise the extent to which parties' decisions are influenced by society and other people. Neglecting this wider context could also lead to the assumption that parties voluntarily entered into a prenup, when a deeper consideration of the balance of power between the parties could produce a different conclusion. As a result, enforcement based on compliance with requirements like disclosure and independent legal advice suggests that prenups are driven by fact-based consent. As McLean puts it, 'while consent is heralded as the legal equivalent of autonomy, in fact it is close only to that part of autonomy that relates to status—to the question of competence'.[116]

Furthermore, though the law considers it to be important that both parties consented to a prenup, the idea of consenting at a particular moment when the agreement is signed is different from the idea of autonomy over a more prolonged period. As circumstances will likely change after the agreement is signed, especially if the marriage is lasting, it is likely that the intentions of the parties will change

[112] See Law Commission, above n 20, para 5.32.

[113] S McLean, *Autonomy, Consent and the Law* (Routledge 2010).

[114] Ibid, 4.

[115] Case law has emphasised that an agreement should be entered into freely (without duress). See *Radmacher*, above n 9; *Z v Z (No 2)*, above n 90; *V v V*, above n 1.

[116] See McLean, above n 113, 215.

too. Therefore, a more realistic view of autonomy might take into account the respective situations of the parties, if, for example, they have changed their careers. Another contextual view of autonomy considers the circumstances in which an agreement is signed. This book will examine whether these circumstances, such as pressure, emotion and psychological impact, are taken into account by the law regulating prenups in the UK. As Bix has astutely noted, 'the fact is that most people are poor at thinking well about events in the distant future, especially if it involves contingencies contrary to our optimistic assumptions'.[117] This cognitive limitation means that parties are often unable to make autonomous decisions when entering agreements that properly represent what is in their best interests. Eisenberg explains these limitations using the terms 'bounded rationality' and 'rational ignorance'.[118] For instance, parties to an agreement are likely to be 'unduly optimistic about the fate of their marriage',[119] as research from Baker and Emery has established.[120] Thus, people might not make truly autonomous decisions if they do not believe that the agreement will ever need to be enforced. Parties are also unlikely to be able to predict the future effect of their agreement, particularly if circumstances change during the marriage, which was not foreseen by the couple.[121] This often also leads to changing personal expectations, which supports the idea that in reality, the exercise of autonomy relevant to prenups is not limited to the time the agreement is signed.

Moreover, the nature of prenups is such that the power balance between parties is usually unequal if, for example, one party desires the agreement more than the other. In short, they are not 'neutral' agreements.[122] As 'power' in itself is an elusive concept, it is more accurate to describe references to power in this context as expressions or processes of power between parties to a prenup. Considering this particular context is complicated but important, particularly when criticising the court's emphasis on autonomy in recent case law. Indeed, the stories from New York attorneys interviewed for the study on which this book is based, show that prenuptial issues of power are very real, as one interviewee described:

> [O]ne of my favourite prenup cases was when I was a younger lawyer … I got a call from one of the big matrimonial lawyers in New York and he wanted me to represent the wife, some professor was his client. The thing was that the professor had all kinds of money and this agreement gave her nothing … I went over there and I talked to the woman, she said what do you think I should do? I said I wouldn't sign this thing, it's terrible! She said

[117] B Bix, 'Private Ordering and Family Law' (2010) 23 *Journal of the American Academy of Matrimonial Lawyers* 249.

[118] M Eisenberg, 'The Limits of Cognition and the Limits of Contract' (1995) 47(2) *Stanford Law Review* 211, 213.

[119] Ibid, 254.

[120] L Baker and R Emery, 'When Every Relationship Is Above Average: Perceptions and Expectations of Divorce at the Time of Marriage' (1993) 17(4) *Law and Human Behaviour* 439. The median response from interviewees was that the probability of other couples divorcing was 50%, but the probability that they personally would divorce was 0%.

[121] Ibid, 444.

[122] Ibid.

> yea but money is so important to him … do you really think it's bad? Can't you make it a little better? I said I doubt it because it's bad on almost every page, says you get nothing … So we meet in the office of this guy … I said well, she's not going to sign it … That was the end of that. And a long time afterwards I heard from the woman and I said what happened? She said oh well I signed the damn thing because it was so important to him. But everything is going fine! So there is this love, there are these emotions that are not exactly like a contract between two people in commerce. You do the best you can.[123]

The findings from this empirical study will be outlined further in chapter three, but even this short anecdote indicates a number of problems with which this book is concerned. First is the idea that prenups are '*not exactly like a contract between two people in commerce*'. Although this may seem obvious given the intimate relationship between the parties involved, the perspectives of those debating the Divorce (Financial Provision) Bill seem to suggest otherwise:

> We have contracts in this country that are enforceable in law for all kinds of things: employment contracts, sale and purchase contracts, leasing contracts, licensing contracts, exclusivity contracts, partnership contracts and so on. Only gambling contracts are not enforceable under the law in this country. It would be an extraordinary state of affairs to put prenuptial contracts—with all the protections required and that are in the Bill before us … on the same footing as gambling contracts.[124]

This perspective does not allow the uniquely emotional context of prenups to be taken into account, and suggests that such agreements are like any other contract (but gambling contracts are not).

The second idea to emerge from the above anecdote is that the division of power is clearly unequal between the moneyed spouse asking for the prenup and the non-moneyed spouse. The wife 'signed the damn thing'[125] even though it was not financially in her interests to do so;[126] but because she had received legal advice and was aware of the terms of the agreement, it would be enforced in New York *and* (given effect in) the UK, provided she was not going to be left destitute. This in itself is an expression and reinforcement of power, because the agreement of parties in quite different bargaining positions is what Shortall would call a practice which is 'taken for granted' without question.[127] That is, if it is *accepted* that there are frequently disparities of power between parties negotiating prenups, it can be argued that this expression of power is manifest in the regulation of these agreements. Identifying and exploring this particular discourse of power is important, because as Shortall puts it, '[i]f the legitimacy of customs and practices is questioned, it is possible for change to occur. To speak of power implies the possibility for change.'[128]

[123] Practitioner 14.

[124] HL Deb 27 June 2014, vol 754, col 1496.

[125] Practitioner 14.

[126] It may have been in her interests from a non-financial point of view, but the attorney did not know why she signed it other than because it was important to her husband that she did.

[127] S Shortall, *Women and Farming, Property and Power* (Macmillan 1999) 7.

[128] Ibid.

Examining power also enables the view of autonomy posited in *Radmacher v Granatino* to be re-evaluated, because the autonomy of one party can be limited by his or her *partner's* exercise of autonomy, particularly if the partner has more bargaining power. Put simply, in McLean's words, 'the moral worth of decisions is predicted not by the mere exercise of choice but potentially also by the impact of that choice on others. Restrictions on individual autonomy are those required to protect others' individual autonomy.'[129] This idea can be traced into the Law Commission's analysis of autonomy in its consultation paper on marital property agreements:

> [W]e have to be very clear what is the autonomy, or freedom, in question. All couples, under the current law, have the freedom to agree whatever they like by way of financial settlement when their relationship comes to an end. The autonomy that is prayed in aid of binding marital property agreements is not simply the freedom to make an agreement, nor simply the freedom to do as one wishes. It is the freedom to force one's partner to abide by an agreement when he or she no longer wishes to do so. It is freedom of contract, but it is therefore freedom to use a contract to restrict one's partner's choices.[130]

In spite of these concerns, it is not clear that the nuances and complexities of autonomy are recognised in practice. Indeed, if power issues are not addressed by the courts, the 'new respect' for autonomy since *Radmacher* is in reality a respect for a flawed version of this concept.

Conclusion

Since *Radmacher*, the approach of the courts seems to suggest that respect for autonomy is incompatible with a regard for the general inequalities of bargaining position. This will be more apparent once the findings of my empirical project are outlined in chapter three, which can determine sources of prenuptial power and how power is exercised. But even the fact that power imbalances often *exist* between parties to prenups is revealing on a number of levels. Perhaps most patently, it demonstrates that although *Radmacher* says that autonomy should be respected because it allows parties to have power to decide the economic consequences of their separation, this view of autonomy presumes that both parties have an equal say in the matter. Yet this particular emphasis is influenced by a liberal view of choice, and so is based on a neutral, equal and rational process unaltered by context. As Herring argues, '[i]ndependence and freedom have become the icons of our age. Yet … in the context of family law these are false gods.'[131]

[129] See McLean, above n 113, 28.
[130] See Law Commission, above n 20.
[131] J Herring, *Relational Autonomy and Family Law* (Springer 2014) 2.

Unfortunately, for family law anyway, Herring is correct. The liberal idea of autonomy *has* become an icon of sorts, particularly since individuals like Alan Miller have told the press that the court awarded his ex-spouse a 'meal ticket for life'[132] on divorce. But Mr Miller's sound bite from this case completely obscures the complex reasoning behind this award.[133] Thus, to make sense of the current position of prenups and where the 'new' respect for autonomy has come from, the historical development of financial provision must be understood. This is the purpose of chapter two, which will also describe in detail how the court exercises its discretion to award financial provision on divorce, or rather the default principles out of which a prenup can contract.

[132] C Davies, 'Three-year wife's £5 million divorce "a meal ticket for life"', *Telegraph* (London, 31 January 2006), available at <http://www.telegraph.co.uk/news/uknews/1509263/Three-year-wifes-5m-divorce-a-meal-ticket-for-life.html>.

[133] See *Miller; McFarlane*, above n 36.

2

The Developing Landscape of Financial Provision on Divorce

After his third marriage, comedian and actor John Cleese expressed his frustration with the outcome of his divorce settlement. According to the *Telegraph* newspaper he said:

> If we [Mr Cleese and his ex-wife] both died today, her children would get much more than mine ... At least I will know in future if I go out with a lady they will not be after me for my money![1]

It is likely that the changing judicial attitude towards prenups at the time of Mr Cleese's third divorce would not have eased this bitterness. Had he entered into an agreement, the outcome of his divorce would probably have been quite different. A year after John Cleese was ordered to pay his third wife approximately £12 million, *Radmacher v Granatino* clarified that a prenup can be decisive in the process of financial redistribution on divorce.[2]

In contrast to the weight currently attributed to prenups, the history of these agreements has been one of unenforceability. This historical background reveals much about how attitudes have developed, not only towards such agreements, but also towards marriage and divorce in general. Indeed, to properly understand important features of relationships between parties to a prenup, in particular autonomy and power, the wider social, economic and legal context of these agreements must be explored. This is because power (or lack of it) within the prenuptial and marital relationship does not exist independently of wider social norms and legal attitudes.

This chapter will explore attitudes towards financial provision on divorce. The first half will describe a brief history of property ownership during marriage and divorce from the latter half of the nineteenth century to the first half of the

[1] A Pierce, 'John Cleese in £12 million divorce settlement', *Telegraph* (London, 18 August 2009), available at <http://www.telegraph.co.uk/news/celebritynews/6043628/John-Cleese-in-12-million-divorce-settlement.html>.

[2] Unsurprisingly, John Cleese and his fourth wife reportedly entered into a prenup prior to their marriage in 2012: A Singh, 'John Cleese marries for the fourth time', *Telegraph* (London, 13 August 2012), available at <http://www.telegraph.co.uk/news/celebritynews/9470746/John-Cleese-marries-for-the-fourth-time.html>.

twentieth century. A feminist perspective on this history is important, as legal development in this area took place against a backdrop of first-wave feminism, which challenged gender inequalities reinforced by marriage and divorce. Because of the oppressive nature of the law at this time, Smart points out that women's 'economic vulnerability outside the family structure'[3] led to the financial dependence of wives on their husbands post-divorce. This background provides important context for the unenforceability of nuptial agreements (such as separation agreements and prenups), which would not allow husbands to contract out of support if it would cause the wife to be financially dependent on the state. But the divorce laws at this time did not afford women any rights to their husbands' property on separation either, and as most unpaid domestic labour was undertaken by women, the consequences of divorce were very harsh indeed. Thus, the introduction of the court's statutory powers to award financial provision and adjust property ownership on relationship breakdown was a necessary change to address the hardship faced by women post-divorce.

The second half of this chapter will outline the development of financial provision orders on divorce (also referred to as ancillary relief) since the introduction of the MCA 1973, which forms the basis of our current law. The law of ancillary relief controls the redistribution of parties' finances, assets and property on divorce.[4] Driven by judicial discretion, an award of ancillary relief is intended to produce a fair outcome for both parties, which arguably must be paramount when the marriage bond is dissolved. Nevertheless, the court's approach towards fairness has changed significantly over time, illustrating the complexities of basing property division on such an 'elusive'[5] concept. In order to adhere to the court's current notion of fairness, the law of ancillary relief today goes further than making awards based on need. Rather, spouses' awards on divorce are based on entitlement. Yet fairness has not always been epitomised by entitlement, and it is important to understand how the concept of fairness has evolved with regard to asset allocation on divorce. In addition, the judiciary's changing approaches to ancillary relief reveal much about contemporary attitudes towards financial provision. As prenups are enforced as part of the court's discretionary assessment, an understanding of this wider context is also essential when understanding why the position of these agreements has developed in the way it has. Clarification of the default rules of financial provision on divorce is also important in order to appreciate precisely what prenups can contract out of when enforced in the UK.

[3] C Smart, *The Ties That Bind: Law, Marriage and the Reproduction of Patriarchal Relations* (Routledge 1984) 48.

[4] The Law Commission has explained that the term 'ancillary relief' is used because the process is 'ancillary to—that is, subordinate to and exercised as a consequence of—the court's powers to terminate the marriage or civil partnership by granting a decree of divorce or by dissolving a civil partnership': Law Commission, *Marital Property Agreements* (Law Com No 198, 2011) 2.

[5] *Miller v Miller; McFarlane v McFarlane* [2006] UKHL 24 [4].

Financial Provision Prior to the Matrimonial Causes Act 1973

As stated previously, there is no marital property regime in the UK and property ownership remains separate on marriage. Therefore, married couples have the right to obtain property and to manage it independently of their spouses. But separate property has not always been the basis of marital property ownership in the UK, being preceded by the doctrine of coverture. Coverture removed women's separate legal status upon marriage, and a wife effectively became her husband's chattel in the eyes of the law.[6] Separate property was introduced in 1882, but during the first half of the twentieth century the formal equality established by separate property did not, in reality, lead to the financial independence of spouses, serving only to reinforce structural economic dependencies of wives who had no independent income.[7] The following sections will examine these issues in more detail, in addition to exploring the origins and development of financial support post-divorce.

Marriage Settlements and the Common Law Doctrine of Coverture

According to Cretney, '[i]t is not a great exaggeration to say that the common law robbed the married woman of full human personality' for most of the nineteenth century.[8] This is because, under the doctrine of coverture in common law, a woman's property and income became her husband's on marriage. Therefore, the husband could dispose of any money the wife had earned or saved before the marriage as he wished. Furthermore, the wife had no economic independence or responsibility, and could not be liable for breaches of contract or tortious wrongs. Such rights and liabilities were the concern of the husband, who was also under an obligation to support his wife financially. Exactly how these obligations developed is unclear, but Eekelaar and Maclean believe that one of the catalysts that transformed the duty for a husband to support his wife into a legal obligation was the poor laws,[9] which compelled economic support within the family and imposed penalties on members who did not maintain their relatives when they had the means to do so.[10] Coverture also reflects the traditional idea that husband and

[6] D Stetson, *A Woman's Issue: Politics of Family Law Reform in England* (Greenwood Press 1982) 5.

[7] In the Victorian era, men and women occupied separate spheres. Women, depending on whether they were working- or middle-class, either performed or directed the work involved in maintaining the household, whilst men earned money to support the family and meet household expenses. M Shanley, *Feminism, Marriage and the Law in Victorian England* (Princeton University Press 1993) 5.

[8] S Cretney, *Family Law in the Twentieth Century* (OUP 2003) 90.

[9] The Poor Relief Act 1601.

[10] J Eekelaar and M Maclean, *Maintenance after Divorce* (Clarendon Press 1986) 2.

wife became 'one flesh'[11] on marriage.[12] Legally, however, these obligations were not enforced until the statutory introduction of divorce.[13] The legislative provision for this was section 32 of the MCA 1857, which gave the judiciary discretion to make orders for maintenance post-separation. This could be marked as the first evidence of financial support between separated spouses being incorporated into legal principle. A contemporaneous judicial explanation for the introduction of this legal obligation is provided by *Sidney v Sidney*, which said the husband must still support the woman he has 'chosen and … discarded'.[14]

Missing from case law like *Sidney*, however, is the influence of female activists in the fight for secularised divorce and the introduction of the MCA 1857. Although coverture survived this reform, the 1857 Act represented the beginnings of deterioration of this doctrine by providing property rights for women for the first time.[15] Clauses 25 and 26 of the Act restored women's *feme sole*[16] property rights, which had been lost on marriage, on separation; but during marriage, a wife's legal personality was still subsumed within that of her husband. A pioneer of the 1857 reform was Caroline Norton, whose campaign for divorce reform was really a campaign for married women's rights that exposed the oppressive nature of coverture.[17] She alerted the public to her own personal hardship under coverture[18] by writing and pamphleteering, and this had a major impact on the 1857 Act due to the particular organisation of government at that time.[19]

In spite of this, married women still did not have any power to control their own property in common law. As a result, upper- and middle-class women resorted to marriage settlements to obtain some financial independence. Marriage settlements were an early form of private ordering, and were conventional among the upper classes in early modern England, Wales and Ireland. These marriage settlements were most commonly made by affluent families in order to ensure that their daughter's assets would not be lost to the husband[20] on marriage. At their most

[11] P Ward, *Divorce in Ireland: Who Should Bear the Cost?* (Cork University Press 1993) 15.

[12] See G Williams, 'The Legal Unity of Husband and Wife' (1947) 10 *MLR* 16; Eekelaar and Maclean, above n 10, 2; Ward, above n 11, 15.

[13] Prior to the introduction of divorce, the ecclesiastical courts had the power to make a husband pay his wife maintenance. Therefore, the concept of alimony derived from the ecclesiastical courts.

[14] *Sidney v Sidney* (1865) 4 Sw & Tr 178, 34 LJPM & A 122.

[15] See Stetson, above n 6, 18.

[16] *Feme sole* referred to the legal status of single women. Married women were *feme couverte*, which signified loss of separate legal status.

[17] For further detail on Mrs Norton's campaigns for married women's property rights, see KD Reynolds, 'Norton, Caroline Elizabeth Sarah [*other married name* Caroline. Elizabeth Sarah Stirling Maxwell, Lady Stirling Maxwell] (1808–1877)' in *Oxford Dictionary of National Biography* (OUP 2004), available at <http://www.oxforddnb.com/view/article/20339>.

[18] Norton separated from her husband but could not divorce him, and as she had no separate legal status, all of her income from writing and her property were kept by her husband, and he had custody of the children.

[19] See Stetson, above n 6, 50; Shanley, above n 7, 22.

[20] SM Okin, 'Patriarchy and Married Women's Property in England: Questions on some Current Views' (1983) 17 *Eighteenth-Century Studies* 121.

basic, marriage settlements were akin to prenups,[21] allowing the autonomous preservation of premarital property, yet crucially they could not bind post-marital property.[22] The settlements operated on the basis of equity, whereby, on marriage, a wife could retain a beneficial interest in the settled property, and so in principle the husband could not deprive his wife of this entitlement without breaching the trust imposed by the agreement.

Although marriage settlements could be beneficial to wealthy middle-class women, they did not resolve the disparity of treatment between men and women by the law. A wife who had married with a settlement was offered only equitable protection, which did not prevent the husband from exercising his common law right to appropriate his wife's income and savings.[23] In reality, therefore, marriage settlements gave married women very little financial power. Though wives could benefit from the income generated by their assets, they could not sell their property or contract with respect to it.[24] Worse still, marriage settlements were not an option for married women without substantial family capital,[25] who could either accept complete financial dependence on their husbands, or opt for divorce. Even the option of divorce was not a realistic alternative, as although men could petition on the ground of a single act of adultery, women had to prove that their case was one of 'aggravated enormity', which meant that their husbands must have been unfaithful and committed incest, bigamy, desertion or, in certain circumstances, cruelty.[26] Not only was it almost impossible for Victorian women to end their marriage, women were also under huge economic and social pressure to marry in the first place.[27] As Shanley explains, 'Legal rules, social practices and economic structures all worked together to induce a woman to marry, and then insured that once married she would be dependent upon and obedient to her husband.'[28] The dependence and obedience experienced by women at this time was exacerbated by coverture.[29]

This triggered a period of lengthy feminist campaigns, which challenged the injustices of the common law and what Shanley says Victorian feminists regarded as 'society's sentimentalization of family life',[30] in that there was a failure to acknowledge the harsh legal rules which focused property ownership and

[21] There is even evidence that marriage settlements were referred to as 'ante-nuptial agreements' in M Taylor, 'On the Conditions of Women as Affected by the Law' (1862) 10 *The English Woman's Journal* 124–27. This terminology mirrors the modern language of prenups.

[22] See Cretney, above n 8, 92.

[23] Ibid, 93.

[24] This is known as restraint on anticipation: see Stetson, above n 6, 58.

[25] See Cretney, above n 8, 93.

[26] Matrimonial Causes Act 1857, s 27; Cretney, above n 8, 167–68.

[27] In 1871 almost 90% of women between the ages of 45 and 49 in England were or had been married. See Shanley, above n 7, 10.

[28] Ibid.

[29] See also Dicey, who writes that the reality of coverture was that 'the daughters of the poor suffered under the severity and injustice of the common law'. AV Dicey, *Lectures on the Relation between Law and Public Opinion in England during the Nineteenth Century* (2nd edn, Macmillan 1962) 383.

[30] See Shanley, above n 7, 7.

economic power on the husband. The first group to instigate this challenge was the Langham Place Circle, which included Barbara Leigh Smith, a prominent activist for women's rights at this time.[31] This group argued for married women to have the same property rights as married men, and in 1857 it advanced two Married Women's Property Bills into Parliament, both of which were unsuccessful. Auchmuty explains that Langham Place Circle's campaign was halted when the Divorce and Matrimonial Causes Act 1857 was passed, because it was asserted at the time that 'happily married women did not need a law protecting their property from their husbands, while unhappily married women could [pursuant to the 1857 Act] obtain a divorce or judicial separation, and so achieve separation of property'.[32]

The work of Barbara Leigh Smith and her peers was followed by a surge in political activity surrounding the issue of married women's property rights. The formation of pressure groups,[33] pamphleteering[34] and the support of John Stewart Mill,[35] who was elected into the House of Commons in 1865, combined to assert formidable pressure on Parliament to introduce reform. The efforts of these groups were partially responsible for significant developments in the law applicable to married women's property, specifically the Married Women's Property Acts (MWPAs) of 1870 and 1882. Further impetus for this reform came from middle-class men who advocated for legislation that would eliminate the need for marriage settlements for their daughters, which was a costly process.[36] However, some commentators argue that greatest incentive for Parliament to introduce the MWPAs in 1870 and 1882 was to help women in poverty.[37] As Cretney writes, women who had been deserted by their drunken labourer husbands often had to relinquish their own earnings and rely on public assistance, because 'the tiny savings they had deposited for safety in a … Savings Bank [had been] seized by the husband in the exercise of his common law rights'.[38] As a result, it was a combination of different pressures and agendas that persuaded Parliament to pass the 1870 and 1882 Acts.[39]

The MWPA 1870 did not introduce separate property for husbands and wives, and fell significantly short of what feminist pressure groups had campaigned for.

[31] See P Hirsch, 'Bodichon, Barbara Leigh Smith (1827–1891)' in *Oxford Dictionary of National Biography* (OUP 2004), available at <http://www.oxforddnb.com/view/article/2755>.

[32] R Auchmuty, 'The Married Women's Property Acts: Equality Was Not Enough', in R Hunter (ed), *Rethinking Equality Projects in Law: Feminist Challenges* (Hart Publishing 2008) 21.

[33] For example the Manchester Circle and the Married Women's Property Committee. See Shanley, above n 7, 50–67.

[34] Auchmuty, above n 32, 21, notes the significant influence of Frances Power Cobbe's writing, for instance: F Cobbe, 'Criminals, Idiots, Women and Minors' in S Hamilton (ed), *Criminals, Idiots, Women and Minors: Victorian Writing by Women on Women* (Boardview Press 1995).

[35] John Stewart Mill published *The Subjection of Women* (1869), which, as Cretney explains, 'gave power and intellectual stimulus to the reform movement'. See Cretney, above n 8, 96.

[36] See Shanley, above n 7, 14.

[37] Ibid, 15.

[38] See Cretney, above n 8, 93.

[39] For a detailed history on this area, see L Holcombe, *Wives and Property: Reform of the Married Women's Property Law in Nineteenth Century England* (University of Toronto Press 1982).

It did not enable a married woman to control property as if she were single, and she had the legal right to remove only specific types of property from her husband's control.[40] The Act was therefore disappointing, because it did not give married women the independent legal personality for which they had fought.[41]

Against this background of inequality, the introduction of the MWPA 1882 was a triumphant victory for the property rights of married women, and was a significant step towards eradicating coverture altogether. The 1882 Act effectively replaced unity of spousal property in the husband's name on marriage, by introducing the doctrine of separate property for married couples, which still applies today. Thus, married women were no longer invisible in the eyes of the law, and could control their own property and earnings. This new legal status for women also meant that contracts between husband and wife would be recognised. It is important to note, however, that coverture was not completely removed by the 1882 Act, because although a proprietary claim could be made on a wife's separate property,[42] she could not be sued personally. Therefore, unlike men and single women, married women were not personally responsible for their own financial dealings.[43]

The absence of personal liability for married women was finally addressed during the early part of the twentieth century through the Law Reform (Married Women and Tortfeasors) Act 1935,[44] the Married Women (Restraint on Anticipation Act) 1949[45] and the Law Reform (Husband and Wife) Act 1962.[46] The 1935 reform was particularly significant, because it assimilated the rights of married and unmarried women in contract and tort for the first time. Essentially, the cumulative effect of this legislation was to ensure that the doctrine of separate property really meant separate property interests for spouses, and the doctrine of coverture could be put to rest. This development had a profound impact on the perceived utility of prenuptial-type agreements, as the removal of coverture also removed the need for marriage settlements. Yet the fact that marriage settlements (traditionally conceived) had become practically obsolete does not fully explain

[40] This included: money acquired through the exercise of literary, artistic or scientific skill (s 1); inherited money up to a limit of £200 (s 7); property which the wife had applied and had registered as separate property (ss 2–5).

[41] See Shanley, above n 7, 58; also Cretney, above n 8, 96.

[42] MWPA 1882, s 1.

[43] See Stetson, above n 6, 55.

[44] This Act provided that a married woman could deal with property, be liable, sue and be sued, and be subject to bankruptcy proceedings as if she were unmarried (s 1). It also provided that a husband would not be liable for his wife's torts or ante-nuptial contracts, debts and obligations (s 3).

[45] Prior to this Act, when property was settled on married women, they were restrained from anticipating it. This meant that for the duration of the marriage, they were prevented from disposing of the property, and could only benefit from the income generated by that property. The Married Women (Restraint on Anticipation Act) 1949 abolished this rule, so that married women had autonomy to manage their property as they saw fit.

[46] This Act supplemented and extended the rights of married women to sue their husbands in tort by providing that husbands and wives were to have a right of action in tort against the other as if they were not married (s 1).

why nuptial agreements (a slightly different beast from marriage settlements) were irrelevant for most of the twentieth century. A possible explanation is that agreements were relatively useless to wealthy husbands because the doctrine of separate property meant their wives had limited legal interest in their property anyway. As most wives also had little property of their own, the court refused to take notice of nuptial agreements in so far as they purported to contract out of support post-divorce.[47] Problematically, therefore, this series of legislative reform only addressed specific inequalities at common law. Although the blow to coverture dealt by the MWPA 1882 was a huge achievement for feminists in the late nineteenth century, for some women, keenly aware of their own structural and economic disadvantage in society, the effects of formal equality and separate property were to be feared, not welcomed.[48] Importantly, however, the realisation of formal equality was a crucial development in the economic relationship between husband and wife. Even though wives did not have the same opportunities to earn money as men did, married women first had to be able to *possess* property[49] before they could challenge the opportunities open to them to *acquire* it. In this way, Auchmuty explains that the feminists who sought to eradicate coverture did not accept the structural inequalities bound up in the unequal social roles of men and women. Rather, equal legal status was an important precondition of further change.[50]

The Effects of Separate Property Prior to the Matrimonial Causes Act 1973

Whilst the importance of the MWPA 1882 cannot be underestimated, husbands and wives' individual control over their property did not lead to economic equality within marriage. This is clear when examining the different outcomes for husband and wife on separation and divorce, which highlighted the need for laws which reflected the 'realities of social power structures'[51] contributing to economic hardship for divorcing women. The MCA 1973, which is still the source of our divorce laws, had a huge impact on the property interests of married women because it gave spouses the ability to acquire a share in their partner's property in order to become economically independent, without relying on their ex-spouses' support indefinitely. Examining the consequences of maintenance prior to the 1973 Act demonstrates the structural economic power that husbands historically have had over wives, and why reform was so important.

In the decades preceding the 1973 Act, married women were generally not free to work outside the home. In the 1950s, it was presumed that marriage would be

[47] In *Bennett v Bennett* [1952] 1 KB 249 the court explicitly stated that the law takes no notice of prenups.

[48] See Stetson, above n 6, 93.

[49] See Shanley, above n 7, 58.

[50] See Auchmuty, above n 32, 17.

[51] S Fredman, *Women and the Law* (Clarendon Press 1998) 15.

upper- and middle-class women's primary goal and occupation,[52] and so married women faced social pressure to leave their jobs and assume responsibility for household duties. Even in the 1960s, when the economy was expanding and women's educational opportunities were improving,[53] the range of career options available to women was limited because, as Auchmuty explains,

> training was thought to be wasted on a girl who was only going to give up work when she married. Many women were delighted to escape from a low-status, routine job into marriage, devoting themselves to further their husband's career, and though him their own economic and social standing.[54]

Women's lack of economic power outside the home was mirrored inside the family home. Husbands had an obligation to support their wives financially, because married men were able to earn money when married women generally could not, particularly when involved with child bearing and home making. This support was provided by maintenance, which gave the husband the upper hand, because wives were dependent on their support on separation and divorce. Furthermore, a wife's maintenance depended on her 'good' behaviour. In *M v M*,[55] for example, the wife was denied maintenance by the court because she had a child by a man who was not her husband 11 years after her marriage had broken down.[56] Ironically, she had divorced her husband on the ground of his adultery. But the husband's actions did not matter, as a *woman's* claim to matrimonial property was a moral right, not a legal one.[57]

The process of the provision of maintenance before the MCA 1973 also placed a significant burden on husbands,[58] because they were bound to provide lifelong support, making a true financial break impossible unless the wife remarried. The doctrine of separate property exacerbated this need for continuing support even more, by failing to recognise that married women were not free like men to work outside the home and acquire assets. If they had been, the burden on husbands to provide maintenance would undoubtedly have been reduced. But instead, women did not have the opportunity to claim an interest in shared assets like the marital home if those assets were in the sole name of the husband. Women could not even keep the housekeeping money they had saved during their marriage; it was considered to be the husband's property because it was paid from his wage.[59] Thus in

[52] As Auchmuty writes, '[u]p to the 1950s upper- and middle-class girls might properly have assumed that marriage was their only occupation': R Auchmuty, 'Law and the Power of Feminism: How Marriage Lost its Power to Oppress Women' (2012) 20(2) *Feminist Legal Studies* 71, 73.

[53] For instance, there was a significant increase in the number of women attending university: M Ingham, *Now we are thirty: Women of the breakthrough generation* (Eyre Methuen 1981) 100, cited in Auchmuty, above n 52, 73.

[54] See Auchmuty, above n 52, 74.

[55] *M v M* [1962] 2 All ER 895.

[56] See Smart, above n 3, 90.

[57] Ibid.

[58] See Cretney, above n 8, 372.

[59] See Smart, above n 3, 47. This was reformed by the MWPA 1964, which permitted wives in England and Wales to keep half of their housekeeping allowance (s 1). This Act was not extended to Northern Ireland.

practice, separate property disadvantaged divorced women and, as Smart explains, served to reinforce the financial vulnerability of women outside the family, as economic security could realistically be achieved only through remarriage or 're-entry into the patriarchal family structure that had in part created her insecurity'.[60]

The effects of the institutionalised inequality that resulted from separate property started to become apparent with changing economic conditions in the late 1930s and 1940s. The introduction of stringent rent controls preventing rent increases and tenancy terminations[61] led to a decline in the availability of rented accommodation, because property owners were deterred from leasing their property. This had a knock-on effect on those separated and divorced women who could have paid for rented accommodation using their maintenance payments, but who could not afford to purchase a new home. Furthermore, women generally did not have any interest in the marital home, as property tended to be in the husband's sole name[62] and the court could not transfer a share in the home to the wife on separation.[63] As Cretney writes, 'once a wife lost possession of a house, the process of acquiring another place to live could be painful and prolonged'.[64]

Given the paradoxical dependency created by separate property and the subsequent burden placed on husbands to maintain their wives, it is unsurprising that some couples resorted to private ordering by nuptial agreement. These agreements typically sought to prevent the wife from applying to the court for an award of maintenance from the husband.

Hyman v Hyman[65] is commonly referred to as the first substantial judicial commentary and precedent on issues relevant to prenups, even though a separation deed was the subject matter of the case. The separation deed was executed in 1919 and precluded Mrs Hyman from attaining maintenance above the amount stipulated in the deed.[66] When the agreement was made, Mr Hyman was living in adultery with another woman; however at this time the ground of adultery did not enable Mrs Hyman to petition for divorce unless an additional offence had been committed, such as bigamy or incest.[67] Being unable to divorce also meant

[60] See Smart, above n 3, 48.

[61] Rent and Mortgage Interest Restrictions Act 1939.

[62] Cretney explains that at this time, a building society would have been more likely to have the husband as the mortgagor. See Cretney, above n 8, 118. See also *Rimmer v Rimmer* [1953] 1 QB 63.

[63] See Cretney, above n 8, 118.

[64] Ibid, 119. In addition, owner-occupation began to increase rapidly, particularly from the 1950s onwards. However, acquiring property was more difficult for divorced women than for divorced men, because divorced women generally did not have enough capital on relationship breakdown. For statistics on owner occupation, see Office of National Statistics, 'A Century of Home Ownership and Renting in England and Wales' (2013), available at <http://www.ons.gov.uk/ons/rel/census/2011-census-analysis/a-century-of-home-ownership-and-renting-in-england-and-wales/short-story-on-housing.html>.

[65] *Hyman v Hyman* [1929] AC 601.

[66] The amount was £20.00 per week for life to the wife.

[67] Although the wife could not petition for divorce on the ground of adultery, the husband could petition on the ground of adultery by the wife.

the validity of Mr and Mrs Hyman's separation deed could not be considered in court.

After the MCA 1923 was introduced, which equalised the grounds of divorce to enable women *and* men to divorce on the ground of adultery alone,[68] Mrs Hyman was finally able to petition for divorce in 1926. In 1929, the wife's case reached the House of Lords, and the principal issue was whether the covenant limiting her maintenance should be upheld. The Law Lords decided that the agreement was invalid because, Lord Atkin said, any agreement limiting provision on divorce would be contrary to public policy due to a risk that parties could be made dependent on the state.[69] Lord Atkin also held that agreements seeking to control the powers of the court to make appropriate financial provision on divorce would be invalid.

Over 20 years later, Denning LJ (as he then was) reiterated Lord Atkin's reasons against enforcing nuptial agreements in *Bennett v Bennett*.[70] It was not in the public interest for a divorced husband to agree to a level of support which would leave his ex-spouse dependent on the state if he had the means to provide for her.[71] Even if a divorced wife were to receive an adequate level of financial support on divorce, Denning LJ said prenups potentially could induce the parties to separate later.[72] Lastly, the powers of the court to award maintenance should not be constrained, and a divorced wife should not be denied the opportunity to apply to the court for support from her ex-husband. As Denning LJ said:

> When husband and wife are separated or divorced, it is often found that they have entered into a deed whereby the husband covenants to pay his wife an annuity and she in turn covenants not to apply to the courts for maintenance … there is nothing wrong in the husband's covenant to pay the annuity … but there may be something wrong … in the wife's covenant not to apply to the courts.[73]

The concerns articulated by the higher courts in *Hyman* and *Bennett* have been labelled in later judgments as public policy objections to prenups,[74] and interestingly, as we saw in chapter one, these objections have influenced the enforcement

[68] That is, without an additional aggravating factor. For more detail on the context of this Act, see R Probert, 'The controversy of equality and the Matrimonial Causes Act 1923' (1999) 11(1) *Child and Family Law Quarterly* 33.

[69] At this time state assistance was governed by the Poor Relief Acts. Specifically, if a wife did not receive maintenance at the time *Hyman* was decided, Poor Law Guardians would have become responsible for her sustenance (*Hyman v Hyman* [1929] AC 601, 608). Poor Law Guardians governed Poor Law Unions, which administered poor relief pursuant to the Poor Law Amendment Act 1834.

[70] See *Bennett*, above n 47.

[71] When *Bennett* was decided, the Welfare State had been introduced in the UK, and state assistance would have been provided pursuant to the National Assistance Act 1948, which abolished the poor law previously referred to at n 69.

[72] See *Cartwright v Cartwright* (1853) 3 de GM & G 982; *H v W* (1857) 3 K & J 382.

[73] See *Bennett*, above n 47, 260.

[74] For instance *Radmacher v Grantino* [2010] UKSC 42.

of such agreements until relatively recently, in spite of changes in social, legal and political attitudes to marriage and divorce.

At the same time as Denning LJ delivered his judgment in *Bennett*, pressure was beginning to build for reform of financial provision on divorce.[75] Edith Summerskill recalls her own experiences of this change as a Labour MP in her memoirs, which reveal a great deal about attitudes (particularly male) towards the property rights of married women at this time.[76] Lady Summerskill campaigned with the Married Women's Association to improve these rights, the necessity of which was demonstrated by stories like that of Mrs Blackwell. As Lady Summerskill recounted:

> Mrs Blackwell was a hard-working housewife, who by taking in lodgers strove to help her husband to pay off the mortgage of their house. She was a thrifty woman; she shopped at the Co-op and left her dividends to accumulate; and over sixteen years of married life they totalled £103. Then the marriage broke up and Mrs Blackwell left home taking her savings: subsequently Mr Blackwell applied to the County Court for the savings to be transferred to him and the application was successful.[77]

In 1943 the Married Women's Association financed Mrs Blackwell's appeal, which was dismissed.[78] The Court of Appeal held that she should not be allowed to keep her savings, in spite of her economic management of the home, because according to Lady Summerskill, one of the judges said, '[i]f we permitted a woman to save out of the housekeeping allowance, and keep the proceeds, then women would be tempted to give their husbands tinned meat rather than roast meat'.[79] Interestingly, this attitude mirrors the male response to the Married Women's Property Act almost 60 years earlier, where fears were expressed that power to control their own property would transform women from kind and loving wives into domestic tyrants.[80] It is also worrying that these fears can be traced into some modern-day attitudes, which consider prenups to be weapons against 'gold-digging' wives.[81]

However, in Mrs Blackwell's case, what if she *had* entered into a nuptial agreement which made provision for her to keep the savings from her housekeeping allowance? Lord Justice Goddard considered this, and said that '[e]ven if there had been an arrangement between the husband and wife with regard to these savings, I am far from saying that this sort of domestic arrangement can necessarily result in a legal contract'.[82] As Lord Atkin held in *Balfour v Balfour*, a domestic arrangement

[75] The same year *Bennett v Bennett* was decided, a Private Member's Bill entitled the Married Women's Disabilities Bill was introduced in the House of Commons. This Bill proposed reform to prevent a husband from defaulting on his maintenance payments, by requiring his employer to pay the wife directly. It also included a clause which enabled further provision for the wife on divorce, including protection to counteract the hardship experienced by wives who had been forced to leave the marital home.

[76] E Summerskill, *A Woman's World* (Heinemann 1967).

[77] Ibid, 144.

[78] *Blackwell v Blackwell* [1943] 2 All ER 579.

[79] See Summerskill, above n 76, 144.

[80] According to Lady Summerskill, this remark was made by Mr Walton MP: ibid, 149.

[81] See discussion in ch 1.

[82] See *Blackwell*, above n 78, 580 (Goddard LJ).

between husband and wife could not have contractual force because there was no intention to create legal relations.[83] If an agreement between the Blackwell spouses had been made by deed, however, Mrs Blackwell might have been able to keep her savings.[84]

Throughout the 1950s, the campaigns to remedy the injustice experienced by women like Mrs Blackwell led to increased recognition of the shortcomings of the law, with academics such as Ferdynand Zweig arguing that 'real equality of status [between husband and wife] could be attained only if a woman who is staying at home could also become at least partly independent in economic terms'.[85] To become independent, however, would require reform. In 1956, the report of the Royal Commission on Marriage and Divorce highlighted this issue,[86] and in 1964 a Private Member's Bill introduced by Lady Summerskill was passed, which led to the enactment of the Married Women's Property Act. This Act enabled women to save their housekeeping allowance and keep a one half share of it,[87] which was a significant step towards further reform extending the property entitlements of married women. An awareness of the inadequacies of the existing law for the economically weaker spouse led the newly formed Law Commission[88] to report on the matter of reform in 1966,[89] and subsequently the Divorce Reform Act 1969 and Matrimonial Proceedings and Property Act 1970 were introduced. Importantly, the Divorce Reform Act was delayed whilst groups such as the National Council of Women of Great Britain insisted on financial safeguards that would assist those likely to suffer financially.[90] After all, women's economic situation at the end of marriage was a major reason why reform was considered to be necessary in the first place.[91] As a result, the Government was able to diffuse opposition to the 1969 Act only by introducing the 1970 Act to address the financial consequences of divorce.[92]

The 1969 and 1970 Acts were consolidated in the MCA 1973, which provides the legal framework for divorce and ancillary relief today. The legislation gave the judiciary extensive powers to make property adjustment between spouses on divorce, and also changed the fault-based grounds of divorce to a single ground

[83] *Balfour v Balfour* [1919] 2 KB 571, 579–580.

[84] Lady Hale said that the parties' contractual intent could have been expressed (which would circumvent the principle in *Balfour v Balfour*, see above n 83) if the agreement had been made by deed: see *Radmacher*, above n 74, [142].

[85] F Zweig, *Women's Life and Labour* (Gollancz 1952) 155.

[86] F Morton, *Report of the Royal Commission on Marriage and Divorce 1951–1955* (Cm 9678, 1956)

[87] MWPA 1964, s 1.

[88] The Law Commission was created as a result of the Law Commissions Act 1965.

[89] Law Commission, Reform of the Grounds for Divorce—The Field of Choice (Law Com No 6, 1966).

[90] BH Lee, *Divorce Law Reform in England* (Peter Owen 1974) 100; Cretney, above n 8, 373.

[91] See Cretney, above n 8, 372.

[92] Lady Summerskill was a prominent opponent of the 1969 Act. She argued in Parliament that reforming the grounds for divorce whilst neglecting to reform financial provision on divorce would create a 'Casanova's Charter', which would leave wives in an extremely vulnerable situation economically. See Cretney, above n 8, 373; *Official Report* (HC) 12 June 1969, vol 784, col 2034.

of irretrievable breakdown.[93] Establishing that the marriage had irretrievably broken down no longer required proof of a matrimonial offence (ie adultery), as parties would be able to divorce after two years' separation with consent,[94] or five years separation without consent.[95] Though this reform was controversial at the time, it also significantly enabled, as the Law Commission put it, 'the decent burial with the minimum of embarrassment, humiliation and bitterness of those [marriages] that are indubitably dead'.[96] But the Act not only added further grounds for divorce, it also transformed the financial consequences of divorce in a way that vastly improved the economic position of spouses (particularly wives) on relationship breakdown.

Financial Provision Under the Matrimonial Causes Act 1973

Financial provision previously depended on the good and moral behaviour of the spouses. In particular, the wife could lose her right to maintenance if she committed adultery, even after having separated from her husband.[97] But the 1973 Act moved away from this assessment of financial provision based on conduct to a consideration of the needs of the parties post-divorce. This also meant that more couples were able to petition for divorce without having to attribute blame first.

The MCA 1973 provides the judiciary with broad discretionary powers to award financial relief on divorce. Crucially, the legislation recognises the significance of domestic work in the home as a contributing factor in its own right towards the value of marital property.[98] Women no longer suffer the fate of Mrs Blackwell, who (Lady Summerskill recalled) was not entitled to a penny after 16 years of work for her family:

> She was a pathetic little figure in her basement room when I visited her in London, where she worked as a waitress in a restaurant. She was helpless and hopeless, a victim of a legal system which still in the twentieth century treats the wife as a chattel of her husband.[99]

Under the 1973 Act, Mrs Blackwell would not have been a victim of the legal system; her work *would* have been recognised by the court, and property adjustment could have been made accordingly. However, whilst the significance of this should not be underestimated, when the 1973 Act was first introduced, financial provision

[93] MCA 1973, s 1(1).
[94] Ibid, s 1(2)(d).
[95] Ibid, s 1(2)(e).
[96] See Law Commission, above n 89, para 1.5.
[97] See, eg, *M v M*, above n 55.
[98] Specifically s 1(2)(f), which includes 'the contributions which each of the parties has made or is likely in the foreseeable future to make to the welfare of the family, including any contribution by looking after the home or caring for the family'.
[99] See Summerskill, above n 76, 145.

on divorce was still characterised by gendered assumptions based on the perceived dependence of wives on their husbands.[100]

This was plainly evidenced by the minimal loss principle, which originated from the Matrimonial Proceedings and Property Act 1970 and said that, when awarding ancillary relief, the court should consider whether parties could be placed

> so far as it is practicable and, having regard to their conduct, just to do so, in the financial position in which they would have been if the marriage had not broken down and each had properly discharged his or her financial obligations and responsibilities towards the other.[101]

The effect of this provision was to enforce an obligation of life-long financial support, which endured even when the marriage itself did not. Enshrined within this legislative target was the entrenched assumption that once married, the husband had undertaken a duty to support his wife for life. As Singer says, however, the minimal loss objective was unattainable,[102] particularly for husbands with financial responsibilities in subsequent marriages, who did not have the means to maintain their estranged wives.[103] On the other hand, the minimal loss principle could be viewed as a response to an increased awareness of the economic effect of divorce on women at the time, as the principle aimed to ensure that wives receiving ongoing spousal support would not face the same levels of financial hardship they had experienced previously. As Smart puts it, '[t]he courts as a whole … [had] come to recognise that the division of labour in the family adversely affects the economic viability of women, particularly when they have children'.[104]

Yet, unsurprisingly, this approach was not favoured by second-wave feminist groups like the Women's Liberation Campaign for Legal and Financial Independence,[105] who argued that the law's assumption of women's economic dependency only served to perpetuate it.[106] Men's groups, like the Campaign for Justice on Divorce, felt the minimal loss principle was unfair too. And so in 1980, the Law Commission recommended that the minimal loss principle should be removed.[107]

Instead, ancillary relief should be awarded on the basis of whether or not a clean break could be implemented according to the circumstances of each case,

[100] A Diduck, and F Kaganas, *Family Law, Gender and the State* (2nd edn, Hart Publishing 2006) 519.

[101] Matrimonial Proceedings and Property Act 1970, s 5(1).

[102] P Singer, 'Sexual Discrimination in Ancillary Relief' (2001) 31(2) *Family Law* 115.

[103] Law Commission, The Financial Consequences of Divorce: the Basic Policy (Law Com No 103, 1980).

[104] See Smart, above n 3, 113–14. See also Cretney, above n 8, 133–37, for a discussion of the impact of women's groups, which informed the opinion of the Archbishop of Canterbury's group *Putting Asunder* and the Law Commission. This subsequently highlighted the importance of reform of married women's property rights.

[105] See Stetson, above n 6, 251.

[106] This view did not represent the opinion of all feminist groups. As Smart explains, there was (and still is) a tension between those who argue for the equality of women and men so that wives do not have special legal privileges, and those who acknowledge that legal intervention is sometimes necessary in order to protect more vulnerable members in the household sphere: see Smart, above n 3, 226.

[107] See Law Commission, above n 103.

which would allow each spouse to become self-sufficient.[108] The Matrimonial and Family Proceedings Act 1984 inserted this consideration into the MCA 1973, as follows:

> [I]it shall be the duty of the court to consider whether it would be appropriate so to exercise those powers that the financial obligations of each party towards the other will be terminated as soon after the grant of the decree as the court considers just and reasonable.[109]

To achieve a clean break, the court could, for example, order a lump sum to be paid instead of periodical payments. This approach represents a clear shift away from the dependency reinforced by the minimal loss principle, towards the ideal that spouses should be independent and autonomous on divorce. However, the realities of marriage and divorce exposed the difficulties with economic self-sufficiency and autonomy as a result of a clean break. At the time the provision was implemented, a clean break was not a realistic option for families with children, or in situations where only one spouse had an income, unless of course the family was exceptionally wealthy and could satisfy a substantial lump sum order. A policy which assumed independency and autonomy on divorce did not reflect inequalities within the marriage, such as the division of labour between husband and wife, childcare responsibilities and social issues such as the gender pay gap.[110] As Symes put it in 1985:

> [O]nly when a radical change in the marital relationship takes place, when it becomes a partnership of two economically independent individuals through the abolition of marital dependency and when the corresponding changes in the social infrastructure are brought about, will there be any chance of formulating a coherent, clean break divorce law.[111]

It was clear that policies based on minimal losses or clean breaks would not work if they failed to recognise the true economic positions of husband and wife on divorce, and to address economic dependencies *without* reinforcing them. Fortunately, the wide discretion to make appropriate financial provision gave the court flexibility to make an award it considered to be appropriate. But aside from directions for the court to give first consideration to any child of the marriage under 18 and to consider whether a clean break could be achieved, the legislation did not stipulate any overall objective which the court should seek to achieve when exercising its discretion. The MCA 1973 does, however, contain a number of provisions that relate to this discretion, which were inserted by the 1984 Act and are still applicable today. Section 25 of the 1973 Act is of particular importance to

[108] Amendments were also made to s 25 that required the court to give first consideration to the welfare of any child of the family younger than 18.

[109] MCA 1973, s 25A (inserted by the Matrimonial and Family Proceedings Act 1984).

[110] At this time, some second-wave feminist groups campaigned for 'Wages for Housework', which would provide women with direct payment for domestic labour. See Stetson, above n 6, 252.

[111] P Symes, 'Indissolubility and the clean break' (1985) 48(1) *MLR* 44, 60.

the ancillary relief process, as it outlines the following matters which the court should have regard to when exercising its discretion to make financial adjustment on divorce:[112]

(a) the income, earning capacity, property and other financial resources which each of the parties to the marriage has or is likely to have in the foreseeable future, including in the case of earning capacity any increase in that capacity which it would in the opinion of the court be reasonable to expect a party to the marriage to take steps to acquire;
(b) the financial needs, obligations and responsibilities which each of the parties to the marriage has or is likely to have in the foreseeable future;
(c) the standard of living enjoyed by the family before the breakdown of the marriage;
(d) the age of each party to the marriage and the duration of the marriage;
(e) any physical or mental disability of either of the parties to the marriage;
(f) the contributions which each of the parties has made or is likely in the foreseeable future to make to the welfare of the family, including any contribution by looking after the home or caring for the family;
(g) the conduct of each of the parties, if that conduct is such that it would in the opinion of the court be inequitable to disregard it;
(h) in the case of proceedings for divorce or nullity of marriage, the value to each of the parties to the marriage of any benefit which, by reason of the dissolution or annulment of the marriage, that party will lose the chance of acquiring.[113]

The court balances these statutory factors on the basis of its discretion to make financial provision orders (section 23), property adjustment orders (section 24) and orders for the sale of property (section 24A) on divorce.

To reiterate, Parliament did not set out how each factor should be applied by the court when evaluating financial relief.[114] This has been developed in the courtroom, and so, as the law of ancillary relief is found in the case law, the important cases in this area must be explored.

Judicial Discretion to Award Financial Provision (Ancillary Relief)

Judicial opinion has influenced the operation of ancillary relief more than anything else, as financial provision depends on how the judge exercises his or her discretion. When considering the conceptual basis of divorce, that is, why assets

[112] Inserted by the 1984 Act.

[113] The Pensions Act 1995 included additional power for the court to consider the value of spouses' pensions on divorce, and accordingly the court could make pension-sharing orders where appropriate.

[114] See *Piglowska v Piglowski* [1999] 1 WLR 1360, 1370 (Hoffman LJ): '[Section] 25(2) … while listing the various matters to which particular regard should be had, does not rank them in any kind of hierarchy. Which of them will carry most weight must depend upon the facts of the particular case.'

should be distributed between spouses in a particular way, there has been a huge diversity of judicial approach. Though the starting point of this assessment is now the House of Lords decision in *White v White*,[115] prior to this case the judiciary was primarily concerned with section 25(2)(b) of the MCA 1973, which directs the court to consider the financial needs, obligations and responsibilities of the parties to the marriage. This approach meant that paragraph (b) of section 25(2) was at the centre of the judiciary's assessment, even though need is only one of eight matters which must all be balanced according to the particular circumstances of the case. But in the absence of any overarching objective, prioritising needs gave the court a starting point from which to work.[116] This approach was expressed by Ormrod LJ in *Preston v Preston*[117] as meeting the 'reasonable requirements' of the parties, which usually meant that provision awarded to the wife simply fulfilled her needs and nothing more. Unfortunately for the wife, this interpretation became entrenched in common law, as judges treated 'reasonable requirements' as being the touchstone of financial provision on divorce.

One obvious advantage of channelling judicial discretion in a way that prioritises need is that in most cases on divorce, assets are in limited supply, and so property must be divided in a way that eliminates as much economic hardship post-divorce as is possible. On the other hand, even if need was generously interpreted to ensure the non-moneyed spouse received adequate provision on divorce, in 'big money'[118] cases the main income provider would usually retain the lion's share[119] of property on divorce because he 'earned' it. Clearly, therefore, ancillary relief at this time was influenced by what Diduck refers to as a

> language of paternalism/welfare that reinforced the values and obligations of the traditional patriarchal family in which the breadwinner was obliged post-separation simply, in effect, to continue his pre-separation marital obligation to support reasonably his dependants.[120]

By the year 2000 the reasonable requirements approach was no longer favoured in academic and judicial commentary.[121] Financial support that was based on

[115] *White v White* [2000] UKHL 54.

[116] When the MCA 1973 was first introduced, in the absence of an underlying principle the courts adopted a fractional approach; see Cretney, above n 8, 430. This meant that wives' awards were usually limited to one-third of the total assets, pursuant to *Wachtel v Wachtel* [1973] EWCA Civ 10. The one-third approach was justified by Lord Denning MR, who argued that the husband should receive more because he would have a continuing obligation to support his former wife financially. Lord Denning MR also believed that the husband would incur more expense than the wife after the relationship had broken down, whilst he wife, on the other hand, could find another husband to support her; and if she did obtain work, she would not need to employ a housekeeper because she could do the housework herself.

[117] *Preston v Preston* [1982] Fam 17.

[118] This term was employed in *White*, above n 115, to describe cases where parties' wealth exceeds their need for housing and income.

[119] E Cooke, '*White v White*: A New Yardstick for the Marriage Partnership' (2001) 13 *Child and Family Law Quarterly* 81.

[120] A Diduck, 'What is Family Law For?' (2011) 64 *Current Legal Problems* 287, 287.

[121] See Singer, above n 102; *Dart v Dart* [1996] 2 FLR 286 (Gibson LJ).

and limited to dependency only really served to buttress economic inequality in marriage, as limiting the non-moneyed spouse's award to reflect his or her need frequently led to a huge disparity of outcome on divorce. Sociological research has repeatedly found that women are usually more economically vulnerable than men on divorce,[122] and the limitations on provision created by the 'reasonable requirements' approach did not ameliorate this problem. Furthermore, financial provision made entirely on the basis of need could produce paradoxical outcomes in lengthy marriages,[123] as the Law Commission explains: 'An applicant might actually receive less after a long marriage than after a short one, because the older divorcee, with consequently a lower life expectancy, had a lower level of "reasonable requirements" when these were capitalised.'[124]

Thus, projections of the amount needed by the non-moneyed spouse in order to maintain his or her lifestyle on divorce were often inflated. This meant that in big money cases, the level of award was often based on an artificial assessment of the parties' need. This was arguably not compatible with the section 25 factors either, which were not intended by Parliament to assume any hierarchy of importance.[125] Need is not the dominant consideration in section 25, and when spouses' assets are surplus to their needs, other important factors (such as the standard of living enjoyed by the parties, and the contributions made by the parties) merit thorough and equal consideration.[126]

The reasonable requirements approach was also symbolically flawed. By refusing provision to the non-moneyed spouse beyond need, ancillary relief awards were made to parties based on their de facto economic contribution to the marriage—thus the breadwinner received the left-over bread because he or she had provided it in the first place.[127] This approach is arguably misguided, because in reality the breadwinner is usually only able to contribute financially due to the non-financial support of his or her partner in the home. Failing to recognise this was perceived as gender discrimination,[128] because the non-financial contributions made by wives were not compensated on divorce. This also meant that the husband (who was usually the main financial provider in 'big money' cases) received *more* than his reasonable requirements,[129] when the only way for the wife

[122] J Herring, 'Why Financial Orders on Divorce should be Unfair' (2005) 19 *International Journal of Law, Policy and the Family* 218.

[123] This is often known as the 'Duxbury paradox', named after the case *Duxbury v Duxbury* [1992] Fam 62, where this outcome was reached.

[124] See Law Commission, above n 4, para 2.31.

[125] A Diduck, 'Fairness and Justice for All? The House of Lords in *White v White* [2000] 2 FLR 981' (2001) 9 *Feminist Legal Studies* 173.

[126] However, it should be noted that a generous approach to need was adopted. As such, these factors were usually considered as provided for incidentally when reasonable requirements were met.

[127] Examples of cases illustrating the 'glass ceiling' created by the reasonable requirements approach are *Dart*, above n 121; *Conran v Conran* [1997] 2 FLR 615; *A v A (Financial Provision)* [1998] 3 FCR 421.

[128] See Singer, above n 102.

[129] For instance, in *Dart v Dart* [1996] 2 FLR 286, the husband was worth an estimated £400 million on divorce, but the wife was awarded only £8.5 million and was ordered to pay the husband's costs.

to accumulate a share in the assets beyond that which met her needs was for her to show that she had made an exceptional contribution to the acquisition of such assets.[130] The worrying parallels between this approach and historical patriarchal views influencing financial provision were not unnoticed by Singer, who saw new concepts being forced into old stereotypes, 'where the expectation was that the former wife would be, as it were, pensioned off with an allotment sufficient to meet her requirements, a dowager put out to graze.'[131]

Although there was clearly discomfort with the reasonable requirements approach at the turn of the century, this approach was not jettisoned until *White v White* reached the House of Lords. In this case, Mr and Mrs White were farmers and business partners who had assets of approximately £4.6 million. Mr White held the majority of the assets,[132] and the award of ancillary relief made to Mrs White was £800,000 at first instance,[133] which was increased to £1.5 million[134] by the Court of Appeal. On appeal, the Law Lords decided that Mrs White's award should not be increased, but significantly they abandoned the reasonable requirements approach. Consideration of the contrasting *ratio decidendi* at each stage of the proceedings in *White v White* is demonstrative of the seminal shift which took place in the House of Lords. The sum of £800,000 was initially awarded in recognition of the amount required to meet Mrs White's reasonable requirements. Yet the appellate court noted that this application of principle was illogical, as it meant that Mrs White received less as a business partner and wife of 34 years than she would have received had she been a business partner and nothing more.[135] However, recognition of such absurdity did not outlaw the reasonable requirements approach: the increase to £1.5 million reflected Mrs White's role in the business rather than her role in the marriage. This led Cooke to ask:

> What of the spouse who is not legally a partner, as Mrs White was, but makes just as much practical contribution to the business? Will the courts be astute to spot that contribution? And what of the wife who has no opportunity to engage in the family business—she has not the skills, or she and her husband have, in happier times, been well content for her to be the homemaker?[136]

Prior to the House of Lords decision, the answer was that the wife in these scenarios would still only receive an award calculated to meet her reasonable requirements. Crucially however, the House of Lords decided that assets should be divided differently in recognition of the different types of contribution noted by Cooke. Thus their Lordships reasoned that Mrs White should be entitled to the £1.5 million award, even if she had not been involved in the business. The marriage alone was

130 *Gojkovic v Gojkovic* [1990] 1 FLR 140.
131 See Singer, above n 102.
132 Specifically 96% (4% of the assets were in Mrs White's sole name).
133 This award represented 17% of the total assets.
134 This represented 32% of the total assets and a percentage increase of 15% from first instance.
135 See *White v White* [1999] Fam 304, 312 (Thorpe LJ).
136 See Cooke, above n 119.

enough to generate such entitlement, and the fact that the Whites were business partners was incidental to Mrs White's overall entitlement. Thus Mrs White's award was not increased, although the reasoning for her award was different because it was not based on reasonable requirement. By eliminating the reasonable requirements approach, it was no longer necessary to attempt to distinguish need from reasonable requirement; instead, *White v White* introduced an entirely new approach to ancillary relief. The decision meant that parties' entitlement is not only defined by their need and financial contribution. Rather, parties' entitlement is generated by taking part in the joint enterprise of marriage, or as Lady Hale later said, by 'sharing the fruits of the matrimonial partnership'.[137] As a result, in big money cases the non-moneyed spouse is entitled to a share of the surplus assets in recognition of his or her contribution (financial and non-financial) to the partnership, instead of in recognition of his or her dependency or need. However, ousting the reasonable requirements agenda meant the Lords had to identify a new starting point when considering how property should be divided. For Lord Nicholls, the answer to this issue was 'obvious'—that 'the outcome ought to be as fair as is possible in all the circumstances'.[138]

Recognition that ancillary relief provision should be based on fairness is not revolutionary in itself. Indeed, provision reflecting each spouse's reasonable requirements arguably reflected the judiciary's perception of the fairest outcome on divorce at that time. However, the revolutionary aspect of *White v White* was that Lord Nicholls attached a new meaning to fairness. Whilst recognising that different judges may have different views as to what fairness requires, he decided that fairness within the context of financial provision under the MCA 1973 could be achieved through the application of two principles: non-discrimination and equality. This statement of principle was significant for two reasons: it was the first time the Law Lords had considered how the discretion conferred by the 1973 Act was to be applied on divorce; and the new principles effectively wiped the slate clean by ruling out the line of precedent before *White*.

This meant a new start when interpreting section 25 in big money cases. In *White v White* and the cases that followed it, the judiciary attempted to outline the new approach as clearly as possible. This must be considered in order to understand how prenups are given effect by the court in the UK.

Non-discrimination and Equality

According to the Law Lords in *White*, fairness cannot be achieved without a clear stance against discrimination between the respective roles of husband and wife during the marriage. As Lord Nicholls explained, '[i]f, in their different spheres, each contributed equally to the family, then in principle it matters not which of

[137] See *Miller; McFarlane*, above n 5, [154].
[138] See *White*, above n 115, [1].

them earned the money and built up the assets'.[139] As a result, husband and wife should be reimbursed for their investment in the relationship. This reimbursement does not depend on the means of investment, and so parenting, homemaking and breadwinning roles should be viewed as being equally valuable to the success of the marriage. The reasonable requirements approach did not equally value each role—thus it was eliminated because it was discriminatory. Diduck notes that prior to *White v White*, the value of non-financial contribution was implicitly undermined because the court failed to fully recognise the balance of contribution made inside and outside the home.[140] This failure was discriminatory, and so the introduction of the non-discrimination principle ensured that the value of home-making and child care would not be underestimated in future. Therefore, eliminating discrimination required dissolving the reasonable requirements approach as it did not coincide with the House of Lords' idea of fairness.

Whilst this was an important development in the law of ancillary relief, Diduck has said it was not really radical for the Law Lords to associate fairness with non-discrimination. However, it *was* radical, she says, to decide that non-discrimination could only be achieved through equality.[141] Importantly, reference to equality did not mean the Lords were advocating an automatic 50:50 division of property on divorce. Equal division had been rejected previously by Parliament[142] and the judiciary.[143] Furthermore, equal division is not only inconsistent with the separate property ideology of the UK; it resembles a community property regime,[144] which, though prevalent in Continental jurisdictions, is not part of UK law. As a result, the equality principle introduced by *White v White* promotes equitable, not equal, distribution on divorce. Application of this principle is intended to give equal weight to the respective contributions to the marriage of husband and wife, whilst also attempting to ameliorate inequities between parties post-separation by giving each party what Lady Hale calls an 'equal start on the road to independent living'.[145]

In practice, this means the court must check its decision against a yardstick of equality to ensure that the principles of non-discrimination and substantive equality are adhered to. Lord Nicholls emphasised that the application of the

[139] Ibid, [24].

[140] A Diduck, 'Dividing the Family Assets' in S Sclater and C Piper (eds), *Undercurrents of Divorce* (Ashgate 1999) 230.

[141] See Diduck, above n 125.

[142] The Law Commission of England and Wales issued a report in 1973 which considered whether a community of property system should be implemented. The Commission concluded that it should not, but recommended automatic joint ownership of the family home. Parliament did not implement this recommendation: Law Commission, *Family Law: First Report on Family Property—A New Approach* (Law Com No 52, 1973).

[143] N Wilson, 'Ancillary Relief Reform: Response of the Judges of the Family Division to the Government Proposals (made by way of submission to the Lord Chancellor ' s Ancillary Relief Advisory Group)' (1999) 29(3) *Family Law* 159.

[144] The distinction between community property and separate property was explained in ch 1.

[145] See *Miller; McFarlane*, above n 5, [144].

yardstick of equality does not create a presumption of equal division, as this would 'be an impermissible gloss on the statutory provision'.[146] This is because a presumption of equal division would oust the discretionary jurisdiction granted to the court by section 23 of the 1973 Act, and thus would be incompatible with Parliament's intent under the legislation.[147] Nevertheless, whilst a presumption was not introduced, the equality principle did mean that the court should provide 'good reason' if equality was departed from on divorce. The good reason which justified an unequal split in the *White v White* case was the fact that a large proportion of the assets held by Mr White had been inherited by him.

However, as Eekelaar noted, *White* did not clarify exactly what would justify a departure from equality,[148] and so subsequent case law had to answer this question. Since *White*, the reasons articulated by the court justifying unequal division are usually that the marriage has been short, or that one party owns non-matrimonial property. Non-matrimonial property includes assets acquired before the marriage, or through gift or bequest. The court has also considered unequal division when one party has made an outstanding contribution to the total pool of assets through his or her talent and success.[149] As later sections of this chapter will show, after *White* the judiciary also began to view prenups as a reason to depart from equality, but unless and until Parliament makes such agreements binding under legislation, ancillary relief principle still has some influence on their enforcement. In particular, the three strands of fairness developed after *White* remain significant to prenup cases.

The Three Strands of Fairness

The conjoined case of *Miller v Miller; McFarlane v McFarlane* was the Law Lords' next opportunity to consider ancillary relief procedure at the highest level.[150] They redefined the concepts of equality, non-discrimination and fairness by specifying three sub-categories to be taken into account, referred to as the 'three strands of fairness': need, compensation and sharing.

[146] See *White*, above n 115.

[147] It is for this same reason that Lady Hale considered the decision of the majority to enforce prenups presumptively to be incompatible with the 1973 Act, in *Radmacher*, above n 74.

[148] J Eekelaar, 'Back to Basics and Forward into the Unknown' (2001) 31(1) *Family Law* 30.

[149] *Cooper Hohn v Hohn* [2014] EWHC 4122; *Lambert v Lambert* [2002] EWCA Civ 1685; *G v G (Financial Provision: Equal Division)* [2002] EWHC 1339 (Fam); *H v H (Financial Provision-Special Contribution)* [2002] 2 FLR 1021. It is doubtful that a spouse will successfully prove exceptional non-financial contribution, although there must be potential for different forms of exceptional contribution, as an entirely financial conception of contribution would risk the gender discrimination the courts have sought to avoid: *Charman v Charman* [2007] EWCA Civ 503. However, as Thorpe LJ has said, this could lead to the 'invidious comparison' of business contributions to a spouse's care for a child or spouse who is disabled: *Cowan v Cowan* [2001] EWCA Civ 679, [166].

[150] See *Miller; McFarlane*, above n 5.

Need

Meeting the needs of the parties is an important part of every ancillary relief case, but in the absence of any overarching objective, the judicial interpretation of need has been uncertain and unpredictable. And understandably so, as an assessment of needs in a case involving few assets is based on compromise;[151] but where spouses have lived an affluent lifestyle, an assessment of needs is likely to be much more subjective. This lack of clarity is problematic when understanding the enforcement of prenups, which may be set aside if the needs of the parties are not met.

The complex matter of what needs are was addressed by the Law Commission, which described needs as encapsulating income needs, housing needs and future needs.[152] To meet income needs, the court often makes periodical payments orders when one party has left work during the marriage.[153] By making this provision, the court recognises that it is often difficult to re-enter the labour market after a lengthy period of absence from it. The housing needs of the parties are also very important, and so the court will often prioritise division of the capital value of the marital home. For owner-occupiers,[154] resolving ownership of the home is usually one of the most important issues on divorce, because it is often the main or only asset of value.[155]

Another important aspect of housing needs considered by the court is the ability for each party to have a mortgage loan. Something the courts will strive to do, but cannot always be successful in doing, is to prevent the parties from becoming dependent on state benefits. Spouses' future needs are also an important consideration, and the court might order the value of a spouse's pension to be shared in order to ensure such needs are met.

In spite of this, the judiciary's evaluation of needs is unpredictable and, at times, inconsistent. In *Miller; McFarlane*, for example, Lord Nicholls considered that the judiciary should adopt a broad view of needs arising within and independently of the marriage,[156] but Lady Hale argued that needs should be restricted to those generated by the marriage.[157] This difference in opinion has not been resolved,

[151] In *Milller; McFarlane*, Lord Nicholls said that '[i]n most cases fairness begins and ends at this stage [because] … the available assets are insufficient to provide adequately for the needs of two homes'. Ibid, [12].

[152] See Law Commission, above n 4, para 2.28.

[153] Periodical payments orders require payment to be made in instalments to the party in whose favour the order has been made. The court has discretion to order payment to be made for the period it considers appropriate. This kind of order does not achieve a clean break.

[154] Recent statistics show that the number of owner-occupiers in England is at its lowest since the 1980s, at 14.3 million or 65.2% (Department for Communities and Local Government, *English Housing Survey 2012–2013: Household Report* (2014), para 1.15).

[155] Particularly since the recent rise in house prices in the UK: S O'Connor, 'Regional housing price disparities increased following the economic downturn' (Office of National Statistics, 28 May 2014), available at <http://www.ons.gov.uk/ons/rel/hpi/house-price-index/march-2014/sty-regional-house-prices.html>.

[156] See *Miller; McFarlane*, above n 5, [26].

[157] Ibid, [138].

and it is unclear how long these needs must be provided for after divorce. Whilst each party must try to live independent of support after divorce, pursuant to the clean break principle, this is not always possible, and so need, as Lady Hale has said, 'is a convenient shorthand for a rather more complicated concept'.[158]

Compensation

The second strand of fairness, compensation, has been described by the Law Commission as an extension of need.[159] Indeed, it is difficult to identify whether an order has been made under the compensation heading, or whether the provision is simply representative of a generous interpretation of need. The purpose of the compensation strand is to ameliorate, as far as possible, the economic disparities which may arise on divorce, or to compensate for relationship-generated disadvantage.[160] This strand is a development of the *White* principles of non-discrimination and equality, in that it highlights disparities that may not have been noticed before this case. Often the homemaking spouse has not had the same opportunities to earn as much as the moneyed spouse, and the financial disadvantage she would have suffered on divorce as a result of the court's approach to financial provision before *White* was discriminatory.

A problem with the compensation strand is that it is unclear how it interacts with need. Distinguishing between need and compensation is confusing, as disadvantage is often compensated for when need is met.[161] Indeed, the Law Commission believes compensation has perhaps always been part of needs-based provision.[162] Therefore, considering compensation separately means that need may be considered more narrowly as a result of the compensation strand.

Another issue when interpreting the compensation strand is how far the courts should compensate one spouse for loss of opportunity at the expense of the other. Eekelaar argues that speculation as to the value of one party's hypothetical alternative life will often be inappropriate: either because such valuation would be arbitrary, or because that party might not have led the 'alternative life' had he or she not married his or her partner.[163] Clearly, the uncertainties stemming from this approach have meant that the compensation principle has been treated with caution by the courts. In *Miller; McFarlane*, Mrs McFarlane's periodical payments order was extended by the House of Lords to last for the rest of her lifetime. This order was made to compensate her for the disadvantages she incurred by giving up an extremely lucrative career and an income which at one time far surpassed that

[158] See *Radmacher*, above n 74, [187].

[159] Law Commission, Matrimonial Property, Needs and Agreements: A Supplementary Consultation Paper (Law Com No 208, 2012), para 2.18.

[160] See *Miller; McFarlane*, above n 5, [140].

[161] Lord Nicholls referred to this as double counting: ibid, [15].

[162] See Law Commission, above n 4, para 2.56.

[163] J Eekelaar, 'Property and Financial Settlement on Divorce—Sharing and Compensating' (2006) 36(9) *Family Law* 754.

of her husband. However, since this case the courts have been reluctant to award compensation to a wife who has given up her career to undertake homemaking or parenting roles.[164] Thus compensation will be awarded only in exceptional circumstances.[165] Application of the need principle is usually viewed as adequate compensation for any disparity of financial outcome on divorce.

Sharing

The sharing strand is arguably most indicative of the change brought about by *White v White*, as it embodies the concepts of non-discrimination and equality. Importantly, it is also the strand of fairness out of which a prenup may contract.

The sharing strand of fairness is an extension of the equality principle developed by *White*. Although the Law Lords in *Miller; McFarlane* said this emphasis on sharing did not make equal division on divorce a rule, Cretney has said that the sharing principle developed the yardstick of equality into a starting point,[166] and he speculated as to whether the UK has now adopted a community property system in all but name.[167] The judiciary has insisted that this is not the case.[168] There are some fundamental differences between the community property system and our system of ancillary relief, the most pertinent distinction being the discretion afforded to the judiciary under the 1973 Act. In community property jurisdictions, financial provision on divorce is made according to the rules of the property regime in place; but as noted previously, there is no property regime in the UK. Furthermore, the House of Lords in *Miller; McFarlane* emphasised the importance of flexibility to make appropriate provision on divorce, and this flexibility does not exist in a community property system. Lastly, community property jurisdictions define exactly what types of property should be divided: the sharing principle does not—it is simply another judicial tool to assist in the ancillary relief exercise.

When applying the sharing principle, the judge should consider whether there is non-matrimonial property that would justify a departure from equal division. This has proved to be problematic, as defining non-matrimonial property is often an onerous task, particularly if during a long marriage, non-matrimonial assets have become intertwined with marital assets. In *Miller; McFarlane*, Lord Nicholls said that the distinction between matrimonial and non-matrimonial property is less relevant in longer marriages, thus the fusion of assets that may take place over time will not necessarily be problematic,[169] and in these cases, all assets are susceptible to the sharing principle. The distinction will be more pertinent in short

[164] *CR v CR* [2007] EWHC 3334 (Fam); *VB v JP* [2008] 1 FLR 742.

[165] This was explicitly stated by Mostyn J in *SA v PA (Pre-marital agreement: Compensation)* [2014] EWHC 392 (Fam) [36].

[166] S Cretney, 'Community of Property Imposed by Judicial Decision' (2003) 119 *LQR* 349.

[167] Ibid.

[168] See *Miller; McFarlane*, above n 5, [151] (Baroness Hale); see also *Radmacher*, above n 74, [107] (Lord Phillips).

[169] See *Miller; McFarlane*, above n 5, [23].

marriages, where it may be easier to categorise the different types of property. However, the protection and entitlement afforded by the sharing principle may also be necessary to achieve fairness in short marriages, particularly if there are children in the marriage. Thus to achieve fairness, an application of the sharing principle will depend on the circumstances of the parties. Indeed, Lady Hale has said it is fairer for some assets to be kept separate in dual career partnerships where the parties have made a conscious effort to separate their property.[170] The court in *Charman v Charman* also considered that the future approach of the judiciary to ancillary relief may accord with how the parties have agreed to hold property during the marriage.[171] The nexus between this view and the changing attitudes towards prenups is obvious—both show a shift towards priority being given to autonomy and the intentions of the parties.

An understanding of the three strands of fairness is also important when examining the court's assessment of prenups, as in *Radmacher v Granatino* the Supreme Court Justices considered these principles to be relevant to the fairness of the agreement.

Prenuptial Agreements and the Three Strands of Fairness

Although the detail of the *Radmacher* decision has already been explored, the judgment also provided clear guidance as to precisely how the judge should consider a prenup as part of the ancillary relief exercise. An outcome that the court considers to be fair when a prenup is in place is of course different from what the court would consider to be fair in the absence of an agreement. But the fairness assessment still relies, to an extent, on the three strands of fairness articulated in *Miller; McFarlane*, though they are applied differently in cases where there is no prenup.[172]

Of the need, compensation and sharing strands, Lord Phillips said the needs of the parties should be met. He also said if a spouse is entitled to compensation, the compensation strand should apply. However, the Supreme Court has said that by signing a prenup, the parties have implicitly contracted out of sharing each other's property, and so the sharing principle should not apply. Therefore, if a prenup is in place, it will be enforced unless the court concludes that the needs of the parties have not been sufficiently met.[173] How need will be assessed by the court in these cases is not entirely clear. In *Radmacher*, Lord Phillips said that an agreement could not leave a party in the position of 'real need', suggesting that 'need' will

[170] Ibid, [150].

[171] See *Charman*, above n 149, [86].

[172] S Thompson, 'Radmacher v Granatino [2010] UKSC 42' (2011) 33(1) *Journal of Social Welfare and Family Law* 61.

[173] This includes provision for the needs of any child of the marriage. Thus a prenup cannot evade the court's discretion to make an order that considers the welfare of minor children. See also the Child Support Act 1991, which gives the court power to make ancillary relief provision with respect to relevant children.

be assessed more conservatively than if there is no agreement. However, it is not apparent how much a prenup will limit the interpretation of need. This lack of clarity indicates that such an agreement does not necessarily avoid the uncertainty surrounding the three strands of fairness.

Still, considering the particular facts of *Radmacher* provides some guidance on how the three strands are applied, and also emphasises that fairness as understood for a prenup is different from the concept of fairness in *Miller; McFarlane*. That is, the majority said specifically that *full* compensation is not part of the fairness test; and in any case there was no compensation factor to consider in *Radmacher*, as Mr Granatino's change of career 'reflected his own preference'.[174] The fairness strand of 'sharing' was also deemed irrelevant by the Court (and thus not considered to be part of the fairness test for prenups), as the existence of the agreement indicated that the husband had renounced any share in the wife's wealth. Lastly, it was concluded that the husband was not in a situation of real need, therefore it was not necessary to make provision in consideration of this strand of fairness either.

In her dissenting opinion, Lady Hale considered the *Miller; McFarlane* strands of fairness on a different basis. She did not apply the sharing principle due to a lack of matrimonial assets (the couple had not acquired any property together), rather than because Mr Granatino had waived his entitlement on divorce. Furthermore, she was not persuaded that the compensation principle could not apply because Mr Granatino's change of career was a personal choice—his decision could have been 'taken for the good of the family as a whole'.[175]

Cases since *Radmacher* have reinforced the approach of the Supreme Court, in that the sharing strand will not apply to the ancillary relief assessment when a prenup has been entered into. When enforcing the prenup in *Z v Z (No 2)*,[176] the court limited the wife's provision to meet her reasonable needs, and so departed from equal sharing.

As a result of these consequences, an awareness of financial provision on divorce is essential in order to appreciate what a couple is capable of contracting out of by signing a prenup. Another reason why it is important to understand the approach of the courts towards financial provision is that there appears to be a direct causal link between dissatisfaction with awards made on divorce (particularly awards made on the basis of equal sharing) and a greater push for prenups to carry more weight on divorce.[177]

Reform of Financial Provision

Cases like *Charman v Charman* (where the wife was awarded £48 million) have been used by the press as evidence that the assets of the moneyed spouse

[174] See *Radmacher*, above n 74, [121].
[175] Ibid, [194].
[176] *Z v Z (No 2)* [2011] EWHC 2878 (Fam).
[177] See Law Commission, above n 4, para. 3.58.

would be imperilled should the couple decide to divorce.[178] Yet these reports fail to convey the judiciary's reasoning for making these awards, and that changing the law in *White v White* was a positive move against gender discrimination.[179] Instead, newspapers like *The Times* have described the Law Lords in *Miller; McFarlane* as 'hammering a rich husband simply to fund an ex-wifes lavish lifestyle'.[180] This perpetuates the very assumptions their Lordships sought to move away from in *Miller; McFarlane*, whereby matrimonial property does *not* belong only to the spouse who has directly earned it, whilst the other spouse must establish a share in that property. Rather, the matrimonial property is viewed as belonging to *both* parties, because in the court's view it has been acquired as a result of financial and non-financial contributions. Eekelaar asserts that the misconception that the husband is unfairly deprived of his property on relationship breakdown has the propensity to 'be exploited by those who believe that the law excessively favours wives and that it undermines marriage'.[181] This fear has provoked the media and the wealthy to press for binding prenups that are able to contract out of a law they do not view as being fair. But those who view the *White* approach to ancillary relief as being inherently unfair are missing the point. Unless there are relevant children who must be provided for, a non-moneyed spouse in a short marriage will not have generated enough entitlement to share equally in the fruits of his or her partner's achievements. The concept of sharing epitomises the nature of marriage itself; a joint enterprise that requires the input of both parties to bear fruit. Thus recognising non-financial contributions empowers women because they are viewed as entitled to share in the assets because of their equal role in the relationship, not just because they are needy or dependent. From this perspective, it is difficult to sympathise with parties who enter prenups to deprive the non-moneyed spouse of an entitlement on divorce.

The court's approach to financial provision in the UK has also been criticised for being uncertain, as since *White v White* it is often difficult to predict the outcome in big money cases. According to Morley, the fairness standard employed on divorce is 'purposefully vague, almost indefinable and completely subjective'.[182]

[178] N Britten, '£48 million for my ex-wife is grotesque and I'm going to fight it, says magnate', *Telegraph* (London, 4 August 2006), available at <http://www.telegraph.co.uk/news/1525533/48million-for-my-ex-wife-is-grotesque-and-Im-going-to-fight-it-says-magnate.html;> Baroness Deech also cited *Charman v Charman* when criticising the effect of the equal sharing principle: Baroness Deech of Cumnor, 'What's a Woman Worth? The maintenance law' (The Gresham Lectures, 13 October 2009), available at <http://www.gresham.ac.uk/lectures-and-events/what%E2%80%99s-a-woman-worth-the-maintenance- law>. See E Saner, 'The myth of the kept woman', *Guardian* (London, 19 September 2009), available at <http://www.theguardian.com/lifeandstyle/2009/sep/19/divorce-settlements-law-deech> for opinion on the reaction of the press to high-profile divorce settlements.

[179] See Law Commission, above n 4, para 3.57.

[180] D Rowan, 'Til dosh do us part', *The Sunday Times* (London, 9 October 2005), available at <http://www.ejfi.org/family/family-25.htm>.

[181] J Eekelaar, '*Miller v Miller*: the Descent into Chaos' (2005) 35(11) *Family Law* 870.

[182] J Morley, 'Enforceable Prenuptial Agreements: Their Time Has Come' (2006) 36(9) *Family Law* 768.

This is problematic for couples trying to bargain in the shadow of the law.[183] Furthermore, the lack of clarity often means high court costs. Morley describes ancillary relief as being 'not unlike entering a casino, except that some games of chance have a more predictable result and the "house" percentage in a casino is modest when compared to the enormous legal fees in a high-stakes, big assets divorce case'.[184]

It is most difficult to predict how the court will apply the three strands of fairness and, specifically, how the strands will be applied to non-matrimonial property in each case. This is because the case law insists that whilst inherited, pre-acquired and gifted property will be less susceptible to equal sharing, the court will not ring-fence it from the ancillary relief exercise. *Charman v Charman* provides some guidance on this matter, as it stated that non-matrimonial property is generally not shared unless it is required to meet needs.[185] However, case law indicates that there are two different ways of reaching this outcome. *Robson v Robson*[186] argued that even if there is non-matrimonial property, all property is susceptible to division, though the non-matrimonial property may give reason to depart from equality. But *Jones v Jones*[187] disagreed, and said that non-matrimonial property should be taken out of the pot of assets before the remaining property is shared equally. The second approach is considered to be clearer, and has been endorsed by the Law Commission of England and Wales, as it generates more predictable results.[188] Nevertheless, the ambiguities in this area demonstrate that applying the three strands of fairness can sometimes be an arbitrary exercise. Furthermore, since legal aid has been removed for private family law cases,[189] financial provision cases which go to court are potentially catastrophic for those who cannot afford legal representation. Litigants in person must attempt to navigate complex principles underlying the law on financial provision, which are not set out in statute and, as we have seen, require a detailed understanding of case law.[190]

The uncertainty surrounding financial provision orders is also problematic in the context of prenups. As the Supreme Court has said that a prenup cannot

[183] That is, to make agreements knowing what a judge would order on divorce in the absence of an agreement.

[184] See Morley, above n 182.

[185] See *Charman*, above n 149.

[186] *Robson v Robson* [2010] EWCA Civ 1171.

[187] *Jones v Jones* [2011] EWCA Civ 41.

[188] Law Commission, *Matrimonial Property, Needs and Agreements: A Supplementary Consultation Paper* (Law Com No 208, 2012).

[189] Legal Aid, Sentencing and Punishment of Offenders Act (LASPO) 2012.

[190] Reports of the consequences of litigants in person have been reported in B James, 'Unintended Consequences of Family Justice Reform' (Family Law Week, 27 June 2014), available at <http://www.familylawweek.co.uk/site.aspx?i=ed130634>. The Judicial Executive Board's evidence to the Commons Justice Select Committee's enquiry into the effect of LASPO also details the negative effects of the cuts in legal aid: Judicial Executive Board, Written evidence from the judicial executive board (MSC 84, April 2014), available at <http://data.parliament.uk/writtenevidence/committeeevidence.svc/evidencedocument/justice-committee/impact-of-changes-to-civil-legal-aid-under-laspo/written/9472.html>.

prevent the needs of the parties being met, the concept of needs must be ascertainable so that parties know what they can and cannot contract out of. The Law Commission recognised this issue, and in its report on marital property agreements it recommended that the concept of needs should be made clearer and that the Family Justice Council should produce guidance on the meaning of 'financial needs'.[191] Though this guidance has not yet been produced, the Government is taking this recommendation forward.[192] It is not clear, however, whether the Law Commission's recommendations regarding qualifying nuptial agreements (as discussed in chapter one) will be implemented; but if they are, it would mean that needs would be the *only* strand of fairness that could not be contracted out of.

Conclusion

An awareness of how the economic relationship between spouses has changed, and how attitudes towards the property interests of spouses on divorce are determined, is important when understanding the current ethos of financial provision on divorce. As this chapter has explored, the property interests and financial power of married men and women has historically been characterised by inequality, often resulting in economic hardship for women. This has corresponded with a system of financial provision that did not address women's needs on divorce, or produce equal outcomes for husbands and wives. In the Victorian era, when the struggle of married women was at its worst, marriage settlements, which were similar to prenups in many ways, were women's only means of economic independence. Today, married women's economic situation is completely different, as is their level of participation in the workplace. Furthermore, women's financial independence is strengthened by the judiciary's recognition of non-financial contributions made in the home, which means that the value of domestic labour is acknowledged, thus enabling women to be economically independent on divorce. At the same time, however, the status of prenups has gone through significant change, and these agreements are now given effect so that couples can avoid having a judge decide how their property will be divided on divorce. Whether this emphasis on individual power and autonomy is for better or for worse is a valuable but complex enquiry.

It is not possible to explain definitively why judicial attitudes towards financial provision on divorce have developed in the way they have, but a number of different phases are apparent in the cases and approaches explored in this chapter. Prior to *White v White*, the reasonable requirements approach championed

[191] Law Commission, *Matrimonial Property, Needs and Agreements* (Law Com No 343, 2014), para 9.1

[192] Ministry of Justice, 'News Release: Divorce Myths to be Dispelled' (17 April 2014), available at <http://lawcommission.justice.gov.uk/docs/lc343_matrimonial_property_government_initial_response.pdf>.

the clean break principle by artificially prioritising needs above other section 25 considerations. But *White v White* signalled the beginning of a new mind-set, which recognised the entitlements generated by non-financial contributions to the family. Though *White* is still the leading authority in ancillary relief proceedings, there has been some speculation as to whether financial provision is beginning to enter a new 'post-*White*' phase due to a series of cases which return to a pre-*White* assessment. One of the main devices for enabling the *White* principles to be side-stepped has been the prenup, whereby, in cases such as *Z v Z (No 2)*, the court has ruled that enforcement of the agreement requires a pre-*White* assessment of needs.[193]

Indeed, exceptions to equal sharing in big money cases are becoming increasingly common, which George has identified as a 'broader pattern of retreat from the non-discriminatory approach demanded by *White*'.[194] The reduction in the protection of equality and sharing, together with the increased emphasis on private ordering by prenups, is, according to Eekelaar, evident of a policy he calls 'directed self-help'.[195] With escalating court costs and cuts to legal aid in private family law cases,[196] prenups are much more politically appealing than before, as they shift the responsibility of deciding the economic consequences of marriage on to the parties themselves. This may also be partly why the perceived need to respect couple's autonomy to enter a prenup has gained so much momentum in recent years, particularly as these agreements were relatively recently only one part of the ancillary relief procedure, yet now more or less determine the economic outcome for parties on divorce.

The development of financial provision on divorce has been conceptualised by Diduck as a change in discourse or, as she puts it, as a shift from a language of equality and rights towards a language of autonomy and individualism.[197] The latest predilection for individual choice is clearly not so new when it refers back to pre-*White* approaches, and is, as Diduck says, 'infused with traditional family discourse as much as … with equality/rights'.[198] This implication that traditional norms are seeping into current attitudes suggests that the old liberal ideas of formal equality, which historically have masked gender disadvantage within the family, are coming to the fore through ideas of individualism and autonomy. This is particularly problematic where issues of power between parties to a prenup are not recognised and addressed. As chapter one explained, prenups are increasingly

[193] See *Z v Z (No 2)*, above n 176.

[194] R George, 'Family Finances and the Corporate Veil: *Prest v Petrodel*' (2013) 43 (8) *Family Law* 991, 994. As part of this broader pattern, George refers to *Prest v Petrodel* [2013] UKSC 34, *Jones v Jones* [2011] EWCA Civ 41 and *Imerman v Tchenguiz* [2010] EWCA Civ 908, in addition to *Radmacher* (above n 74).

[195] J Eekelaar, 'Then and Now—Family Law's Direction of Travel' (2013) 35(4) *Journal of Social Welfare and Family Law* 415, 424.

[196] See *Q v Q; Re B (A Child); Re C (A Child)* [2014] EWFC 31 for a detailed discussion by Sir James Munby of the impact cuts in legal aid have had on family law.

[197] See Diduck, above n 120, 287.

[198] Ibid.

being given effect where there has *not* been independent legal advice or full disclosure of assets, even though the choice to enter into such an agreement is clearly influenced by these factors. But even if the choice of the non-moneyed spouse has arguably been affected, the agreement, perhaps ironically, is enforced on the basis of autonomy. What this means in reality, however, is that the choice of the moneyed spouse, who is usually the husband, is prioritised.[199] He can choose to contract out of the sharing principle, which also means contracting out of the concepts of equality and non-discrimination this principle represents. This is of especial concern for the spouse who has made non-financial contributions to the family through childcare or otherwise during the marriage. By ring-fencing the assets of the moneyed spouse, a prenup can potentially ignore the value of this unpaid work, which George, Harris and Herring view as 'remarkable':

> There are few, if any, other areas of law where a person can engage in gender discrimination because the other person has consented to the treatment. For so long, marriage has been a vehicle for oppression and disadvantage for women, and it is unfortunate that, so soon after having amended the law on ancillary relief so that marriage can be a tool for protecting women's interests, the court should allow men to create agreements which remove that protection.[200]

It is indeed alarming that the substantive equality achieved by *White* can be taken away by a prenup, particularly if the 'autonomy' on which such an agreement is assumed to be based is actually a smokescreen for inequality of power. Importantly, however, this does not mean that prenups must inevitably be perceived as permitting gendered economic oppression between spouses. If a different view of autonomy is employed, whereby the court takes into account the context in which the agreement is signed, and the circumstances and relationship of the parties involved, a prenup could empower the non-moneyed spouse to secure terms that do not limit her award. If this is possible, it is preferable to the protection provided by *White*, because, as Auchmuty puts it, '[p]rotection is not the best way forward for women; what we need is a world where they never find themselves in this kind of predicament in the first place, and we are well on the way to achieving this'.[201]

If women can use prenups to counteract what appears to be an increasingly apparent trend towards economic inequality on divorce, the protection and achievements established in *White v White* are not undermined. To ascertain whether this is possible, it is first necessary to examine the results of empirical research to understand how prenups are enforced in practice, and how attitudes in practice influence the way autonomy and power are and could be conceived.

199 See also A Murray, 'Are our Higher Courts Prejudiced against the Role of the Married Woman? The Need for Reform' (2013) 43(1) *Family Law* 66.

200 J Herring, P Harris and R George, 'Ante-nuptial agreements: fairness, equality and presumptions' (2011) 127 *LQR* 335, 338.

201 See Auchmuty, above n 52, 84.

3

Attorneys' Experiences of Prenuptial Agreements in New York

In 2010 I travelled to New York to interview attorneys about their experience of prenups. This chapter considers the results of this research, which provides an empirical basis for the issues of power that have been examined so far. Drawing on New York practitioners' in-depth experience of prenups produces a valuable comparative perspective that can inform approaches to such agreements in the UK, where there is much less experience of them because historically the court has not attributed much weight to them. A comparative approach can also be a valuable means of exploring ways to reform the law. Even in the absence of reform, it helps to perceive legal issues in a different and often more nuanced way. Indeed for practitioners, the increased globalisation of the legal world means that knowledge of the law in other jurisdictions can be essential. As Lord Steyn observed in *MacFarlane v Tayside*:

> [T]he discipline of comparative law does not aim at a poll of the solutions adopted in different countries. It has the different and inestimable value of sharpening our focus on the weight of competing considerations. And it reminds us that the law is part of the world of competing ideas markedly influenced by cultural differences.[1]

The purpose of a comparative approach is not to transpose the problems and experiences of prenups in New York onto the UK. Rather, the aim is to find out more about issues of power affecting prenups and the long-term effects of these agreements in a jurisdiction where they are routinely enforced, whilst acknowledging the differences between these two jurisdictions.

Why New York?

New York City is synonymous with the rich, and for good reason, as reports state that one of the highest concentration of billionaires in the world live there.[2] Therefore, it is unsurprising that some of the most famous nuptial agreements

[1] *Macfarlane and Another v Tayside Health Board* [2000] 2 AC 59, 81.

[2] C Poladian, 'Billionaires' homes around the world: New York City houses 103 of the richest people on the planet', *International Business Times* (1 October 2014), available at <http://www.ibtimes.com/pulse/billionaires-homes-around-world-new-york-city-houses-103-richest-people-planet-1697132>.

have been created and litigated in New York by individuals like Donald Trump, whose efforts to protect his assets by signing a postnup with his first wife are public knowledge.[3] As a result, New York is an ideal location for an empirical and qualitative study of prenups, because it proffers a rich experience of them. The system of financial provision on divorce in New York also shares many similarities with that in the UK, in that it is based on the courts' discretionary assessment of the circumstances of the case and is guided by a list of statutory factors. Before considering these factors in more detail, it is important to note that not all states in the United States (US) are like New York, as there are no federal laws governing financial provision on divorce in the US and each state has its own rules. These rules differ according to the theory of financial provision applied in each jurisdiction, which is usually based on equitable distribution or community property.

Community property does not operate in New York, but it is the default system of financial provision in nine states, including Washington, California and Texas. It applies when a prenup has not been used to alter the financial consequences of divorce, which means that on relationship breakdown, each spouse retains a one-half interest in all marital property. This includes property acquired during the marriage, but excludes gifted and inherited property. States where community property applies were not chosen for the study because prenups function differently in these jurisdictions than they do in the UK. That is, whilst prenups are used to opt out of an automatic division of assets in community property jurisdictions, in the UK these agreements are used to prevent the court from deciding how spouses' assets will be allocated on divorce.

On the other hand, the system of equitable distribution is similar to the process under which financial provision orders are made in the UK. It is the basis of property redistribution in 41 states, including New York, and typically centres on the exercise of judicial discretion according to a list of statutory factors. The statutory factors in New York are especially comparable to the applicable law in the UK (specifically, section 25 of the MCA 1973). These factors to which the court must have regard are listed in the Domestic Relations Law section 236 Part B, as follows:

1. The income and property of each party at the time of the marriage, and at the time of the commencement of the action;
2. The duration of the marriage and the age and health of both parties;
3. The need of a custodial parent to occupy or own the marital residence and to use or own its household effects;
4. The loss of inheritance and pension rights upon dissolution of the marriage as of the date of dissolution;
5. Any award of maintenance;
6. Any equitable claim to, interest in, or direct or indirect contribution made to acquisition of such marital property by the party not having title, including joint efforts or expenditures and contributions and services as a spouse, parent, wage earner and homemaker, and to the career or career potential of the other party;

[3] *Trump v Trump* 179 AD 2d 201 (New York 1992).

7. The liquid or non-liquid character of all marital property;
8. The probable future financial circumstances of each party;
9. The impossibility or difficulty of evaluating any component asset or any interest in a business, corporation, or profession and the economic desirability of retaining such asset or interest intact and free from any claim or interference by the other party;
10. The tax consequences to each party;
11. Wasteful dissipation of assets by either spouse;
12. Any transfer or encumbrance made in contemplation of a matrimonial action without fair consideration;
13. Any other factor which the court shall expressly find to be just and proper.

The court is required to take the first 12 factors into account. The purpose of the thirteenth statutory factor is as what Schechter has called a 'catchall' provision, in solution to a political impasse when the equitable distribution law was passed.[4] The role of fault with regard to property distribution on divorce was mooted by the legislators, and factor 13 represents a compromise so that conduct that shocks the conscience of the court (egregious fault) may be taken into account. Thus, the effect of these specific requirements listed in section 236 is that there is less judicial discretion on divorce in New York than there is in the UK, because the provisions of the former jurisdiction are more prescriptive whilst the latter jurisdiction provides the judge with power to consider all the circumstances of the case.[5]

However, whilst the judiciary might have more discretion in the UK, the basis of equitable distribution in New York is the same: fairness. Another similarity is that equal division is not an automatic outcome, as the New York court has explained that 'although plaintiff's contributions as a homemaker are indeed worthy of full consideration, there is no requirement that the distribution of each item of marital property be on an equal or 50-50 basis'.[6]

The law on prenuptial agreements in New York is inextricably linked to the default rules on financial provision, because it is these rules that a prenup purports to contract out of. The status of prenups in New York is also dependent on the wider context of nuptial agreements in the US, which is examined in the following section.

The Law of Prenuptial Agreements in the United States

Traditionally, agreements regulating spouses' property on death were enforceable but agreements providing for divorce were not. Ellman believes this was expected given that divorce was granted only in limited circumstances; it was based on fault and required the consent of both parties.[7] Prenuptial agreements were also viewed

[4] S Schechter, *New York Family Law* (2nd edn, Delmar Cengage Learning 2006) 266.

[5] MCA 1973, s 25(1).

[6] *Arvantides v Arvantides* 64 NY 2d 1033 (New York 1985).

[7] I Ellman, 'Marital Agreements and Private Autonomy in the United States' in J Scherpe (ed), *Marital Agreements and Private Autonomy in Comparative Perspective* (Hart Publishing 2012) 411.

as being contrary to public policy for encouraging divorce and therefore destabilising the institution of marriage.[8]

Attitudes towards prenups were reformed with the introduction of no-fault divorce in the US in the 1970s. As the stigma attached to divorce dissipated, previous hostilities towards such agreements also faded. The turning point for prenups was in 1970, with a case that could perhaps be viewed as America's *Radmacher*.[9] *Posner v Posne*r declared that the enforcement of prenups on divorce was no longer contrary to public policy:

> With divorce such a commonplace fact of life, it is fair to assume that many prospective marriage partners ... might want to ... agree upon, if possible ... the disposition of their property and the alimony rights of the wife in the event their marriage, despite their best efforts, should fail.[10]

This represents the modern stance on prenups in the US. Every state has made prenups enforceable since this decision, through case law or legislation. Initially states followed what Bix called 'the fairness approach',[11] whereby courts scrutinised the procedural and substantive fairness of agreements at the time of signing and enforcement. However, the trend towards enforceability became quite clear when the National Conference of Commissioners of Uniform State Laws enacted the Uniform Premarital Agreement Act (UPAA) in 1983. As Bix observes, though the provisions of the Act at first appear to be influenced by the fairness approach, their effect makes vitiation of prenups much less likely. In short, prenups were assimilated to a much greater extent with 'normal' contracts made in the course of business.

At the time the study examined in this chapter was carried out, the UPAA had been introduced in 31 states[12] but New York had not subscribed to the legislation.[13] But even though the uniform premarital agreement laws are not directly applicable in New York, the study revealed that the provisions in the UPAA are used as a guide in practice. Thus, some noteworthy elements of the UPAA will be briefly outlined. Pursuant to section 6(a)(1) of this Act, voluntariness is a procedural requirement of enforcement, which, as Ellman notes, 'imposes a test for premarital agreements that goes beyond what is required by standard doctrines, such as duress, that apply to all contracts'.[14] The spouse challenging the prenup must show that that the agreement was not executed voluntarily in order for it to be set aside, although the meaning of 'voluntariness' is not defined in the Act. However, the UPAA also

[8] B Atwood, 'Marital Contracts and the Meaning of Marriage' (2012) 54 *Arizona Law Review* 11, 22; *McCarthy v Santangelo* 78 A 2d 240 (Connecticut 1951).

[9] *Radmacher v Granatino* [2010] UKSC 42.

[10] *Posner v Posner* 257 So 2d 530 (Florida 1972).

[11] B Bix, 'Bargaining in the Shadow of Love: The Enforcement of Premarital Agreements and How We Think About Marriage' (1998) 40 *William and Mary Law Review* 145.

[12] Most recently: Mississippi, Missouri, South Carolina and West Virginia.

[13] Since the study, the UPAA was amended in 2012 by the Uniform Premarital and Marital Agreements Act (UPMAA).

[14] See Ellman, above n 7.

requires disclosure of assets,[15] and the disclosure of this information assists in persuading the court that an agreement was made voluntarily because it is assumed that knowledge of each another's assets indicates an understanding in part of the effect of an agreement. Still, the disclosure requirement does not provide as much protection as one might have thought. The UPAA allows the right of disclosure to be waived, and also requires spouses wishing to challenge an agreement to show that they 'did not have, or reasonably could not have had, an adequate knowledge of the property or financial obligations of the other party'.[16] In addition, a claim of non-disclosure will not be successful unless it is coupled with proof that the agreement was unconscionable.[17] Unconscionability in itself is difficult to prove as it requires a high degree of unfairness,[18] and so the operation of these provisions indicates that those seeking to set aside a prenup have an onerous burden of proof. Ellman summarises the difficulties as follows:

> [N]either non-disclosure nor unconscionability alone will affect the agreement's validity. Indeed, the waiver provision in … the UPAA creates the stunning possibility that an unconscionably unfair agreement could be enforced against a party who was uninformed because he or she waived disclosure, because having lost the non-disclosure objection to the agreement, he or she necessarily also loses the unconscionability objection.[19]

At least three states have amended the language of the UPAA after adopting it so that disclosure and unconscionability are separate requirements.[20] However, it is clear that the UPAA advocates strict enforcement of prenups. There is no requirement in the Act that parties entering an agreement obtain independent legal advice. As a result, even though it may seem that the UPAA has several protective requirements enabling a prenup to be set aside, in reality, an agreement made in a state which has adopted the UPAA will be enforced rigorously.

In the summer of 2012, the Uniform Law Commission in the US approved the Uniform Premarital and Marital Agreements Act (UPMAA), which amends the UPAA slightly. Though it still does not require the parties to obtain independent legal advice, parties must at least have had access to independent legal representation. To fulfil this requirement, it must be established that parties had adequate time to consider whether to obtain independent legal advice. There must also have been enough time for parties to find a lawyer and consider the advice provided. In addition, the UPMAA adds a requirement that was not in the UPAA, for each party to disclose its property value and income. This means that parties must make a good faith attempt to provide accurate financial disclosure. Lastly, the Act provides that an agreement can be set aside if the agreement was unconscionable

[15] UPAA, s 6(a)(2)(i).
[16] Ibid, s 6(a)(2)(iii).
[17] UPAA, s 6(a)(2).
[18] B Atwood, 'Ten Years Later: Lingering Concerns about the Uniform Premarital Agreement Act' (1993) 19(2) *Journal of Legislation* 127.
[19] See Ellman, above n 7.
[20] Ibid.

when signed *or* if financial disclosure was inadequate, instead of requiring evidence of both as the UPAA did. However, the meaning of 'unconscionability' is not defined in the Act.[21] At the time the interviews for the study were carried out, the UPMAA had not been introduced, and so practitioners' references to the uniform laws on prenups are in relation to the UPAA.

The Law of Prenuptial Agreements in New York

As was noted above, the default rules that apply on divorce in New York follow the doctrine of equitable distribution. Equitable distribution is considered to be an extremely onerous procedure, and is light-heartedly referred to by practitioners as the 'Full-Employment Act for Accountants, Actuaries, and Appraisers'.[22] The process is expensive and labour intensive,[23] as an inventory must be created of all property owned by the spouses separately and jointly. 'Property' is real and personal, and Schechter also notes that any tangible or intangible asset which may produce an income is viewed as property. Intellectual property (like copyrights and patents), contingent interests (like prospective inheritances), pension rights, professional licences and even careers are considered to be assets. Therefore, if one spouse attains a degree or professional licence, for example, that spouse's enhanced earning capacity as a result of that qualification is a marital asset to be considered on divorce.[24] Unsurprisingly, valuing assets like enhanced earning capacity and intangible property can be exceedingly complicated.

Once the property has been ascertained, marital property must be distinguished from non-marital property so that it may be subjected to equitable distribution. This process generates problems similar to those described in the previous chapter on financial provision in the UK. For example, non-matrimonial property such as inherited assets may become susceptible to equitable division if they have actively increased during the marriage.[25] This could happen if such assets are invested during the marriage or are merged with marital property. Furthermore, a business set up before marriage is separate property, but an increase in the value of a business during the marriage is viewed as active appreciation. Thus the non income-producing spouse is entitled to share in the business profits in recognition

[21] For more information on this reform, see B Atwood and B Bix, 'A New Uniform Law for Premarital and Marital Agreements' (2012) 46 *Family Law Quarterly* 313; T Oldham, 'Would Enactment of the Uniform Premarital and Marital Agreement Act in All Fifty States Change US Law Regarding Premarital Agreements?' (2012) 46 *Family Law Quarterly* 367.

[22] See Schechter, above n 4, 265.

[23] Ibid.

[24] *O'Brien v O'Brien* 66 NY 2d 576 (New York 1985).

[25] This is known as active appreciation, which means the increase in the value of the asset can be attributed to one of the spouses. The increase in value becomes marital property, even if the original asset was separate before the marriage. On the other hand, assets remain separate if the appreciation is passive, the increase having occurred incidentally through circumstances like inflation.

of his or her homemaking contribution.[26] In cases like this, of which there are many, there is no clear dividing line between marital and non-marital assets due to commingling.[27]

Against this complicated backdrop of equitable distribution, the enforcement of prenups is viewed as being an important way of attaining certainty in the event of divorce. As Schechter maintains, 'many people … attempt to forestall unhappy contingencies, even as they enter marriage with hope in their hearts',[28] because of the perception that in New York, divorce rates are high and equitable distribution is complex (and therefore costly).

Prenuptial agreements in New York are enforced according to the Domestic Relations Law, section 236B(3), which provides as follows:

> 3. Agreement of the parties. An agreement by the parties, made before or during the marriage, shall be valid and enforceable in a matrimonial action if such agreement is in writing, subscribed by the parties, and acknowledged or proven in the manner required to entitle a deed to be recorded. Notwithstanding any other provision of law, an acknowledgment of an agreement made before marriage may be executed before any person authorized to solemnize a marriage pursuant to subdivisions one, two and three of section eleven on this chapter. Such an agreement may include (1) a contract to make a testamentary provision of any kind, or a waiver of any right to elect against the provisions of a will; (2) provision for the ownership, division or distribution of separate and marital property; (3) provision for the amount and duration of maintenance or other terms and conditions of the marriage relationship, subject to the provisions of section 5-311 of the general obligations law, and provided that such terms were fair and reasonable at the time of the making of the agreement and are not unconscionable at the time of entry of final judgment; and (4) provision for the custody, care, education and maintenance of any child of the parties, subject to the provisions of section two hundred forty of this article. Nothing in this subdivision shall be deemed to affect the validity of any agreement made prior to the effective date of this subdivision.

In summary, the scope of a prenup includes financial distribution on death and divorce, and custody of children, subject to the legislative provisions relating to child support. To be clear, agreements can make provision for child support and custody in the event of separation, but carry little weight, as the court can override this provision on divorce. The principal requirements for enforceability can also be noted in this section: an agreement must be signed, in writing and acknowledged in the manner required to record a deed.[29] Like the UPAA, there is no explicit requirement in this Law for disclosure or independent legal advice. The statute only asks that the terms of an agreement are fair and reasonable when the agreement is made, and that it is not unconscionable when enforced. There is no

[26] *Price v Price* 69 NY 2d 8 (New York 1986). This mirrors the ratio of the House of Lords in *White v White* [2000]UKHL 54.

[27] Commingling occurs when non-marital property and marital property are mixed.

[28] See Schechter, above n 4, 265.

[29] Meaning it must be witnessed by a notary public (distinguished from a notaire).

further explanation as to the meaning of fairness, reasonableness or unconscionability. Thus exploring the meaning of these terms has been a judicial task.

The following section presents the findings from the research carried out in New York, which includes practitioners' views on how the Domestic Relations Law is interpreted. The empirical findings that are examined also facilitate a deeper level of comparative analysis when juxtaposed with the position of prenups in the UK.

Summary of Findings

Background to the Study

The findings considered in this section are taken from a study carried out in September 2010 in the Manhattan area of New York City. Twenty attorneys were interviewed, and as a qualitative study it was not intended to be representative of all practitioners in the state. Interviewees were located through the American Academy of Matrimonial Lawyers (AAML) organisation via the AAML online database.[30] Thirty randomly selected practitioners were contacted by letter, and 15 appointments were made from this initial contact. The remaining five interviewees were located using snowball sampling whilst in New York.[31] The study's objective was to seek the most experienced attorneys for interview, and several interviewees had been drafting prenups since equitable distribution (and the Domestic Relations Law) was introduced. The interviews were semi-structured, so that it was possible to probe attorneys' responses using open-ended questions in order better to understand their personal experiences.

Attorneys' Experiences of Prenuptial Agreements in New York

In this section, the findings from the study are arranged according to the themes discussed during interviews, to summarise the salient issues raised by the 20 practitioners. The findings also reflect the aim of the study, which was to ascertain whether there is empirical support for the concerns raised in earlier chapters surrounding prenuptial issues of autonomy and power. Following this, the implications of the interview findings are analysed in the context of the UK position on prenups.

[30] The database may be accessed online at <http://www.aaml.org>.

[31] The purpose of snowball sampling is to establish new connections through existing contacts. For a thorough consideration of snowball sampling in a different context, see N Cohen and T Arieli, 'Field research in conflict environments: methodological challenges and snowball sampling' (2011) 48 *Journal of Peace Research* 423.

Reasons for Entering into an Agreement

Considering why couples enter into prenups arguably sheds some light on the allocation of power within these partnerships. It also shows that there can be practical advantages to such agreements, particularly when both parties are entering second marriages, as one interviewee explained:

> [A client will] ... say it's a horrible process and I never want to do that again. If they do it with a prenup the next time around, it divides the money ... very quickly. Sometimes, these things are very fair. [Clients say] ... anything we acquire jointly is split. We each get back the money we put into [the marriage]. It's very simple and saves a ton on litigation costs. There can be some major benefits to the prenup.[32]

Those who have experienced divorce in the past are keenly aware of its financial consequences, and for some of these couples, it is important to safeguard their assets and prevent litigation if they marry a second time. This reasoning has contributed to the UK court's attitude that prenups should be given effect out of 'respect for individual autonomy':[33] in the Court of Appeal in *Radmacher*, Thorpe LJ did not accept that prenups are made by 'the predominantly male super-rich' where power imbalance is likely; instead, those seeking agreements are in many instances 'mature couples ... each contemplating a second marriage'.[34]

Unfortunately, in New York the general consensus among the attorneys who were interviewed was that this does not accurately represent the typical context in which agreements are entered into. Interviewees identified three types of clientele seeking prenups: people with family money; people who have established a great deal of wealth (or expect to in future); and people entering second and third marriages (usually with children). Of these, the clients most commonly referred to were those with family wealth. A typical response was as follows:

> As to the client base ... it generally used to be the older second marriage issue ... or they had been older people who had worked ... Well I've seen that's changed, it honestly has. So many people coming in for prenups with ... a lot of family money ... young people who are getting married, their parents are saying you must have a prenup and whether they like it or not they do it. That's really been the focus.[35]

Indeed, several interviewees said that the family of the wealthier spouse was often more eager than the parties for a prenup to be made. A typical reason given for the creation of an agreement was to 'protect the family in the event that something went wrong somewhere along the line'.[36] Therefore, it cannot be assumed that the prospective husband and wife are the only parties involved in an agreement because it is their names alone on the paper.

[32] Practitioner 10.
[33] See *Radmacher*, above n 9, [78].
[34] *Radmacher v Granatino* [2009] EWCA Civ 649, [27].
[35] Practitioner 15.
[36] Practitioner 14.

Interviewees also said that clients entered into agreements to avoid the uncertainty of how their property would be divided under the equitable distribution laws. In particular, one interviewee said that clients often expressed a 'desire to not have to go through what can be in New York at least a long, difficult process of determining for the process of equitable distribution … the value of everything'.[37] As was noted earlier in this chapter, in New York the pot of assets for division on divorce is not simply tangible property. Qualifications, skills and licences may also be divided, an onerous process which often requires specialist forensic accountants. For example, one interviewee referred to a lawyer with a law practice who was getting divorced. That person's business and licence were valued and subsequently divided according to equitable distribution. According to this interviewee:

> The problem with that is once you divide it up you are dividing up futures because in New York you can't sell your practice, you can't sell your law licence … It is based on a projection of what you are going to earn during your normal earning life … It's a torturous process. It can be a costly legal exercise.[38]

From this perspective, it is easy to sympathise with clients who want to avoid sacrificing their future earning potential and their future business, and who seek prenups because they risk losing millions at the discretion of the court on divorce. In the words of one interviewee, an agreement will 'involve people who have significant wealth … it's rare that you have something involving less than a million dollars. Our average agreement ranges from $5 million to a billion.'[39] Equally, however, the sacrifices being made by both spouses must be taken into account. Every interviewee was absolutely clear that prenups are usually entered into because there is a gap between the income or wealth of the two parties. In reality one spouse is not in the same economic position as the other. Thus it is not surprising that interviewees also said that the main reason people enter into prenups is because one party wants to protect the finances he or she currently possesses, or to protect the finances he or she expects to possess in future. The consequence of this was summarised by one attorney: 'Infrequently are both parties looking for the prenup agreement.'[40] This illustrates precisely why it is important to explore people's reasons for entering into such agreements. If we know that people enter into these agreements because one person wants to, then there may be underlying issues of power between the parties.

The Balance of Power Between Parties to a Prenuptial Agreement

During each interview, attorneys' views were probed about this power dimension. Each attorney believed that prenups tended to be conceived on an unlevel playing field. Several interviewees felt that the desire for an agreement was often one-sided: 'Usually it is one party I think presses for it. I haven't seen too many

37 Practitioner 18.
38 Ibid.
39 Practitioner 2.
40 Practitioner 12.

people at least in my practice who both say, "I think it's a mutual best interest to execute a prenuptial contract."'[41]

Yet the experience that a prenup is typically suggested and set up by one party does not mean it can be assumed that one party holds the lion's share of negotiating power. On the other hand, interviewees explained that there is a link between the allocation of wealth between parties to an agreement, and the balance of power within these relationships:

> Oftentimes, there is a moneyed party, or a more moneyed party coming into the marriage and it's the more affluent party that is going to look for the agreement and preserve what he or she has coming into it and then dictating also what may happen in the event that the marriage doesn't work out ... [W]hen you have the money you have leverage I think.[42]

Similarly, when describing a pressured negotiation process, another respondent specifically described the moneyed party as the person with the leverage:

> The duress element comes to play when one party has the strong financial advantage, where they say, if you want to marry me and my money you better sign ... I have seen women crying in my office before they are signing a prenup, and sometimes I have seen clients of mine treat their soon to be wife quite harshly because they say this is a business deal: 'I told you when we got engaged I had to have a prenup agreement. This should be no surprise to you ... I need it in order to marry you.'[43]

Aside from revealing the emotional tension in these situations, the above quotation demonstrates that wealth allocation is closely related to the way power is distributed between parties to a prenup. As it is the wealthy spouse who wants such an agreement to safeguard his or her wealth, the agreement is, at least in theory, intended to benefit the wealthy spouse. It is the wealthy party who is seeking an agreement; and it is therefore the wealthy party who substantively has the power to bargain on his or her own terms. In cases of family wealth there is often additional third-party pressure on the non-moneyed spouse to sign an agreement. However, it is important not to oversimplify matters by concluding that the power imbalance between couples is based purely on who has more money. As interviewees disclosed, there are a multitude of reasons why couples enter into prenups. Such reasons may be personal and unique to each individual couple. Interviewees also said that the power dynamic between parties may be influenced by a combination of factors, such as disparity in backgrounds, age and experience, views of marriage and, importantly, gender. In particular, interviewees identified a gender dimension to prenups, even though they were not asked directly whether gender affected the balance of power between parties to an agreement. For example, interviewees employed phrases like 'non-moneyed spouse' and 'wife' interchangeably, typically qualifying these statements by adding, 'I say the woman because it almost always is'.[44] The experience of attorneys is that even if both parties are financially

[41] Practitioner 7.

[42] Practitioner 12.

[43] Practitioner 8.

[44] Practitioner 20. Practitioners 2, 8, 12, 15 and 17 also made similar statements.

independent, the wealthy party is still usually male, and according to one attorney, 'comparing the two net worths [is like comparing] apples to oranges'.[45] Interviewees said the gender dimension was most apparent in cases where assets were not generated through family money, 'but [in] the ones where people have already built money … societally speaking [the wealthy party] is still more often male than female'.[46]

From the outset, inequality of bargaining power is potentially problematic in the context of prenups. The most obvious consequence is that the agreement will likely benefit the party who holds the most bargaining power. As one attorney said, '[n]o one who signs a prenup who is on the short end wants that prenup or is happy with it'.[47] This is because the party on the 'short end', usually the lesser income-producing spouse, is agreeing to waive his or her right to an award of equitable distribution or maintenance should the marriage break down. Whilst it is not uncommon for one party to a contract to benefit more than the other, an unequally bargained prenup could lead to hardship for one spouse on divorce. This is more likely in long-term marriages, as the circumstances between the parties often change and the lesser income-producing spouse becomes more dependent on the moneyed spouse. As one attorney summarised:

> One thing I've seen is what you plan for never really happens, it's always something you've never really thought about or circumstances change, so what sounded fair and reasonable at one point is no longer [fair] 10 or 15 years later because circumstances change.[48]

As a result, the real impact of an agreement that benefits one party at the expense of the other is often unforeseeable. When an agreement like this is implemented, however, the manifestation of this inequality is problematic. Yet because New York law assumes that both parties have freely entered the agreement (when they often have not), the non-moneyed spouse will be forced to accept the consequences of the prenup and change (usually) her lifestyle, living situation and employment, after years of sharing a different life with her partner.[49] In addition, some interviewees expressed concern that people are not aware of these repercussions, as not enough agreements have been implemented yet:

> I think that we're going to see more and more over the next 5, 10, 15 years a lot of these bad deals that have been made by a lot of people … they're in their late twenties and thirties with seven figure incomes, marrying people who are going to get divorced and a lot of them have signed prenuptial agreements where their spouse will get nothing or next to nothing. And I think that the courts will have some issues on their hands about how to deal with all of that.[50]

[45] Practitioner 15.
[46] Practitioner 1.
[47] Practitioner 13.
[48] Practitioner 15.
[49] See *Cron v Cron* 780 NYS 2d 121 (New York 2004).
[50] Practitioner 17.

Therefore, as the number of divorces where these 'bad deals' have been made increases, the problems contingent on inequality of bargaining power become more apparent.

In spite of this, several attorneys felt that not enforcing agreements was 'infantilising'[51] the spouse who happens to be younger, less wealthy or female. One interviewee recalled a case where he represented a husband who wanted to enforce a prenup. The wife's attorney argued that the husband 'wanted to revert to some male centred world where he gets all the money and she gets nothing'.[52] But he also implied that the wife was incapable of signing an agreement and being held to it. Whilst it might have been harsh to enforce the agreement strictly in favour of the moneyed spouse, this interviewee believed it was much worse, and in fact 'sexist', for the wife not to be bound by the agreement because she 'is just a woman'.[53] This argument was made in several interviews, which indicates a perception that the only alternative to power inequality is non-enforcement, which is also problematic because it restricts the agency of both parties. As a result, even though interviewees recognised that prenups are affected by unequal bargaining power, accepting this inequality was considered preferable to preventing women with less power from making enforceable choices. It seems that attorneys did not believe it was feasible for the court properly to account for contextual power imbalances whilst still enforcing an agreement. This response summarises the views expressed by several interviewees:

> [I]f it's equality you want then I don't think we will ever enforce any contract … we are not going to go all the way to treating the person as a minor incapable of contract … there are times when I think we could use a little more [protection] but I don't know how much more. I don't know how you would do it.[54]

The effect of this tension between enforcement and equal power represents an unfortunate dilemma and will be considered in further detail later in this chapter. The following section summarises findings from another theme that was discussed during interviews, which was whether the law in New York recognises issues of power between parties to an agreement and, if so, how the law addresses these issues.

Addressing Issues of Power in Practice

Judicial Interpretation of the Domestic Relations Law

As all interviewees identified a power imbalance between parties entering prenups, they were subsequently asked how the law addressed this issue. There are legislative safeguards contained within the Domestic Relations Law that say that an agreement should not be unfair when made and must not be unconscionable

[51] Practitioner 1.
[52] Ibid.
[53] Ibid.
[54] Ibid.

when enforced.[55] However, these terms are open to judicial interpretation. One interviewee was an attorney who had formerly been a chief matrimonial judge in New York state, and so had experience of the kind of circumstances in which a judge would set an agreement aside. For an agreement to be found unconscionable, the former judge said 'it would really have to be terrible, she is being left penniless … something that shocks the conscience of the court'.[56]

There is no legislative requirement for independent legal advice or full financial disclosure, yet the former judge said an absence of these elements could influence the court's decision if it does not like the agreement. That is, if the non-moneyed party was not represented by independent counsel then the former judge said that an agreement would not have to shock the conscience of the court to be set aside. The interviewee used the example where 'he is making $2 million a year and has a load of assets and he is giving her maybe $20,000 a year for maintenance for two years when they have been married ten years'.[57] According to this interviewee, a court might consider this agreement to be unconscionable if the non-moneyed spouse had not received independent legal advice when the agreement was negotiated. However, she opined that the agreement would not be deemed to be unconscionable if both parties had received independent legal advice. This is also evidenced by the fact that all interviewees stressed the importance of ensuring that both parties are independently advised when entering prenups, as without this advice there is more of a risk that the agreement will be set aside. Needless to say, it is in the attorney's interests to draft an agreement which is not susceptible to challenge on divorce.

In addition, the fact that emphasis is placed on ensuring that both parties were independently advised illustrates that the courts are aware of the potential problem of unequal bargaining power. On the other hand, if both parties are independently advised, the interviewees stressed that those parties are presumed to have exercised free choice when entering a prenup. The court will neither look for a disparity of power between the parties, nor will it be influenced by the argument that there were such disparities if both parties have been appropriately advised. Unless an agreement is unconscionable, for an agreement to be vitiated, it must be established on normal contractual grounds that there has been duress or undue influence.

A pertinent finding from the research is that, without exception, every interviewee said that it was very rare for an agreement to be deemed to be unconscionable by the court. Most said the claimant would have to show that the agreement would make him or her dependent on state welfare. The following quotation

[55] *Christian v Christian* 365 NE 2d 849 (New York 1977) states that this should apply to property waivers as well as maintenance waivers.

[56] Practitioner 9.

[57] Ibid.

illustrates the typical response of interviewees when asked what a court would consider unconscionable:

> I haven't seen many things declared unconscionable by a court. That's sort of the point. I suppose if someone was wandering around Madison Avenue with a cup looking for people to put quarters in it, then that would be declared unconscionable but there aren't many cases out there. I can't tell you if I've seen any … My sense of it is that the person almost has to give up everything. I mean it's got to be a complete wipe-out for it to be unconscionable.[58]

Interviewees have said that the court will look more sceptically at an agreement that moves the non-moneyed spouse from a huge house into a one-room apartment, even if the parties had been properly advised. However, if one of the parties gave up his or her career during the marriage to support the family, but had received appropriate legal advice, an agreement would not usually be varied (although the court could ensure that the children do not experience any lifestyle change by granting an appropriate level of child support).[59] It would be even less likely for the court to intervene if the claimant was under the age of 50, as the court would then expect that person to seek employment.[60]

Steps Taken by Individual Attorneys

Disclosure

As noted above, prenups in New York will be set aside only in exceptional circumstances. Therefore, a badly negotiated agreement or an unfair agreement will not be set aside by the court on divorce. Interestingly, however, all the interviewees said that they take deliberate steps to ensure not only that an agreement is fair when made, but also that it will not later become unconscionable. For example, when a prenup is being drafted, clients are encouraged to provide adequate disclosure of their assets. This includes listing underlying financial documents, business entities, bank account statements, stock brokerage statements, trust agreements and documents of a similar nature. Indeed, one attorney said that it is better for the moneyed spouse to overestimate his or her net worth than to underestimate it when entering a prenup.[61] This is because inaccurate financial disclosure arguably means that neither party will be able to understand the precise financial consequences of the agreement.

[58] Practitioner 17.

[59] This influenced the outcome of *Cron*, above n 49. In this case, the court modified the agreement to increase the housing allowance allocated to the wife, so that the children would not experience a drastic change in lifestyle.

[60] Practitioner 9.

[61] Practitioner 2.

Timing

Unlike other US states, there are no legislative timing requirements in New York. However, a number of interviewees referred to section 1615 of the California Family Law Code, which states that prenups must be signed at least 30 days before the marriage. There must also be a seven-day period between the time when the agreement is first presented to the parties and when the agreement is signed. The ethos behind these provisions, according to the respondents, is to provide a 'cooling-off period' for the parties before the wedding. However, the courts have made it very clear that pressure to sign before the marriage will affect the enforcement of the agreement only in extreme circumstances, because of the argument that parties are free to walk away from the agreement and, in some cases, the marriage. Indeed, interviewees recalled situations where people decided they would like an agreement only days before their wedding. As one an attorney said, 'you would be surprised how many people do [this] … because they are scared to broach it or they have waited until their families have said wait a minute … you've got to do one'.[62] But in these situations, the effect of bargaining inequalities and other pressures is heightened. Therefore, a fair and considered agreement is less likely to be drafted. The fact that all interviewees refused to provide legal advice to couples requesting prenups days before the wedding indicates an awareness that a cooling-off period is necessary to ensure meaningful negotiation.

Most interviewees did not suggest that the mandatory period of 30 days, required by Californian law, should be introduced in New York, because bringing the date forward in this way created a 'false deadline'. That is, the pressure that this provision seeks to avoid on the eve of the wedding is simply moved to a different date. Furthermore, some interviewees recalled agreements they had drafted that were signed in the week, or even on the day, of the wedding, but which they considered to be fair because of the months of negotiation that had preceded them. Thus the general consensus among respondents was not that there should be a mandatory cooling-off period. Instead, a competent attorney should ensure that the parties have a satisfactory period of time to negotiate and redraft agreements that are, as much as possible, mutually beneficial to both sides. The reasons for this were explained by one respondent as follows:

> Think of it … as a business deal. Throw out the emotions. If you let the emotions get in the way your judgment is not going to be good unfortunately. We can't control our client's emotions and their future spouse's emotions, so I know that particularly in the case of a woman who is getting married for the first time and seeing that this is going to be the dream of marriage that little girls think about maybe more than little boys, she wants to walk down the aisle in three days, doesn't want to be embarrassed when all those guests who flew in from all over the country … hear that [she is] not going to get married. There is a level of duress there that you can't avoid. But if you start out negotiating long before

[62] Practitioner 1.

> you have to send out wedding invitations you have the advantage to see whether this is the marriage that you want to go through because you will deal with compromises.[63]

From this perspective, having time to consider an agreement before the wedding has been booked and paid for might be crucial in reducing pressure during negotiations.

Independent Legal Advice

During interviews, attorneys most frequently emphasised the importance of independent and competent legal advice.[64] In particular, they considered independent counsel to be the best way of ameliorating unequally bargained agreements. One attorney recalled that after advising a client on 'what [he] thought was reasonable', she did not sign the agreement on the basis of this advice and said, '[I]f I was going to marry a control freak who really thought that that was the limit of my self-worth, I guess I'm glad I found out now before I married him right?'[65] This is an example of when legal advice made a positive difference and indicates that independent and competent legal advice can enable the parties to be open and honest about their expectations before marriage.

However, whilst independent advice was propounded by some attorneys as being definitively indicative of arm's length negotiations, other attorneys recognised that independent representation did not always make a difference. As one interviewee said:

> Sometimes I can see it in their eyes, they think, I have to sign it to get married and that's sometimes true and I know I'll convince him to tear it up, or he'll change or something and my experience is that's not what happens.[66]

Thus independent counsel is not always enough to ensure that both parties have complete autonomy when entering prenups. Indeed, several interviewees recounted incidents where clients entered agreements in spite of being expressly advised not to. Interviewees said that to avoid later malpractice suits, they often ask clients to sign a letter stating that their lawyer has recommended that they should not enter the agreement in question. But evidence from discussions with almost all interviewees suggests that many clients sign unreasonable agreements in spite of what their lawyer has told them. As one attorney recalled, 'I have been in a few situations where I have actually withdrawn from representing a woman who I felt was not agreeing to something that was even remotely fair.'[67] Even though this attorney felt that the agreement was completely unreasonable, the court would likely conclude that it was still voluntarily signed and would be unlikely to make a finding of unconscionability.

[63] Practitioner 8.

[64] Independent legal advice is not a requirement, and therefore an absence of it is not sufficient to overturn the agreement unless there are other corroborating factors: *Werther v Werther* 9 Misc 3d 1114 A (New York 2005).

[65] Practitioner 10.

[66] Practitioner 15.

[67] Practitioner 8.

Sunset Clauses

In addition to considerations of timing, independent legal advice and full financial disclosure, some attorneys advocated the insertion of a 'sunset clause' when drafting a prenup.[68] The effect of a sunset clause is that once a defined period of time has elapsed, the award to the non-moneyed spouse increases, or alternatively the prenup is no longer enforceable. Several interviewees felt that this clause represented a compromise between the parties, as the non-moneyed spouse will not waive his or her equitable distribution rights if the marriage lasts, yet the moneyed spouse's assets are protected in the short term.[69] Other interviewees, however, preferred to avoid the insertion of sunset clauses, as they had been involved in multiple cases where the moneyed spouse ended the marriage before the clause came into effect.[70] Indeed, one attorney felt that the true effect of sunset clauses is to cause spouses to re-evaluate their marriage and think about divorce.[71]

The Influence of the Uniform Premarital Agreement Act[72]

A number of attorneys said that although the UPAA had not been adopted by New York, the terms of this legislation provide a useful guide. As one interviewee explained:

> [W]e try to meet the provisions anyway on the theory that if the couple gets divorced in New Jersey, even though … the agreement says it should be interpreted under New York law … I don't want them to throw out the agreement … [because] we need [to meet] the Uniform Premarital Agreement Act … most of the provisions that strike you as being the ones that are there to protect fairness you know we try to meet.[73]

Therefore, the safeguards within the UPAA are often applied in practice, even though they do not officially apply to prenups in New York. Adhering to these safeguards arguably does more to show that the attorney has sufficiently represented his or her client. For example, the voluntariness requirement in the UPAA is satisfied if steps have been taken to ensure independent legal advice and the proper disclosure of assets.[74] But respondents' assertion that unreasonable and unequally bargained agreements are enforced suggests that in practice these safeguards might not be adequate.

[68] Practitioner 18 and Practitioner 11.
[69] For example Practitioners 1, 3, 7 and 20.
[70] For example Practitioners 8, 12 and 15.
[71] Practitioner 20.
[72] After the interviews were carried out, the UPMAA 2012 was introduced, the effect of which was considered earlier in this chapter.
[73] Practitioner 1.
[74] The question of voluntariness is based on these facts rather than the actual context in which the agreement was signed.

Other Steps

Given the fact that an agreement will rarely be deemed unconscionable by the court, interviewees admitted to 'working the system'[75] when representing the non-moneyed spouse on divorce. In their experience, interviewees said that the moneyed spouse is usually more willing to increase the share of assets to the non-moneyed spouse on divorce if it means avoiding the expensive threat of litigation. In effect, the non-moneyed spouse often has some leverage on divorce to seek a little more than he or she would receive under the agreement, but interviewees emphasised that the award will 'clearly not [be] as much as they would get if there was no agreement at all'.[76] Thus the bargaining power in this situation hinges on the threat of litigation costs to the moneyed spouse, as there is rarely any threat that the court would vary or set aside an agreement, or order equitable distribution to be paid to the non-moneyed spouse. A moneyed spouse unwilling to adjust the terms of the agreement will decide to face the risk of litigation, and in these situations it is the non-moneyed spouse who must pay if unsuccessful in his or her challenge.

Interviewees also said they would take steps during the drafting process to improve an agreement for the non-moneyed spouse or make it less one-sided. Whilst these efforts might assist the interests of both parties, it does not necessarily mean there is a level playing field. Nevertheless, one respondent described how he would attempt to iron out inequalities as much as possible:

> A good prenup, the one I did today actually, had good benefits for both parties. Yes, it doesn't give the wife nearly as much as she might get if the parties did not have an agreement, but it guarantees a certain level.[77]

In this scenario, the non-moneyed spouse's lawyer can at least prevent her from entering an agreement that would preclude any entitlement to her spouse's assets on divorce.

Remaining Issues

Whilst the safeguards taken in relation to prenups in New York undoubtedly contribute to a higher overall standard of fairness, they arguably do not ameliorate the power imbalance between parties to these agreements. The unconscionability threshold is extremely high, and interviewees indicated that the standard is made even more difficult to satisfy by the judiciary's inherent reluctance to overturn these agreements. According to interviewees, this reluctance stems from a fear that the courts will become congested with prenup cases if such agreements are easily challenged. Therefore, it is presumed by the court that such agreements are entered into freely. This is particularly problematic if, to quote one interviewee,

[75] For example, Practitioners 1, 2, 3, 12, 17 and 19.
[76] Practitioner 17.
[77] Practitioner 10.

'there is almost never a level playing field'[78] when prenups are negotiated. The party with less bargaining power may not have entered an agreement freely, particularly if it is not beneficial to that party. However, evidence from the interviewed attorneys suggests that if the court recognises this issue, it must scrutinise almost every prenup. Ironically, therefore, it appears that inequality of bargaining power is so prevalent within the context of prenups, it is masked and accepted by the court. On this basis, it could be surmised that the majority of prenups cannot be both effectively enforced and evenly negotiated at the same time.

Another issue inherent in prenups is that they provide for future circumstances that are often impossible to predict. The most common change in circumstances referred to by interviewees was a change in lifestyle as a result of the increasing success of the moneyed spouse during the marriage. The moneyed spouse in these examples was typically described by interviewees as being 'exceptionally wealthy'.[79] Interviewees also said that in these situations, the lesser income-producing spouse would often receive a relatively small percentage of this wealth under the agreement, having to scale down his or her lifestyle after separation. Although the attorneys often perceived the effect of these agreements as unfair, this would not amount to unconscionability. Interestingly, interviewees speculated that if the non-moneyed spouse received a small fraction of the partner's wealth, but the amount was large when compared to a judge's salary, the court would be very unlikely to make a finding of unconscionability.

Advice for the UK

In the final stage of discussion with each attorney in New York, the interviewees were asked their views on the position of prenups in the UK. All interviewees agreed that couples in the UK should be able to make enforceable agreements. However, there was a difference in opinion as to how the law in the UK should be reformed. Some interviewees expressed satisfaction with the current operation of the law in New York, and suggested that the UK could adopt provisions similar to those under the Domestic Relations Law. Some interviewees recommended the New York law with some slight amendments, but when probed did not specify what these amendments should be. Several attorneys proposed a system in the UK modelled on the UPAA. This is interesting, given that New York does not subscribe to that Act. Other interviewees suggested more specific methods of reform. A number of interviewees felt the threshold of unconscionability required to set a prenup aside is too high and proposed a different standard in the UK, such as unfairness. Other interviewees did not like the unconscionability standard but were not sure what the alternative would be. An example of this response was the opinion that 'unconscionable is a pretty high standard … fair and reasonable

[78] Practitioner 17.

[79] Practitioner 1.

seems a little low, I don't know what words you would find that are somewhere in between those two'.[80]

One interviewee said that in the UK the court should apply a 'smell test'.[81] The point of this is that rather than applying a prescriptive set of safeguards, the individual merits of the case could be considered. The following example was used to explain the 'smell test' from a judicial point of view:

> If the agreement was fair and it was signed two days before the wedding it wouldn't bother me, it wouldn't knock me out at all if she had good legal advice, but if you told me that the first day she got the agreement was two days before the wedding, how competent could the legal advice be? … I want to see that there have been drafts exchanged … really serious negotiations going on …[82]

Interestingly, interviewees' views as to how prenups should be enforced depended on their classification of these agreements. Those advocating strict enforcement believed that such agreements were akin to any other business deal. As one attorney opined, 'I don't know why they should be treated differently from other contracts … [D]on't be sentimental about contracts in family situations, at that point in the marriage these are financial issues.'[83] This view is also apparent in New York case law, which distinguishes between unmarried parties entering prenups and married parties entering postnuptial agreements. In *Christian v Christian*,[84] the court held that spouses are in a fiduciary relationship. However, interviewees said that parties to a prenup are not ordinarily viewed as fiduciaries (although, as Bronstein has said, the reported case law has not clarified when this relationship *would* be considered fiduciary).[85] Nevertheless, the experience of attorneys is that it is much more difficult to set aside a prenuptial than a postnuptial agreement. This is because the court has reasoned that the consequences of being pressured to sign a prenup are less serious, because the parties have the choice not to marry and not sign an agreement. Parties who are already married do not have this option. As an interviewee explained, 'when you are entering into a prenup agreement you have a different relationship with your future spouse than you would have with that person if you were married to them'.[86] The practical effect of this is that marital property agreements entered into by spouses (for example postnuptial or separation agreements) are subjected to a much higher level of scrutiny by the court, because it recognises that the parties are not ordinary business partners. For example, a higher level of financial disclosure must be provided than would be required for a prenup.

[80] Practitioner 1.
[81] Practitioner 9.
[82] Ibid.
[83] Practitioner 3.
[84] See *Christian*, above n 55.
[85] P Bronstein, 'The pre-nuptial agreement in the United States of America' in D Salter *et al*, *International Pre-Nuptial and Post-Nuptial Agreements* (Jordans 2011) 473.
[86] Practitioner 8.

In *Matter of Greiff*,[87] the question of whether parties to a prenup are in a fiduciary relationship was not clearly answered. Ultimately, however, it was held that if the court found that one party had a distinct advantage over the other, the burden of proof would shift. Thus, the party trying to uphold the agreement would have to persuade the court that there had not been any undue influence, duress or fraud when the agreement was made. This case shows that a fiduciary relationship may exist between parties to a prenup but, unlike postnuptial agreements, this relationship is not automatic. The court must first find a real imbalance between the parties before they are deemed to be in a special relationship. A participant in the study under consideration was a lawyer in this case, and he initially formulated the argument that it should be possible for the burden of proof to shift between parties to a prenup. To clarify, this would mean that the party seeking to enforce the agreement would have to show that he or she did not have a distinct advantage over the other party. However, when asked what the court would consider to be a distinct advantage, he said 'the courts have not really gone into it'.[88] Indeed, the legal characterisation of the relationship between parties to a prenup has not been developed much through jurisprudence. It seems that *Matter of Greiff* was exceptional in recognising that parties to such an agreement could have a special relationship. Interviewees said that the court instead tends to view the parties as bargaining at arm's length. As a result, New York law equates the relationship of engaged parties entering a prenup and entering a marriage in the same way as that of parties entering any other contract.

Nevertheless, not all attorneys agreed that a prenup is like any other business agreement. Whilst they felt that parties should take responsibility for their own decisions, they also said it should be recognised that the circumstances in which prenups are conceived are different from the normal course of business. In short, these interviewees appreciated the complications of enforcement:

> [T]he reason these agreements are difficult is this is a clash of two rights … she is right to say, 'Well we love each other, why should I have to give up my rights before we get married? Why shouldn't I get what the law says a woman should get or spouse should get in these situations and why should I have to go to sleep at night and every time I look at you I think that I have waived all these rights?' The husband says 'Look I went through a 3 year divorce, cost me half a million dollars, I had to give away half my assets, it was brutal, I'm not doing that again.'[89]

Both parties have equally legitimate interests when entering the marriage, but reconciling these interests by a prenup will often overlook the rights of the non-moneyed spouse. The disparity of power underlying the creation of so many agreements makes compromise between these clashing rights near impossible.

[87] *Matter of Greiff* 90 NY 2d 341 (New York 1998).
[88] Practitioner 17.
[89] Practitioner 13.

One attorney said he made an effort to ensure that the agreement recognises the sacrifices being made by the non-moneyed spouse:

> Sometimes there's a present payment of money as consideration for the relinquishment of future rights. We do a lot of prenuptial agreements for instance where there is what I would call a wedding present. You know at the time they go through the marriage ceremony a cheque is written for a significant amount of money and therefore the person getting the money waives any future claims.[90]

New York law does not require this kind of consideration, but it could be argued that this kind of practice helps reduce the inequalities resulting from unequally bargained agreements. The attorneys who advocated this practice did not view prenups as basic contracts, and were influenced by the marital context with which these agreements are associated. This perspective was most apparent when interviewees explained why they felt the unconscionability standard is too harsh after a lengthy marriage, and why a different standard, like unfairness, might be more appropriate:

> I don't have as much of a problem with unconscionability at the time an agreement is made, but I think on the support issue it's very hard to look at a crystal ball and say what life is going to be like for people over a long period of time. You know short marriages, the concept that you want parties to be restored to the status quo that existed at the time of the marriage makes a lot of sense, but in long marriages where people have sacrificed their ability to establish a career, they've been a homemaker or parent, or simply the spouse who has tagged along, doing whatever it was hosting dinners, attending functions, travel for business, was the person they confided to and pillow talk, what have you. There is something to be said for making that contribution and people should not be left in the lurch in terms of support after a lengthy period of time, and asked to live on significantly less money. Unfair, I think it means that the concept of marriage is a partnership, and both partners in fact harvest the fruits of what is going on, so if you're going to ask somebody to waive their rights of support in future then … there is not a substitute for an alimony waiver that approaches in value what the alimony would have been if there wouldn't have been an agreement.[91]

This view was held by several interviewees, who seemed to believe that the importance of autonomy, certainty and contractual force in relation to prenups is diluted as the marriage progresses and circumstances between parties change. In light of these changing circumstances, it is conceivable that parties' intentions change over time too. However, if the court accommodates these changes when an agreement is enforced, it risks being viewed as unduly paternalistic from a traditional contractual perspective. Thus, an agreement in New York is rarely varied when the parties' circumstances have changed. The result of this is that problems with prenups are not addressed, because conventional contract law struggles to recognise them. When considering the development of such agreements in the UK, therefore, contract theory must be assessed in a way that does not overlook the rights

[90] Practitioner 2.
[91] Ibid.

of the non-moneyed spouse, the nature of the marital partnership (particularly in longer marriages) or the disparity of power between the parties. It is also interesting to explore whether considering the concept of autonomy only at the moment a prenup is signed is realistic, when intentions and circumstances are, as the New York experience shows, extremely susceptible to change. Therefore, a more fluid notion of autonomy, which develops with a couple's circumstances and relationship, will be considered in later chapters.

Comparative Analysis

'Prenuptial Contracts'

The first theme to be considered as emerging from these findings is the perception of prenups as contracts. There was a consensus among interviewees that the Domestic Relations Law set such agreements apart from ordinary business contracts because they must be fair and reasonable when signed and not unconscionable when enforced. But interviewees also revealed that in reality this terminology does little to distinguish these agreements from any other contract. The meaning of 'unconscionability' is narrowly constrained, so that enforcement is stringent even in cases where interviewees believe the agreement was not fair. As a result, New York jurisprudence arguably perceives prenups as being contractual in nature. This is reflected in cases like *Eckstein v Eckstein*, where the court stated that

> a duly executed antenuptial agreement is given the same presumption of legality as any other contract, commercial or otherwise, and is not, regardless of the fairness and reasonableness of the agreement, burdened by a presumption of fraud arising from the subsequent confidential relationship of the parties.[92]

In some contexts, the New York courts have said that a prenup may be subjected to a higher level of scrutiny than is afforded to contracts in general.[93] However, the court in New York has also emphasised that 'there is a heavy presumption that a deliberately prepared and executed written instrument manifests the true intention of the parties and that, therefore, a high order of evidence is necessary in order to overcome that presumption'.[94]

[92] *Eckstein v Eckstein* 129 AD 2d 552 (New York 1987), 553.

[93] *Kessler v Kessler* 33 AD 3d 42 (New York 2006), 45. See also *Cioffi-Petrakis v Petrakis* 960 NYS 2d 152 (New York App Div 2013), where a New York court held that the prenup in question had been induced by fraud. The husband allegedly made assurances before the marriage that the agreement would be destroyed if the parties had children. The parties subsequently had children, and the wife successfully challenged the prenup on divorce.

[94] *Brassey v Brassey* 154 AD 2d 293 (New York 1989), 294–295.

One interviewee attempted to explain why a prenup is viewed in this way:

> [T]he courts in New York and in a lot of America treat it as just another contract. We believe in the sanctity of contracts. People are allowed to choose how they want to contract and we're not going to interfere with that and we're not going to second guess them … The problem, from my perspective, is that it's not a regular business transaction. Where you are dealing with prenups, you are dealing with something special. You are dealing with people's emotions … there is this basic assumption that, yeah I might be signing this document, but I'm never going to actually use it. And, as a result … you know, the economic bargaining is not always equal. And the problem is the results can be highly inequitable.[95]

But although prenups are recognised as having particular problems, it seems that these problems cannot be addressed at the same time as requiring parties to abide by what they have agreed. Thus the court's approach is to presume the autonomy of the parties once it is satisfied that routine conditions have been complied with. On the other hand, acknowledging that an agreement was not equally bargained, or that the choice of one party was not made freely, is viewed as 'disempowering'[96] because the power to enter a binding prenup is taken away. As a result, agreements are treated as contracts, because there is a perception that the alternative, when resolving issues of power, is non-enforcement.

Some interviewees suggested that marriage is also a contract, because when people get married there are financial consequences that are dictated by the state:

> [W]hether you like it or not, you are entering into an economic contract when you get married … The only difference with a prenup is you are setting the terms of the contract instead of just saying whatever terms the state imposes on me are fine.[97]

Interestingly, this perspective has also been considered by the judiciary in the UK. In *Radmacher v Granatino*, Lady Hale stated as follows:

> Marriage is, of course, a contract, in the sense that each party must agree to enter into it and once entered both are bound by its legal consequences. But it is also a status. This means two things. First, the parties are not entirely free to determine all its legal consequences for themselves. They contract into the package which the law of the land lays down. Secondly, their marriage also has legal consequences for other people and for the state. Nowadays there is considerable freedom and flexibility within the marital package but there is an irreducible minimum. This includes a couple's mutual duty to support one another and their children.[98]

Lady Hale's argument is persuasive. Marriage cannot simply be described as a contract, because in reality the nature of marriage is much more complex than this. Prenuptial agreements, which regulate the financial consequences of marriage and divorce, are more than just contracts. Yet the empirical study indicates that

[95] Practitioner 10.
[96] Practitioner 1.
[97] Ibid.
[98] See *Radmacher*, above n 9, [132].

in New York, prenups *are* treated as contracts. In the UK, though agreements are not enforced as stringently, the Supreme Court also believes that prenups should have contractual validity.[99] This is not problematic, as long as the wishes of the non-moneyed spouse are not overlooked in favour of strict enforcement. The next chapter examines the law of contract more closely, to assess whether it is capable of recognising the power inequalities associated with prenups.

Fiduciary Relationship

It was noted earlier in this chapter that *Matter of Greiff*[100] found a way for the context of the premarital relationship to be taken into account if a fiduciary relationship is established. To reiterate: in normal circumstances the person challenging the agreement must persuade the court why it should not be enforced. This onus is reversed if a fiduciary duty is proved in circumstances where the agreement has been the product of fraud, duress or other inequitable conduct. Unfortunately, the possibility of establishing this duty has not been developed by case law. An application of *Matter of Greiff* has not always helped to ameliorate unfair agreements either, as was the case in *Cron v Cron*.[101] An interviewee who mentioned *Cron* said, 'I thought the prenup was awful … [I]f any case was going to be the case where the agreement would be set aside, that would be it and the appellate division … said it's a good agreement.'[102] The agreement was upheld and a fiduciary duty was not proved, because the non-moneyed spouse was aware of her husband's assets and was held to have understood the agreement, even though her lawyer had advised her not to sign it. Therefore, there is a huge difference between recognising that parties to a prenup are fiduciaries and recognising the potential for a fiduciary relationship in limited situations. Interviewees seemed to agree that an automatic fiduciary relationship is not recognised in the way it is between spouses. As one attorney explained:

> I think fiduciary relationships exist between spouses and [engaged persons] are not spouses. They are two independent people who are not married entering into a contract … I have seen it argued [that engaged couples are fiduciaries]. I think that the law is otherwise … I think the law finds fiduciaries between … spouses. But not between two [people who are engaged]. I mean, you're not granted any rights. If you're dating, and you're in a relationship with an individual, but that isn't solemnised by marriage, you have no obligation to support that person. You have no obligation to provide that person with health insurance. You know, if the relationship ends tomorrow, then there are no obligations between those two people. So, simply because those two people decide to enter into a contract, I don't think that there are rights or obligations that all of a sudden

[99] Ibid.
[100] See *Greiff*, above n 87.
[101] See *Cron*, above n 49.
[102] Practitioner 12.

> arise because they have entered into this contract, I don't see it any different to two people dating. You know, it's like any other contract. You don't have to enter into it.[103]

The problem with this perception is that parties to a prenup are considered to be more like business partners than spouses. The reality of the emotions and inequalities of power they face is overlooked because a fiduciary relationship is present only in extreme circumstances, for example a situation of fraud or duress. Put simply, instead of considering the reality of parties' relationships, the basis of a fiduciary duty is dependent on exceptional circumstances.

Comparing New York with the UK

There are many important distinctions between the law applicable to prenups in New York and that in the UK. Though both default systems share conceptual similarities, such as fairness, there are differences in how property is distributed in these jurisdictions. One important difference is that in New York property division and maintenance are considered separately, but they are not in the UK. This has an effect on prenups, as one practitioner explains:

> I [have] been troubled sometimes that in New York we look at the property warrants when signed but maintenance warrants when signed *and* when entered … I do think property is subject to a higher burden to overcome the agreement because it's not embedded so deeply in the core of the marital relationship.[104]

Therefore, property provisions in an agreement will be more stringently enforced than maintenance provision, for the court is more likely to conclude that a spouse is at risk of becoming destitute if insufficient maintenance provision has been made. However, in the UK, there is no evidence that some aspects of an agreement will be set aside more easily than others.

The best source of information on practitioners' experience of prenups in this jurisdiction is Hitchings' empirical study in England of the views and approaches of family practitioners concerning marital property agreements.[105] Respondents were purposely selected based on their experience of prenups. The focus groups and interviews were conducted before the Supreme Court judgment *Radmacher v Granatino* was published, and so the study reflected attitudes towards marital property agreements at this time.[106] The responses of interviewees in Hitchings' study were quite different from those in the study discussed in this chapter. But any comparisons made between the New York findings and Hitchings' findings in

[103] Ibid.

[104] Practitioner 1.

[105] E Hitchings, *Law Commission Report: A study of the views and approaches of family practitioners concerning marital property agreements* (2011). For empirical research on public perceptions of prenups, see A Barlow and J Smithson, 'Is modern marriage a bargain? Exploring perceptions of pre-nuptial agreements in England and Wales' (2012) 24(3) *Child and Family Law Quarterly* 304.

[106] My project was on a much smaller scale than Hitchings' research, geographically and otherwise. This difference in methodologies is considered when conducting the comparative analysis.

England should be approached with caution. This is not simply due to legislative differences: practitioners also have different experiences of prenups in England because these agreements have been given effect by the judiciary only relatively recently. Indeed, when asked about the number of prenup cases undertaken in a year, the average response from practitioners in the New York study was between 10 and 15, but in England it was between 1 and 5. Though the high numbers of wealthy clients in Manhattan might contribute to the demand for agreements, the difference in popularity still means a difference in experience. Furthermore, although prenups are enforced stringently in New York, at the time Hitchings conducted her research, practitioners in England explained that they could not guarantee that their clients' agreements would be enforced on divorce. These contextual differences must be borne in mind when comparing the experience of practitioners in each jurisdiction from both sets of empirical findings.

Across both jurisdictions, the reasons practitioners' clients seek prenups are similar. Like in New York, in the UK the most commonly cited motives are family wealth, earned wealth and second marriages. In New York and England, practitioners specifically described some clients as 'trust fund babies', whose families were extremely wealthy and were pushing for agreements to be made. In Hitchings' sample an international marriage was also an important factor, as a spouse from another jurisdiction where prenups are routinely enforced is more likely to want an agreement. As in the New York study, the term 'crystal ball' was used in Hitchings' report to describe the uncertainty and difficulty with drafting agreements that control the division of future assets. Furthermore, there was a similar disparity of opinion about the use of sunset clauses,[107] and about timing issues (such as how long before marriage the agreement should be signed).

There also seemed to be some consensus between the New York and English studies as to the steps taken by practitioners when ensuring a 'good' agreement. Like practitioners in New York, respondents in England felt that full disclosure was important. Clients' qualifications and professions are not given an economic value in the same way in the UK as they are in New York. However, practitioners within Hitchings' sample varied as to the level of disclosure they believed to be sufficient. In my project, all practitioners insisted that a comprehensive level of disclosure was necessary to prevent any future problems with enforcement. Interestingly, one of the respondents in Hitchings' report said it was important that the wealthy party did not misstate his or her wealth, and would recommend clients to 'overstate their wealth'[108] to ensure the agreement protected them. This response echoed that of several interviewees in New York, which shows that disclosure is considered to be a necessary part of ensuring a fair agreement.

[107] Sunset clauses are referred to as 'review clauses' in Hitchings' research, see above n 105.
[108] Ibid, 50.

Independent legal advice was considered important by practitioners in both samples, but in New York the respondents were more certain as to what truly independent legal advice meant. As one respondent explained:

> [L]et's say 5 lawyers independently get a suite and they share a secretary, receptionist … they are independent lawyers but nevertheless they are together and he sends them to someone three doors down from him, that is problematic.[109]

It was also emphasised that the lawyer drafting the agreement must be an experienced matrimonial lawyer. It was not considered to be sufficient if the lawyer was experienced in a different area of law. In England, however, practitioners' responses varied as to the level of experience required to draft an agreement. Some respondents said the firm's partners would draft agreements, and other respondents said junior solicitors had drafted them.

With regard to the enforcement process, in New York it is clear that agreements are enforced routinely. In Hitchings' project, responses varied, with some agreements being enforced completely and some not at all. What is clear from Hitchings' study is that at the time the interviews were conducted, the enforcement of prenups was fairly inconsistent. Indeed, respondents in England had limited experience of any enforcement at all. As prenups have only gained prominence in recent years, many have been drafted only relatively recently too.

Issues with Power

The comparisons made between the empirical projects undertaken in New York and England thus far have related to practicalities with the drafting process rather than more conceptual issues. However, the issue of bargaining inequalities did emerge in Hitchings' project. An illustration of these inequalities was as follows:

> He (prospective husband) was putting an enormous amount of pressure on her. His solicitors had drafted the document with assistance from counsel and it was presented to me for approval, and I sought to make a number of amendments and advised her accordingly, and why we needed to make the amendments, and each time we did that, she would go back to him and I would then be told subsequently 'we're not making those amendments, we're leaving them in.' So, after a number of meetings, a number of attempts to amend the document—we did get some tweaks in—and a huge disclaimer from her, the parties signed the document. This was not before he had cancelled one wedding date. So you can see, there was a huge imbalance between the two of them.[110]

Other examples of power inequality included situations where advice and disclosure were limited, due to the 'unequal bargaining position' of the parties.[111] As in New York, it was also common for pressure to come from the family of the wealthy party. But the question for Hitchings in her research was whether these different

[109] Practitioner 9.
[110] See Hitchings, above n 105, 60.
[111] Ibid, 61.

kinds of pressure could be considered to be duress, to be taken into account at the time of enforcement. Her conclusion was that, 'apart from third party involvement, there appears to be very little evidence of duress going beyond the standard "I won't marry you, if you don't sign this agreement"'.[112] The only exception was a case where the wife received limited legal advice because her fiancé would not pay for more. In cases where the threat not to marry was used as leverage during negotiations, or where other bargaining inequalities were present, some respondents in Hitchings' project said they would note this in a narrative that would form a preamble to the agreement. At the point of enforcement, the court would then be made aware of the context in which negotiations took place. In spite of this, the majority of Hitchings' respondents did not seem to think this kind of pressure amounted to duress. As Hitchings notes, prenups now must meet a higher standard of 'I won't marry you + an additional factor'.[113]

A similar process was not described by attorneys in New York. Indeed, the findings from New York make it clear that threats to cancel a wedding unless a prenup is signed are irrelevant at the time of enforcement.[114] Whilst Hitchings' sample discussed the incidence of duress, respondents did not appear to approach the issue of power in a way that considered how it limited the individual autonomy of parties to an agreement. The examples of pressure explored in this chapter may not fit within the concept of contractual duress (and whether they do or not is considered in chapter four). Furthermore, it is understandable why some practitioners in New York were dismissive of the prospect of a level playing field for prenups. The unfortunate fact is that prenuptial power inequalities are so ubiquitous that in practice courts are desensitised to most instances of pressure because they are 'normal'.

Postnuptial Agreements

Perhaps the clearest contrast between the British and American perspectives was their difference in approach to postnuptial agreements. It is noted above that prenups are much more difficult to set aside than postnuptial agreements in New York, due to the perception that spouses are more susceptible to duress than people who are engaged to be married. When asked why, one attorney considered matters from the clients' point of view:

> I would sign anything my wife put in front of me if she said this is important, not even if she threatened to leave me, if she just said this is important, you know, I'd sign anything. So to me a marital agreement … is so much more duress.[115]

112 Ibid, 62.

113 Ibid.

114 This is corroborated by case law such as *Colello v Colello* 780 NYS 2d 450 (New York 2004), which says that a threat to cancel the wedding unless an agreement is signed does not amount to duress.

115 Practitioner 1.

Thus there is a general perception that postnuptial agreements should be more difficult to enforce for reasons of public policy. The effect of using the marriage as leverage is perceived to be more serious:

> In New York if two people do a prenup, the consideration is we are getting married, each has the right not to get married. So you are getting married and that's the consideration. So you can do various things, but in a postnup agreeing to stay married meaning, 'honey if you don't sign this postnup I'm going to leave you', that is not consideration, that's not good public policy.[116]

As such, postnuptial agreements are treated with caution in New York, and a higher level of disclosure is required. The position of postnuptial agreements in the UK is very different. According to Hitchings, there is a belief that duress is less likely to occur during negotiations for postnuptial agreements, because the 'bargaining element of the impending marriage [has] been taken away'.[117] It is likely that Lady Hale's judgment in the Privy Council case *Macleod v Macleod*[118] influenced this perspective, as she suggested that unequal bargaining power was a trickier issue for prenups than postnuptial agreements:

> Post-nuptial agreements, however, are very different from pre-nuptial agreements. The couple are now married. They have undertaken towards one another the obligations and responsibilities of the married state. A pre-nuptial agreement is no longer the price which one party may extract for his or her willingness to marry.[119]

The public policy concerns, evident among interviewees in New York, that continuation of the marriage could be consideration for the postnuptial agreement, were also dismissed by Lady Hale:

> There may also be occasional problems in identifying consideration for the financial promises made (now is not the time to enter into debate about whether domestic services constitute good consideration for such promises). But both of these are readily soluble by executing a deed, as was done here.[120]

As a result of the *Macleod* decision, Hitchings has said that a two-tiered system has developed in England, whereby couples who have signed a prenup are advised to return after the wedding and enhance its chances of enforcement by signing a postnuptial agreement too.

It is interesting how these contrasting views of postnuptial agreements have influenced the drafting process for prenuptial and postnuptial agreements in both jurisdictions. Postnuptial agreements in England will conceivably not be drafted with as much caution as they would be in New York, because the balance of power between parties to these agreements is viewed differently. On this basis, practitioners in the UK could be more amenable to recognising the existence of a fiduciary

116 Practitioner 13.

117 See Hitchings, above n 105, 111.

118 *Macleod v Macleod* [2008] UKPC 64.

119 Ibid, [36].

120 Ibid.

relationship between parties to a prenup, because of the way power imbalance prior to marriage is viewed. At the time of writing, there is no evidence in the limited series of cases on prenups since *Radmacher* to suggest that a fiduciary duty could be recognised (which reverses the onus of proof and places it on the party seeking to enforce the agreement). In *V and V*,[121] for example, it was found that there was inequality of bargaining power and pressure on the wife, but the agreement was 'willingly and honestly entered into by both parties'.[122] Charles J (applying *Radmacher*) overturned District Judge Cushing's decision that the weight of the agreement should be reduced to account for the wife's much weaker bargaining position.[123] However, he did emphasise that, pursuant to *Radmacher*, 'unconscionable conduct … can result in an agreement not being given any weight or not being given full weight'.[124] Unfortunately, as the research from New York has shown, there is some difficulty with the concept of unconscionability in this area. Whether the meaning of 'unconscionability' will become similar to how it is perceived in New York is unclear, but appreciating the effect of power issues on party autonomy will be difficult if only extreme circumstances deemed to be unconscionable are taken into account. If anything is to be learned from the New York experience, it is that unconscionability will not recognise the majority of power inequalities in relation to prenups. As was explained by one interviewee, it is an exceptional standard:

> [Unconscionability—] that's such a hard threshold to meet. You effectively have to be destitute and it's just not going to happen. It's not my experience in … the types of cases this office handles. You had a lawyer, you had disclosure, you entered into it. Unless you are going to be a ward of the state it is going to be upheld.[125]

Evidently, a prenup is often entered voluntarily, willingly and knowingly in the eyes of the court, even when there have clearly been significant power imbalances between the parties.

Conclusion

The study under consideration has revealed some interesting findings as to how prenups operate in practice. Unequal bargaining power is not properly taken into account, because to do so would limit the ability of the parties to make agreements without state intervention. Yet without any state intervention, agreements are potentially tainted by significant imbalances of power. As the study concluded,

[121] *V v V* [2011] EWHC 3230 (Fam).

[122] Ibid, [64].

[123] The husband presented the agreement as a precondition to marriage. The wife was 10 years younger than the husband, had a child and was keen to get married after having been engaged for some time.

[124] See *V v V*, above n 121, [58].

[125] Practitioner 12.

the problem with the prenuptial context is that power imbalance is so ubiquitous it is not recognised. Furthermore, to recognise the reality of the premarital relationship, attempts have been made to impose a fiduciary duty on the party with the upper hand, but there are no reported cases where this has been successful. Prenuptial agreements in New York are contracts, through and through. Stringent enforcement leaves no room for anything other than specific criteria based on unconscionability; and even without independent advice and full disclosure, agreements can still be enforced.[126] Thus the New York experience demonstrates that autonomy is something which *both* parties to an agreement almost never have but are almost always presumed to have, as if the prenup evenly reflects the wishes of both parties. The next chapter will look at the operation of contract law more closely to see how this happens, and whether it is capable of recognising a more realistic notion of autonomy that does not mask bargaining inequalities.

[126] See *Christian*, above n 55; also *Werther*, above n 64.

4

Remedies in Contract for Prenuptial Agreements

Introduction

The theme of autonomy has appeared consistently throughout this book and also within the general debate on the position of prenups in the UK.[1] Respecting autonomous decisions made by parties to such agreements has been considered by the judiciary to be of paramount importance. However, if decisive weight is to be accorded to prenups on this basis, the judiciary must also be able to recognise when decisions made by parties to a prenup have not been autonomous. Previous sections of this book have demonstrated that this is often the case, as many agreements are made in the context of inequality of bargaining power. In these situations, the decision of the non-moneyed spouse to relinquish his or her rights to the moneyed spouse's property means that he or she will receive a much smaller share of the assets on divorce. As earlier chapters have explained, in the absence of an agreement the court can divide property equitably, in a way that will reflect the contributions made by both parties during the marriage. But if an agreement has been made, the outcome on divorce will be greatly influenced by the terms of that agreement. Moreover, if prenups are made legislatively binding, the judiciary's discretionary power to regulate unfair agreements (which was reserved by the Supreme Court in *Radmacher v Granatino*)[2] will be ousted.

Accordingly, an integral question in this book is: How can the court recognise and ameliorate issues of power between parties to prenups? The starting point when addressing this issue must be to assess the existing legal tools available to the judiciary. As a result, this chapter will consider the remedies available in contract law to those who are disadvantaged by an uneven playing field when entering agreements.

The relevance of contract law to prenups in the UK ought to be stated more clearly, as these agreements have not typically been characterised as contracts in this jurisdiction. Indeed, as chapter two noted, the courts have historically been

[1] See *V v V* [2011] EWHC 3230 (Fam), where Charles J applied *Radmacher v Granatino* [2010] UKSC 42.

[2] See *Radmacher*, above n 1.

reluctant to enforce prenups, and would not regard contracts between husband and wife as containing adequate intention to create legal relations.[3] However, the Supreme Court and the Law Commission have both noted that a prenup will be set aside if it is not contractually valid. This means that a vitiating factor, such as duress, undue influence, mistake, misrepresentation or frustration, is present that renders an agreement void or voidable. The Law Commission did not think that the protection offered by these vitiating factors was sufficient in the context of prenups and proposed further safeguards due to the 'special nature' of these agreements.[4] This indicates that the Law Commission does not view prenups as ordinary contracts. However, if these agreements are not contracts, what are they? Discerning the nature of these agreements is difficult, for as Bix has noted, they span many areas of law.[5]

There are many differences between the 'normal' contract made in the course of everyday business and the 'special' agreement conceived between parties to a prenup. Lady Hale has repeatedly emphasised that prenups differ hugely from agreements between business partners,[6] as the former type of agreement is characterised by issues of power completely different from those that apply to the latter. Indeed, the close relationship shared by parties to prenups is habitual within family law.

Yet prenups are not exactly family law agreements either. This is because their purpose is to contract out of the normal consequences of marital status, which are controlled by the MCA 1973 and by judicial discretion to make financial orders on divorce. When explaining his initial reticence towards taking a prenup into account, Thorpe J (as he then was) described these agreements as contractual terms that should not influence the rights and responsibilities imposed by the 1973 Act.[7] Whilst the majority of the Supreme Court said that the question of whether prenups have contractual status is a 'red herring',[8] Lady Hale has said extra-judicially that the majority viewed such agreements as legally binding, or as having contractual status.[9]

From this perspective, it is more appropriate to consider issues of power associated with prenups within a contract law context, whilst adopting an approach that also incorporates family law elements like flexibility and fairness. This is more logical than attempting to fit contractual concepts within family law, which would require a reconceptualisation of extremely complex issues like the nature

[3] *Balfour v Balfour* [1919] 2 KB 571.

[4] Law Commission, *Marital Property Agreements* (Law Com No 198, 2011), para 6.49. Refer to ch 1 for a summary of the safeguards recommended by the Law Commission.

[5] B Bix, 'Bargaining in the Shadow of Love: The Enforcement of Premarital Agreements and How We Think About Marriage' (1998) 40 *William and Mary Law Review* 145.

[6] See *Radmacher*, above n 1; B Hale, 'Equality and Autonomy in Family Law' (2011) 33 *Journal of Social Welfare and Family Law* 3.

[7] *F v F (Ancillary Relief: Substantial Assets)* [1995] 2 FLR 45, 66.

[8] See *Radmacher*, above n 1, [63].

[9] See Hale, above n 6.

of marriage and whether it is rooted in status or contract.[10] The utility of prenups is also arguably undermined if they are siphoned off as a particular type of family law agreement, and are thus denied contractual status. Indeed, Mulcahy has said that the status of prenups 'has been largely relegated to the sphere of family law, despite the fact that the majority of such contracts involve those concerned to protect proprietorial interests in acquired capital, as well as non-commercial expectations'.[11] For these reasons, contract law is relevant to the enforcement and characterisation of such agreements.[12] Thus the task of addressing the issues with prenups should not be consigned only to the area of family law.

The aim of this chapter is to situate prenups within the context of contract law in the UK, to assess whether prenuptial issues of power can be recognised within this framework. To clarify, 'issues of power' in this book does not simply mean inequality of bargaining power when the agreement is made (although this is an important issue). Rooted in the concept of power are other issues, like future disadvantage to the disempowered spouse as a consequence of the agreement; the relinquishment of rights like sharing conferred by marital status; and the gender dimension attached to prenups.

The structure of this chapter is as follows. First, duress and undue influence will be considered in the context of prenups to determine whether these contractual doctrines are able to recognise issues of power connected to these agreements. The chapter will also explore whether duress and undue influence can provide sufficient protection to the party vulnerable to power imbalances resulting from the circumstances of a prenup. Following this, unconscionable bargaining will be explored. There is no general doctrine of unconscionability or inequality of bargaining power in English law, and whether there should be is outside the ambit of this book. But in some circumstances the courts have set aside agreements for being unconscionable bargains. To clarify, unconscionability is examined in this chapter as a contractual vitiating factor, and so is distinguished from the concept of unconscionability underpinning constructive trusts and estoppel.

Vitiating factors such as mistake and misrepresentation might be applied to prenups in certain situations, but these doctrines are not based on power imbalances between contracting parties. For an agreement to be void for mistake, a mistake must have been made about the nature of the transaction. The Law Commission has said this could only be argued if one party did not know the agreement was a prenup. The only other way of claiming mistake in contract would be if one party was mistaken about the identity of the other party (which is highly unlikely in the context of a prenup).[13] The Law Commission also found that the majority of

[10] See D McLellan, 'Contract Marriage—The Way Forward or Dead End?' (1996) 23 *Journal of Law and Society* 234; also *Radmacher*, above n 1, [132] (Lady Hale).

[11] L Mulcahy, 'The Limitations of Love and Altruism—Feminist Perspectives on Contract Law' in L Mulcahy and S Wheeler (eds), *Feminist Perspectives on Contract Law* (Routledge 2005).

[12] Although it is emphasised that this does not mean that treatment of prenups should be aligned with ordinary business/commercial agreements.

[13] See Law Commission, above n 4, para 6.19.

misstatements made when an agreement is being negotiated would not be considered material to the formation of a prenup and therefore would not constitute misrepresentation.[14] Hence these doctrines have limited capacity to account for prenuptial issues of power.

In contract law the resolution of pressure, coercion and exploited bargaining positions is assigned to duress and undue influence. Therefore, these doctrines are the most relevant contractual solutions to issues of power between parties entering prenups. Indeed, the rationale of these doctrines is to protect the vulnerable party from being bound by contracts into which he or she did not enter voluntarily, and where the other party has behaved improperly.[15] However, whether this rationale can recognise these issues against the intimate backdrop of prenups must be explored. This is difficult to ascertain without adopting a comparative approach, as the courts in the UK have not yet had the opportunity to consider duress and undue influence comprehensively in the prenuptial context. Therefore, this chapter will consider case law from the US when assessing the effectiveness of existing contract law.[16]

The law in the US is different from the law in the UK. Furthermore, the application of contractual principle varies from state to state. An illustration of the diversity of judicial approach is provided by Ellman,[17] who compares *Button v Button*[18] with *Simeone v Simeone.*[19] *Button* is situated at one end of the spectrum, as it stated that to be enforceable, nuptial agreements must be fair when made and fair at the time of divorce. At the other end of the spectrum, *Simeone* exemplified a harsh pro-enforcement approach,[20] as the court strictly applied contract law to the enforcement of the agreement with no regard for substantive fairness. Ellman maintains that the approach of most states is situated between these opposing approaches, and so whether vitiating factors should be applied to prenups as to any other contract appears to be a recurring debate in US case law. Providing a complete picture of how different courts treat prenups is not possible within the constraints of this chapter. The purpose of considering these cases is simply to provide a guide as to the kind of circumstances in which the courts might find duress, undue influence or unconscionable bargains.

[14] Ibid, paras 6.20–6.23.

[15] J Beatson, *Anson's Law of Contract* (28th edn, OUP 2002) 276.

[16] The case law referred to in this chapter was obtained by searching for decisions at <http://www.findlaw.com> and <http://www.lexisone.com>, and from reading secondary sources that have highlighted important cases in this area.

[17] I Ellman, 'Marital Agreements and Private Autonomy in the United States' in J Scherpe (ed), *Marital Agreements and Private Autonomy in Comparative Perspective* (Hart Publishing 2012) 403.

[18] *Button v Button* 388 NW 2d 546 (Wisconsin 1986).

[19] *Simeone v Simeone* 581 A 2d 162 (Pennsylvania 1990).

[20] J Grossman, 'Prenuptial Agreements: The Iowa Supreme Court takes a Strong Pro-Enforcement Stance' (*FindLaw's Writ*, 6 January 2009), available at <http://writ.lp.findlaw.com/grossman/20090106.html>.

Duress

Background

There are three established categories of duress: duress to the person (threats or acts of violence);[21] duress to goods; and economic duress.[22] These categories have developed in response to incidents of commercial pressure, and so applying each category prescriptively to pressure in the context of prenups arguably misses the point of the duress principle. Thus, it is better to consider the underlying objective of duress in relation to prenuptial contracting. This is to vitiate contracts where one party has been a victim of illegitimate pressure that forced him or her to enter into the contract.

In *Pao On v Lau Yiu Long*, Lord Scarman described duress as 'a coercion of the will so as to vitiate consent'.[23] One interpretation is that contracts tainted by duress are voidable, because if the consent of one party was not given freely, that party arguably did not consent at all. Conversely, commentators like Phillips[24] and Trebilcock[25] argue that consent under duress is more forthcoming due to the extreme pressure being exerted. Thus in *The Universe Sentinel*,[26] Lord Scarman clarified that the law intervenes through the medium of duress because the claimant has not truly consented, he has 'realis[ed] that there is no other practical choice open to him'.[27] In other words, it is imperative that the claimant must have had no alternative but to enter a contract. On this basis, successfully vitiating a prenup for duress might be almost impossible, for unless the victim has a gun held to his or her head, he or she can refuse to sign the agreement and refuse to marry. However, there are varying degrees of consent, which may affect the level of coercion experienced when entering agreements.

According to *Halsbury's Laws*, duress is not really about absence of consent at all.[28] Rather, the basis of duress rests on pressure, and so it is the nature of this pressure that is a crucial consideration of the court. Illegitimate pressure is therefore a key ingredient of duress.[29] The requirement of illegitimacy means that normal commercial pressure is insufficient.[30] Thus 'normal' pressure in the context

[21] *Barton v Armstrong* [1976] 1 AC 104.

[22] *The Sibeon and The Sibotre* [1976] 1 Lloyd's Rep 293.

[23] *Pao On v Lau Yiu Long* [1980] AC 614, 635.

[24] J Phillips, 'Protecting those in a disadvantageous negotiating position: unconscionable bargains as a unifying doctrine' (2010) 45 *Wake Forest Law Review* 837.

[25] M Trebilcock, *The Limits of Freedom of Contract* (Harvard University Press 1993).

[26] *Universe Tankships Inc of Monrovia v ITWF, The Universe Sentinel* [1983] 1 AC 366.

[27] Ibid, 400.

[28] *Halsbury's Laws* (5th edn, LexisNexis Butterworths 2010) vol 9, para 5.

[29] See *DSND Subsea Ltd v Petroleum Geo-Services ASA* [2000] BLR 530, where the pressure was not illegitimate because the defendant acted in good faith.

[30] See *Barton*, above n 21.

of prenups will presumably not justify court intervention either. Unfortunately, the line between normal and illegitimate pressure in the context of prenups is not conceptually certain. As a result, it is difficult to determine the meaning of illegitimate prenuptial pressure, and also what it means to have no option but to enter such an agreement.

'Prenuptial Duress'

The New York research outlined in chapter three indicated that there is almost always an unlevel playing field when prenups are being negotiated. There is particular pressure when one party wants an agreement more than the other. It is arguably due to this reality that the Law Commission has said:

> [W]e think that the courts will be slow to find duress from circumstances that amount to no more than the inevitable context in which marital property agreements are made. But they will be alert to the possibility of deliberate and improper pressure, which in effect leaves the victim with no choice but to sign.[31]

Put simply, prenuptial pressure is normal when one party is pushing for an agreement, thus the court is unlikely to intervene in these 'ordinary' scenarios. Dyson J has described illegitimate pressure as different 'from the rough and tumble of the pressures of normal ... bargaining',[32] and so the application of duress is restricted to situations of extreme pressure. This makes it difficult to identify pressure that does not occur in an 'inevitable context' of prenuptial contracting. Threats to the person such as domestic abuse clearly constitute duress. But many other instances of pressure will in theory fall short of the high threshold of illegitimacy.

Prenuptial duress has not been discussed in any detail in this jurisdiction, but a number of US cases have considered this area.[33] Pursuant to the Second Restatement of Contracts,[34] duress makes a contract voidable 'if a party's manifestation of assent is induced by an improper threat by the other party that leaves the victim no reasonable alternative'.[35]

It appears that even in the intimate context of marital agreements, only extreme pressure will maintain a claim of duress. In the case *In re Marriage of Balcof*, it was found that duress does not require an illegal act and includes 'whatever destroys one's free agency and constrains [one] to do what is against [one's] will, [and which] may be exercised by threats, importunity or any species of mental coercion'.[36]

[31] See Law Commission, above n 4, para 6.30.

[32] See *DSND Subsea Ltd*, above n 29.

[33] To reiterate, it is not suggested that the approach of the judiciary in the US would be adopted in the UK. However, the US material is useful as a guide as to whether the common law offers parties to prenups adequate protection.

[34] The Restatement of Contracts outlines the general position of contract law in the US. Restatements do not have the force of law and are only persuasive authority as to what the law is.

[35] American Law Institute, Restatement (Second) of Contracts (1981), §175.

[36] *In Re Marriage of Balcof* 141 Cal App 4d 1509 (California 2006), 9.

A successful claim of duress was made in this case because, prior to signing a separation agreement, the husband was screamed at and struck by the wife. She also threatened to divorce him and prevent him from having contact with his children if he did not enter the agreement. In *Lyons v Lyons*, the court provided a similar definition of duress: that the plaintiff must have been 'deprived … of the ability to exercise her own free will'.[37] In this case, however, the court held that there was no duress, even though the husband prevented the wife from leaving the house until she signed the agreement. The evidence in this case suggested that the wife had not been fearful or stressed by the behaviour of her husband.

A study of US cases by Standler concluded that neither the pregnancy of the wife, nor the presentation of an agreement shortly before the wedding will amount to duress in the majority of cases.[38] Furthermore, US courts have not found duress in cases where one party is presented with an agreement and told by his or her partner that if he or she did not sign, there would be no wedding. The Law Commission does not view this kind of ultimatum[39] (in the absence of additional exceptional circumstances) as duress either, because neither party is coerced: he or she has the option not to agree, and not to marry.[40] The courts in the US view cancellation of proposed marriage as a 'natural result'[41] of a prenup's not being signed when one party desires the agreement. The judiciary's reasoning also hinges on the belief that there can be no duress because the threat or ultimatum (isolated from other coercive factors) is not unlawful.[42] Indeed, the common law on both sides of the Atlantic does not seem to recognise much in the way of lawful act duress, and in the context of prenups it appears that in most cases the court will find that the party had a reasonable alternative[43] to entering into the agreement.

If the non-moneyed party is pregnant *and* the moneyed party threatens to cancel the wedding unless a prenup is made, the court is still reluctant to vitiate on the ground of duress. It does not matter that the non-moneyed party might be desperate to marry as a result of the pregnancy and therefore will potentially enter an unfavourable agreement. For example, in *Baumgartner v Baumgartner*,[44] a court in Ohio found that the appellant signed the agreement only because she was pregnant and the defendant had threatened not to marry her unless a prenup was entered into. However, there was no finding of duress, as the court reasoned that the pressure applied by the moneyed party was not wrongful. A court in Pennsylvania[45] reached the same conclusion even though the pregnant party was

[37] *Lyons v Lyons* 289 AD 2d 902 (New York 2001), 904.

[38] R Standler, 'Voluntary Consent in Prenuptial Contracts in the USA' (27 September 2009), available at <http://www.rbs2.com/dcontract3.pdf>.

[39] Economic duress might arise when one party threatens to breach the contract. However, an action for breach of contract is no longer available when an engagement is called off.

[40] See Law Commission, above n 4, para 6.27.

[41] *Howell v Landry* 386 SE 2d 610 (North Carolina 1989), 617.

[42] *In Re Marriage of Spiegel* 553 NW 2d (Iowa 1996).

[43] See *Halsbury's Laws*, above n 28, para 711.

[44] *Baumgartner v Baumgartner*, unreported (Ohio 1989), cited in Standler, above n 38.

[45] *Hamilton v Hamilton* 591 A 2d 720 (Pennsylvania 1991).

18 years old, unemployed and was told that without the agreement there would be no wedding. She had signed the agreement although her lawyers had advised her not to.[46]

In the US, the presentation of a prenup on the eve of the wedding will not necessarily constitute duress. A North Carolina court has said that 'the mere shortness of the time interval between the presentation of the premarital agreement and the date of the wedding is insufficient alone to permit a finding of duress or undue influence'.[47] Therefore, in this case there was no contractual remedy available in the circumstances.[48] Timing, however, was one factor the Law Commission thought might constitute duress in the UK.[49] Consequently, in this jurisdiction the presentation of an agreement at a time that does not allow both parties to consider it properly may lead to the court's finding illegitimate pressure in some circumstances.

The US courts have also recognised that a combination of 'situational monopolies'[50] might lead to extreme pressure to sign a prenup. For example, a Florida court found that the agreement was a product of duress due to a combination of timing issues, lack of financial disclosure and an ultimatum.[51] The prenup was presented to the non-moneyed spouse for the first time two days before the wedding, and it contained no information about the husband's finances. The court reasoned that

> [s]he had only one day to seek counsel from her own attorney, to make an independent evaluation of the contract or to cancel her wedding. The only rational conclusion is that her signature was the product of unwarranted compulsion, and the document should have been set aside on that basis.[52]

As a result, it does not appear to be possible to point to one factor as definitive proof of duress. Rather, a finding of duress will depend on the circumstances of the case, and whether these circumstances have the combined effect of coercion when entering the prenup. Again, it is unclear whether the court in the UK would adopt the same approach as in the US. Nonetheless, it is likely that the scope of duress in relation to prenups in this jurisdiction would be limited. Indeed, the Law Commission has said the claimant would have to show that the alternative to entering the agreement was truly unbearable.[53]

[46] See also *Kilborn v Kilborn* 628 So 2d 884 (Alabama 1993).

[47] See *Howell*, above n 41.

[48] However, see *Matter of Marriage of Norris* 624 P 2d 636 (Oregon 1981), where an agreement presented on the day of the wedding was set aside.

[49] See Law Commission, above n 4, para 6.30.

[50] M Trebilcock, 'An Economic Approach to the Doctrine of Unconscionability' in B Reiter and J Swan (eds), *Studies in Contract Law* (Butterworths 1980) 381.

[51] *Hjortaas v McCabe* 656 So 2d 168 (Florida 1995).

[52] Ibid, 170.

[53] See Law Commission, above n 4.

Difficulties with 'Prenuptial Duress'

Duress will apply to prenups only in extreme situations, and so the disparity of power that often exists between parties to these agreements will almost always fail to be recognised by this doctrine. As the judiciary in the UK currently has discretion to set aside prenups if they are unfair, the judges' assessment of these agreements is based primarily on wider questions of fairness, rather than on whether the agreement was made under duress. Thus there is a dearth of case law on this issue. In the US, however, the judiciary does not have the same discretionary power over prenups, yet there is also a scarcity of cases in which the court has held that an agreement was made under duress. Standler has suggested that this is because judges in the US apply commercial contract rules for duress to prenups, which rules ignore the more subtle power disparities within a non-commercial relationship.[54] However, the American Law Institute has said the courts will scrutinise prenups more than commercial agreements for duress.[55] This indicates that the courts are aware of the unique pressures emerging from the creation of these agreements. In spite of this, the high threshold required of duress in the prenuptial context is arguably harsh. Someone who has finalised wedding plans, who is pregnant or who is simply blinded by love, is more vulnerable to pressure to enter an agreement than he or she would be in a commercial context.

Undue Influence

In cases where the pressure is neither explicit nor extreme enough to constitute duress at common law, relief may be sought in equity through the doctrine of undue influence. This 'equitable doctrine of coercion' also recognises more subtle pressure that falls short of duress but which is contrary to good conscience.[56] According to Lord Nicholls, 'the objective [of undue influence] is to ensure that the influence of one person over another is not abused'.[57] Therefore, if the consent of one party is obtained in a way the law finds unacceptable, the transaction will not be allowed to stand.[58] More than this, Lord Nicholls' assertion suggests that the doctrine of undue influence does more than police an absence of consent. Rather, as other dicta affirm, this doctrine is about preventing 'victimisation of

[54] See Standler, above n 38.

[55] American Law Institute, *Principles of the Law of Family Dissolution: Analysis and Recommendations* (LexisNexis 2002) 947.

[56] See *Halsbury's Laws*, above n 28.

[57] *Royal Bank of Scotland Plc v Etridge (No 2)* [2001] 2 FLR 1364, 6.

[58] Ibid, 7.

one party by the other'.[59] Pawlowski believes that this theory looks to the misconduct of the wrongdoer when the transaction is being entered into, rather than to any contractual imbalance incurred by the actual terms of the contract.[60]

There are two categories of undue influence.[61] The first is *actual undue influence*, which requires proof of illegitimate pressure causing the claimant to enter the contract. Lindley LJ has defined actual undue influence as 'unfair and improper conduct, some coercion from outside, some overreaching, some form of cheating, and generally, though not always, some personal advantage obtained by a donee placed in some close and confidential relation to the donor'.[62] The second category is *presumed undue influence*, which does not require the claimant to prove that illegitimate pressure has been exercised. Therefore, presumed undue influence does not necessarily involve coercion: this doctrine is triggered in situations where there has been an abuse of trust. If the relationship of the parties and the nature of the transaction satisfy certain criteria, undue influence is presumed unless the alleged perpetrator of that influence can produce evidence to rebut the presumption.

Both categories of undue influence will be considered below in relation to prenups.

Actual Undue Influence

Background

Before the doctrine of economic duress emerged, duress was limited to acts of physical coercion. Actual undue influence, therefore, provided an equitable remedy to victims of illegitimate pressure, when threats had been made to property, goods or business. Since the scope of duress has been extended, there is significant overlap between duress and actual undue influence.[63] Indeed, Birks and Yin have argued that elements of duress[64] and undue influence should be assimilated further.[65] Conceptually, however, duress and actual undue influence are distinct concepts. Pawlowski explains that duress has historically been justified in cases where consent is impeded. But actual undue influence is based on constructive fraud[66] (in particular, the idea that one should not benefit from one's own wrongdoing).[67] Slade LJ has described actual undue influence as affirmative proof 'that the wrongdoer exerted undue influence on the claimant in order to

[59] *National Westminster Bank plc v Morgan* [1985] 1 All ER 821, 827 (Lord Scarman); *Allcard v Skinner* (1887) 36 Ch D 145.

[60] M Pawlowski, *Undue Influence and the Family Home* (Cavendish Publishing 2002) 8.

[61] These categories were classified by Cotton LJ in *Allcard*, above n 59, 171.

[62] Ibid, 181.

[63] See *RBS v Etridge (No 2)*, above n 57.

[64] Economic duress in particular.

[65] P Birks and C Nyuk Yin, 'On the Nature of Undue Influence' in J Beatson and D Friedman (eds), *Good Faith and Fault in Contract Law* (Clarendon Press 1995) 57.

[66] See Pawlowski, above n 60, 11.

[67] This view is corroborated by *Halsbury's Laws*, above n 28.

enter into the particular transaction which is impugned'.[68] The party alleging the influence must prove that it has occurred.

Bank of Credit and Commerce International SA v Aboody[69] exemplifies the operation of the doctrine of actual undue influence between husband and wife. In this case, the Court of Appeal found that the husband's behaviour towards his wife constituted bullying. The wife signed company documents after the husband interrupted a meeting she was attending with an independent lawyer and made her cry. The husband was 20 years older than the wife, and she had trusted him with the company documents in question. Even though the wife was experienced in business, the court decided that on the facts she had signed because of the pressure from her husband.

Like other cases of actual undue influence, the bullying behaviour of the husband in *Aboody* was quite extreme. As a result, there must be clear evidence of victimisation for a claim of actual undue influence to be successful.

Application to Prenuptial Agreements

Actual undue influence has not yet been discussed in any prenup cases in the UK. However, in *NA v MA*[70] the court disregarded a postnuptial agreement on the basis of actual undue influence. The agreement was considered as part of the ancillary relief exercise (and therefore, like prenups, would not have been enforced contractually), but Baron J applied contractual principles when deciding on the weight to be attached to the agreement. Her reasoning for refusing to implement the agreement was as follows:

> [T]his post nuptial agreement was offered on a take it or leave it basis at the time of and in the throes of emotional melt down and was stipulated to be the only way in which to save this marriage. It was also in play at a time when the parties were living in the same household, were habitually arguing and where the Wife (on everyone's evidence) was being subject to constant questioning and arguments about her affair.
>
> There was no time for careful reflection. The Wife informed the Court that the Husband pressurised and bullied her to sign from the outset … As the Husband knew that she wanted above all else to save the marriage, felt overwhelmingly guilty and did not want her affair to destroy her or children's lives, his ultimatum about the agreement being a prerequisite to the marriage continuing put her under severe, undue and unacceptable pressure. I find that she was given no effective choice and her free will was overborne. I am absolutely satisfied that the Husband made his position abundantly clear to her whenever the matter was raised. He used his dominant position both emotional and financial (in the sense that he knew she had no financial independence) to ensure that she felt that she had no alternative but to sign the agreement … [H]e told her that she could not come home unless she signed it. She signed the agreement … only because she

[68] *Bank of Credit and Commerce International SA v Aboody* [1990] 1 QB 923, 953.
[69] Ibid.
[70] *NA v MA* [2006] EWHC 2900 (Fam).

> knew that he meant it and she had no realistic alternative if she wanted to return to her home (to be with her children) and to give the marriage a further chance.
>
> The Law … characterises this type of behaviour as undue pressure and undue influence. For these reasons I will not implement the terms of this agreement.[71]

This is a clear example of illegitimate pressure. However, it is not clear whether a prenup created in similar circumstances would be set aside for undue influence, if considered on a purely contractual basis (and not in the context of ancillary relief proceedings). The main justification for the remedy of undue influence in *NA v MA* was that the wife had no 'realistic alternative' to entering the postnuptial agreement, as she would have had to leave her marriage, her home and her children. A court could find that cancelling a wedding might be a more realistic alternative than this, and fail to vitiate the prenup as a result. Indeed, on consideration of wider public interest concerns, threats to end a marriage are much more serious than threats to end an engagement. Vitiating a postnuptial agreement for undue influence is therefore more justifiable on this basis, as the pressure applied is patently illegitimate.

Difficulties with Applying Actual Undue Influence to Prenuptial Agreements

The decision in *NA v MA* is both encouraging and frustrating in equal measure. It illustrates that in certain situations the court will recognise that the reality of negotiating marital agreements is different from contracting in commerce, as Baron J recognised the effect of pressure on the wife 'in the throes of emotional meltdown'.[72] Thus, the law of undue influence enables the court to police cases of extreme pressure. On the other hand, ultimatums like those in *NA v MA* may not evidence undue influence in the context of prenups because the parties have not married yet. However, many couples cohabit and have children before marriage. In this situation, a threat to end an engagement unless an agreement is signed is equally coercive. It is unclear whether the courts would recognise this and find undue influence.

Moreover, for many agreements the pressure is unlikely to be as obvious as it was in *NA v MA*. Hence, there are many instances where agreements have been made under extreme pressure but may not be vitiated according to undue influence. If the victim of the pressure had an alternative to entering the prenup (on an objective assessment) then that party will be held to the agreement, as he or she is considered to have made an autonomous choice. As a result, there could be many instances in which actual undue influence would fail to recognise disparities of power between parties entering prenups.

Indeed, as actual undue influence is comparable to elements of duress (for example, economic duress), the problems and advantages associated with these

[71] Ibid, [128]–[129].
[72] Ibid.

doctrines in relation to prenups are unsurprisingly also similar. Therefore, in situations where one party is warned that the wedding will be cancelled unless the prenup is signed, or if one party is pregnant or if the agreement is signed shortly before the wedding, it is unlikely that a claim of actual undue influence will be successful. If the agreement was presented in a context that truly left the claimant with no time to consider it properly, undue influence may be established. But it is conceivable that the pressure must be glaringly obvious for an agreement to be vitiated on this basis.

Presumed Undue Influence

Background

The rationale of presumed undue influence may be distinguished from duress and actual undue influence because, rather than focusing on any wrongful act that has been committed, the court interferes on the ground of public policy, and also to prevent the abuse of influence arising from certain types of relationship.[73] As Lord Chelmsford put it, presumed undue influence is concerned with situations where 'confidence is necessarily reposed by one [party in another], and … the influence is exerted to obtain an advantage at the expense of the confiding party' by that other.[74] Thus presumed undue influence may be invoked in situations where the extent of the pressure is insufficient to establish duress or actual undue influence, but the effect of that pressure is still coercive due to the confidence and trust existing between the parties to the agreement.

A successful claim of presumed undue influence shifts the burden of proof so that there is a presumption of undue influence (but not a presumption that this influence has been abused)[75] unless it can be rebutted by the respondent. In some cases this presumption arises automatically due to the nature of the relationship, for instance the relationship of solicitor and client.[76] Pursuant to older authorities, a presumption of undue influence arose in cases where the parties were engaged,[77] because 'a young woman engaged to be married … reposes the greatest confidence in her future husband' and 'in many, if not most, cases she would sign anything he put before her'.[78] However, engaged couples are no longer in relevant relationships for presumed undue influence.[79] This is because, as stated in *Zamet v Hyman*, the reliance of a young woman on her fiancé should not be assumed in every case.[80]

[73] See Pawlowski, above n 60, 11, referring to Cotton LJ in *Allcard*, above n 59.

[74] *Tate v Williamson* (1866) 2 Ch App 55, 61 (Lord Chelmsford LC).

[75] See Beatson, above n 15, 289.

[76] See *Aboody*, above n 68.

[77] *Page v Horne* (1848) 11 Beav 227; *Cobbett v Brock* (1855) 20 Beav 524; *Lovesy v Smith* (1880) 15 Ch D 655, cited in Pawlowski, above n 60, 51.

[78] *Re Lloyd's Bank Ltd* [1931] 1 Ch 289, 302 (Maugham J).

[79] *Zamet v Hyman* [1961] 1 WLR 1442.

[80] Ibid, 1446 (Lord Evershed MR).

In addition to engaged couples, spouses are not considered to be relationship cases[81] that create an automatic presumption either. As a result, if unfair pressure has been applied in the context of a prenuptial (or postnuptial) agreement, a presumption of undue influence will arise only if two conditions are met.[82]

First, the claimant must prove that, based on the facts of the case, there is a relationship of trust and confidence in the management of the claimant's financial affairs. This may often be the case between parties to a prenup. In particular, if the couple are cohabiting before the wedding, there may be some level of financial interdependence in the form of joint bank accounts or co-ownership of the home. The Law Commission has said that evidence of reliance or 'something asymmetrical' between the parties would be sufficient to persuade the court that a relationship of trust and confidence exists.[83]

Secondly, the agreement must require explanation in a way that is not readily explicable by the relationship itself.[84] It is more difficult to determine how to satisfy this condition. The Law Commission has said that this will simply depend on 'the terms of the agreement and upon whether or not it obviously puts one party at a disadvantage'.[85] However, it could be argued that power inequalities between parties are usually readily explicable by the relationship they are in. Leverage when negotiating is normally reduced if one party is more dependent on the other for management of finances. Unfortunately the 'normality' of this power imbalance disqualifies prenups from presumed undue influence claims, as such inequities arguably stem from the close relationship the parties enjoy. In order to be successful, the claimant would have to show that he or she did not sign the agreement in accordance with ordinary motives, which preserves this remedy for exceptional cases. Arguably it might be 'ordinary' for someone to sign a prenup without considering the consequences because he or she loves his or her partner. It might also be 'ordinary' to sign an agreement because the wedding has been booked and paid for. Whilst someone's freedom of choice is limited in these situations, it is unclear whether these examples could justify a claim of undue influence.

The operation of presumed undue influence in the context of surety transactions between husband and wife might provide some clarification as to the kind of situations and pressure the court will recognise. In these transactions, the surety is usually the wife, and she provides security (in the form of a second mortgage) over the marital home to a lender for her husband's business debt.[86] The involvement of a third party lender (usually a bank) means that, unlike prenups, these transactions are not contained within the purely private, domestic sphere. Furthermore, this kind of transaction is an example of financial decision making

[81] See *RBS v Etridge (No 2)*, above n 57.

[82] Ibid.

[83] See Law Commission, above n 4.

[84] *RBS v Etridge (No 2)*, above n 57.

[85] Law Commission, above n 4.

[86] B Fehlberg, 'Money and Marriage: Sexually Transmitted Debt in England' (1997) 11 *International Journal of Law, Policy and the Family* 320.

between couples,[87] whereas a prenup is ordinarily viewed as an agreement between individuals to protect their own future financial interests. Despite these important distinctions, the law in this area merits consideration. Presumed undue influence has developed primarily through case law involving second mortgage agreements made by spouses. The relationship between husband and wife when entering these agreements shares similar issues of power with the relationship between parties to prenups. Furthermore, an assessment of the court's ability (or inability) to recognise such issues in the context of surety agreements could be useful when gauging whether the court could recognise similar issues contingent on the enforcement of prenups.

The leading case on the law in this area is *Royal Bank of Scotland Plc v Etridge (No 2)*. The House of Lords heard eight conjoined appeals in this case, where the wife had acted as surety for her husband's debt to the bank. Undue influence was claimed in this context in order to vitiate second mortgage agreements, where the family home was being repossessed by the bank as a result of the couple's defaulting on mortgage repayments. This judgment indicates a concern for imbalances of power between parties, and recognition by the judiciary of the effect of these inequities in the context of intimate relationships. For instance, Lord Nicholls said that 'the court will … note, as a matter of fact, the opportunities for abuse which flow from a wife's confidence in her husband'.[88] Simultaneously, however, the practical outcome of this case suggests that this appreciation does not always translate into practice, as presumed undue influence is often difficult to establish.

In cases where presumed undue influence was successfully established, the wife had not obtained competent and independent legal advice[89] before entering the suretyship transaction. However, in *RBS v Etridge (No 2)*, there was evidence of pressure in some cases that was not sufficient to vitiate the agreement. For example, Mrs Gill and her solicitor were under the impression that the charge on her home was for £36,000 when it was for £100,000. Her testimony was that she felt she had no alternative but to enter the agreement, and declared the following:

> I did sign the documents put in front of me but with time for more reflection, and in less urgent circumstances, with proper advice to think about it, and time to consult a solicitor of my own, I would never have done so.[90]

The court decided that in different circumstances, Mrs Gill would have still entered the agreement, and therefore it did not find undue influence in this case. Furthermore, in Mrs Etridge's case, it did not matter to the court that she claimed not to properly understand the consequences of the surety transaction. The court found no evidence of any abuse or bullying that pressurised Mrs Etridge to act as

[87] Ibid.

[88] See *RBS v Etridge (No 2)*, above n 57, 19.

[89] McKendrick has said that evidence of independent and competent legal advice will usually (but not always) rebut a presumption of undue influence: E McKendrick, *Contract Law* (8th edn, Palgrave Macmillan 2009) 292.

[90] See *RBS v Etridge (No2)*, above n 57, 281.

surety, and so the claim of undue influence was unsuccessful.[91] These examples suggest that unless the surety has been subjected to fairly blatant pressure by his or her partner, or has not obtained independent and competent legal advice, his or her claim of presumed undue influence is unlikely to be successful.

This is disappointing given that there is clearly a gendered power imbalance attached to suretyship transactions, which the court does not appear to ameliorate in most cases.[92] Indeed, when referring to the position of husband and wife in *Barclays Bank plc v O'Brien*,[93] Lord Browne-Wilkinson said:

> [T]he sexual and emotional ties between the parties provide a ready weapon for undue influence: a wife's true wishes can easily be overborne because of her fear of destroying or damaging the wider relationship between her and her husband if she opposes his wishes.[94]

Nevertheless, whilst the potential for unfair pressure is recognised, Auchmuty believes that judges are reluctant to recognise power imbalances commonly attached to this gender dimension because they are desensitised to it.[95] As pressure is arguably an 'ever-present danger'[96] in agreements between husband and wife, Auchmuty has noted that the judiciary views such pressure as an ordinary consequence of intimate transactions, and so will not interfere. As has already been noted, pressure must be exceptional in the view of the court to justify an agreement's being vitiated.

Application to Prenuptial Agreements

As stated previously, the context of surety transactions is very different from the situation of prenups. Whilst husband and wife are the only parties to a prenup, surety transactions are characterised by a more complex web of relationships between husband, wife and the bank. In these cases, a transaction will be called into question when the bank has failed to ensure that the parties obtained independent legal advice. Therefore, the focus of suretyship transactions is on the behaviour of the bank. Clearly this is not the case as regards prenups. The absence of the bank changes the tenor of the relationship and the agreement at issue. In these more intimate situations (where the commercial third party is absent), it is unclear whether the moneyed spouse is burdened with the same responsibility for ensuring that independent legal advice is sought by the non-moneyed spouse. Thus, the court arguably approaches these two situations differently in cases of presumed undue influence.

[91] Ibid, 221.
[92] See Fehlberg, above n 86.
[93] *Barclays Bank plc v O'Brien* [1994] 1 AC 180.
[94] Ibid, 190.
[95] R Auchmuty, 'The Rhetoric of Equality and the Problem of Heterosexuality' in L Mulcahy and S Wheeler (eds), *Feminist Perspectives on Contract Law* (Routledge 2005) 51.
[96] *Royal Bank of Scotland v Etridge* [1998] All ER (D) 408 (Stuart Smith LJ).

There are unfortunately no reported cases in England, Wales and Northern Ireland in which presumed undue influence has been considered in detail in connection with prenups. Therefore, US cases again provide an interesting insight into the application of this doctrine to such agreements. Section 177 of the Second Restatement of Contracts outlines the law of undue influence in the US as follows:

> Undue influence is unfair persuasion of a party who is under the domination of the person exercising the persuasion or who *by virtue of the relation between them* is justified in assuming that that person will not act in a manner inconsistent with his welfare.[97]

It appears that the effect of this provision in many states is a formulation of undue influence that is quite similar to that in the UK. In California, for example, the courts have developed a body of case law surrounding undue influence in a relationship based on trust and confidence.[98] In the case *In Re Marriage of Burkle*, the court helpfully summarised the operation of presumed undue influence in relation to postnuptial agreements:

> A presumption of undue influence does not arise in an interspousal transaction unless one spouse obtains an unfair advantage or obtains property for which no or clearly inadequate consideration has been given. The presumption does not apply to a post-marital agreement in which both spouses obtain advantages.[99]

Applying this case, it seems that a prenup would need to be clearly one-sided for an argument of presumed undue influence to be made.

There does not appear to be an abundance of US case law that expressly considers presumed undue influence. As explained in chapter three, the US courts appear to be more concerned with the concept of 'voluntariness' when enforcing prenups. In spite of this, presumed undue influence was an important consideration in *Lutgert v Lutgert*.[100] The court explained its reasoning for finding a presumption of undue influence:

> There is ample conclusive evidence of [undue influence] in this case. To begin with, the husband sprang the agreement upon [his wife] and demanded its execution within twenty-four hours of the wedding; and it has been said that a woman ought not be 'too much hurried' into such an agreement … passage had been booked for a honeymoon cruise to Europe; rings had been bought; a trousseau had been bought; all invitations to family and friends had been given; all arrangements otherwise had been made; an ultimatum had been delivered by the husband: 'No agreement, no wedding'; and obviously, there arose a sudden stark awareness of the potential immediate loss of a future life of enormous grandeur.[101]

It seems that the combination of factors described in this case persuaded the court that the wife had signed the agreement under a presumption of undue influence.

97 See Restatement of Contracts, above n 34 (emphasis added).

98 A Nievod, 'Undue Influence in Contract and Probate Law' (1993) 10(1) *Cultic Studies Journal* 1.

99 *In Re Marriage of Burkle* 43 Cal Rptr 4d 181 (California 2006), 185.

100 *Lutgert v Lutgert* 338 So 2d 1111 (Florida 1976).

101 Ibid, 1116.

This indicates that the pressure of individual circumstances is often important. On the other hand, a significant disparity of power between the parties themselves does not appear to be as persuasive in the courtroom, according to *Delorean v Delorean*.[102] The New Jersey court explained why a claim of undue influence was not successful in this case:

> While [the wife's] decision may not have been wise, it appears that she had sufficient time to consider the consequences of signing the agreement and, indeed, although she initially refused to sign it, after conferring with her intended spouse and an attorney, she reconsidered and decided to sign it. Concededly, the husband was 25-years older and a high powered senior executive with General Motors Corporation, but she was not a 'babe in the woods.' She was 23-years old with some business experience in the modelling and entertainment industry; she had experienced an earlier marriage and the problems wrought by a divorce; and she had advice from an attorney who, although not of her own choosing, did apparently give her competent advice and recommended that she not sign. While it may have been embarrassing to cancel the wedding only a few hours before it was to take place, she certainly was not compelled to go through with the ceremony. There was no fraud or misrepresentation committed by the husband. He made it perfectly clear that he did not want her to receive any portion of the marital assets that were in his name. At no time did she ever make an effort to void the agreement and, of course, it was never voided. Under these circumstances the court is satisfied that the wife entered into the agreement voluntarily and without any fraud or duress being exerted upon her.[103]

In this case a disparity of power was certainly evident. The husband was much wealthier than the wife and was 25 years her senior. But the court regarded the wife's actions as being completely voluntary. It is likely that the wife's previous divorce was influential, as this was one of the reasons the court did not consider her to be a naive 'babe in the woods'.

If a claimant is in a weak bargaining position and has received neither independent nor competent legal advice before entering a prenup, it might be more difficult to rebut a presumption of undue influence when a relationship of trust and confidence has been established. The court in *Fletcher v Fletcher* said that there might be a presumption of undue influence if the agreement were to be presented a short time before the wedding, and if 'the postponement of the wedding would cause significant hardship, embarrassment or emotional distress'.[104]

Difficulties with Applying Presumed Undue Influence to Prenuptial Agreements

Although prenups and surety transactions are arguably distinct, the prevalence of pressure in surety transactions is also a feature of prenups. Therefore, it is conceivable that in the situations considered above, where the non-moneyed spouse is

[102] *Delorean v Delorean* 211 NJ Super 432 (New Jersey 1986).

[103] Ibid, 436.

[104] *Fletcher v Fletcher* 628 NE 2d 1343 (Ohio 1994) [1348].

pregnant or is faced with an ultimatum, the law of presumed undue influence is unlikely to ameliorate the situation. This is due to a problem that Auchmuty articulates as 'the impossibility of demonstrating "special features" that would mark the proceedings out from ordinary marital interactions'.[105]

Like duress and actual undue influence, a major difficulty with applying presumed undue influence to prenups is distinguishing between abnormal and normal pressure. Hence, it is likely that an agreement will be vitiated on this ground only if there are illegitimate and fairly explicit examples of pressure and coercion. Many prenups made in the context of unfair imbalances of power will not justify intervention by the court. Familiarity with subtle inequities invariably makes these inequities acceptable in the eyes of the law, even if the effect of this is unjust. This is because disparity of power is viewed as a typical consequence of the intimacy of the parties. On this basis, failure to recognise or police these issues masks the fact that the weaker party has not truly bargained freely and autonomously.

Indeed, unequal power between parties to a prenup is so common the Law Commission in the UK has proposed that presumed undue influence should not apply to these agreements at all. It has said that marital property agreements could be 'unduly vulnerable to challenge on the grounds of undue influence',[106] and suggested that requiring independent legal advice would be a reasonable alternative to the equitable remedy of presumed undue influence. This proposal is logical given the fact that McKendrick has said that a presumption of undue influence is normally rebutted by evidence that the claimant has received independent and competent legal advice.[107] However, whilst the value of independent legal advice should not be underestimated, it does not make bargaining inequalities disappear.

The law of undue influence is more sensitive to issues of power in domestic agreements. Conceptually, therefore, it should recognise the bargaining inequalities overlooked by the law of duress, which in principle treats domestic agreements like commercial contracts. But although presumed undue influence is probably the most appropriate contractual remedy for weaker bargaining parties in prenups, it may fail to take less obvious forms of manipulation and influence within the relationship into account.

A major problem with duress and undue influence is that these doctrines focus on factual enquiries into the wrongdoing of the respondent and the consent of the claimant. These enquiries are informed by pressure, and not by the fairness of the situation. This approach is arguably inappropriate when applied to prenups because the wrongdoing of the moneyed spouse is not always apparent. There may be severe issues of bargaining inequality during prenuptial negotiations that have no connection to the conscience of the defendant. Similarly, the claimant is often presumed to have entered an agreement freely because he or she has received independent legal advice. Such advice will ensure that an informed

105 See Auchmuty, above n 95, 66.

106 See Law Commission, above n 4, para 6.40.

107 See McKendrick, above n 89, 292.

choice has been made in many situations. But treating the fact of independent advice as determinative evidence of consent ignores the possibility that parties' decision making might be influenced by other more powerful pressures. Indeed, evidence from New York in chapter three indicates that this is often the case. Furthermore, the manipulation of the non-moneyed spouse by the respondent is only recognised within the traditional boundaries of duress and undue influence. The constrained nature of these doctrines means that the pressure emanating from the wider circumstances of the impending marriage is often overlooked. Therefore, considering unconscionability in principle within the prenuptial context could be useful, as it views fairness as being relevant when setting contracts aside.

Unconscionability

Background

The overarching aim of the doctrines of duress and undue influence is to prevent the stronger contracting party from attaining an unjust advantage over the weaker party by coercive means. In *Lloyds Bank Ltd v Bundy*,[108] Lord Denning MR proposed that this common theme should unify these doctrines under a general doctrine of inequality of bargaining power, or unconscionability. Rather than focusing on aspects like illegitimate pressure and causation, a remedy would instead be based on whether the agreement met a threshold level of fairness.[109] Therefore, in theory the court could recognise

> when the parties have not met on equal terms—when the one is so strong in bargaining power and the other so weak—that, as a matter of fairness, it is not right that the strong should be allowed to push the weak to the wall.[110]

This principle is ostensibly applicable to prenups, as it is unfair to allow the moneyed spouse to dictate the terms of an agreement, even though this often happens. But although the idea of a general doctrine of unconscionablity has triggered a great deal of academic debate,[111] it has been refuted by the judiciary, with steadfast opposition from Lord Scarman in particular.[112] He maintains that Parliament has placed the necessary restrictions on contract law,[113] and that agreements should

[108] *Lloyds Bank Ltd v Bundy* [1975] QB 326.

[109] S Nathan Thal, 'The Inequality of Bargaining Power Doctrine: The Problem of Defining Contractual Unfairness' (1988) 8 *OJLS* 17.

[110] See *Bundy*, above n 108, 336–337.

[111] M Chen-Wishart, *Unconscionable Bargains* (Butterworths 1989); N Bamforth, 'Unconscionability as a Vitiating Factor' [1995] *LMCLQ* 538; SM Waddams, 'Unconscionability in Contracts' (1976) 39 *MLR* 369.

[112] See *Pao On*, above n 23; also *Morgan*, above n 59.

[113] In *Morgan*, above n 59, Lord Scarman rejected a general doctrine of unconscionability on the basis that statute, such as the Consumer Credit Act 1974, provides adequate protection.

not be set aside simply because one party has unfairly exploited its dominant bargaining position.[114] Other critics have said Lord Denning's suggestions are too bold in light of contract law's general reticence towards policing unfairness. For instance, Trietel has said that the scope of unfairness is too difficult to define, and that this uncertainty is unwelcome within the law of contract.[115]

However, principles of fairness and inequality of bargaining power can be traced into the operation of doctrines like undue influence. Lord Scarman has also noted that 'a court in the exercise of this equitable jurisdiction is a court of conscience'.[116] Moreover, there are many uncertainties within contract law, such as ascertaining the scope of lawful act duress, or distinguishing between legitimate and illegitimate pressure in relation to duress and undue influence.

On this basis, it is less persuasive to argue that fairness is an unsavoury concept in contract because it engenders uncertainty. Indeed, the underlying principle of inequality of bargaining power is often influential on judicial reasoning in this jurisdiction. Commentators like Thal and Phillips are in favour of a general doctrine of unconscionability, which could be developed by case law the way other doctrines, like undue influence, have developed.[117] However, the purpose of this chapter is not to assess whether this should be the case: it is to consider how existing contractual principle may ameliorate prenuptial imbalances of power.

Although there is no unifying doctrine of unconscionability in the UK, the courts have recognised an equitable jurisdiction to set aside unconscionable bargains.[118] Agreements will be treated as unconscionable[119] only in limited circumstances. In cases where there is unequal bargaining power between the parties,[120] the court will not find unconscionability unless the respondent is also guilty of wrongful conduct. As with undue influence, it is necessary that the conscience of the stronger party is affected by his or her behaviour.[121] Therefore, if the agreement is unfair but the parties are innocent, no remedy of unconscionable bargaining will be available.

McKendrick has said that articulating the circumstances in which a bargain is unconscionable is problematic.[122] Capper's assessment of the case law is that for an agreement to be unconscionable, the court must be persuaded that the dominant party consciously intended to take advantage of the weaker party.[123] This intention could be evidenced by the imposition of harsh terms in a morally reprehensible

[114] See *Pao On*, above n 23.

[115] G Treitel, *The Law of Contract* (7th edn, Stevens & Sons 1987) 58–61.

[116] See *Morgan*, above n 59, 825.

[117] See Thal, above n 109; also Phillips, above n 24.

[118] *Fry v Lane* (1888) 40 Ch D 312.

[119] To be clear, unconscionability is discussed in this chapter as a vitiating factor and not as a description of the parties' conduct. This distinction is considered in Bamforth, above n 111.

[120] *Alec Lobb (Garages) Ltd v Total Oil GB Ltd* [1985] 1 All ER 303.

[121] It has been mooted whether presumed undue influence and unconscionable bargaining should be assimilated, for they are so similar in nature. M Trebilcock, 'The Doctrine of Inequality of Bargaining Power: Post-Benthamite Economics in the House of Lords' (1976) 26 *University of Toronto Law Journal* 359.

[122] See McKendrick, above n 89, referring to *Boustany v Piggott* (1993) 42 WIR175.

[123] D Capper, 'The Unconscionable Bargain in the Common Law World' (2010) 126 *LQR* 403.

manner, and therefore Capper has said that unconscionable bargaining could be viewed as requiring more overt forms of pressure than undue influence.[124] To behave in a morally reprehensible manner suggests that the party benefitting from the alleged unconscionable bargain must have actively sought out such a bargain, well aware of the unfair advantage being obtained. However, an unconscionable bargain might also be found in cases where the special disadvantage to or impairment of one party leads to the other receiving a *passive* benefit from the transaction. The defendant obtains an unfair advantage passively because he or she only has constructive knowledge of the other parties' disadvantage, and therefore did not actively seek out an unconscionable bargain.[125] Interestingly, the courts in England and Wales are much less willing to find an unconscionable bargain in cases of passive receipt than in other jurisdictions, such as Australia and Ireland.[126] Capper has noted that these common law jurisdictions do not rely on the proof of morally reprehensible conduct,[127] and so there is more flexibility to find an unconscionable bargain when the defendant has merely accepted terms that are very much to his or her advantage from a vulnerable party who did not receive independent legal advice.[128] This scenario is much more akin to the operation of undue influence in surety transactions, which is why in Australia, for example, Sir Anthony Mason notes that 'the unconscionable bargain has relegated undue influence into second place'.[129] But in English law, Lord Denning MR's vision of a general doctrine of unconscionability has not come to fruition, and the case law suggests only *active* extortion of the more vulnerable party's agreement will do for an unconscionable bargain to be found.[130]

Backhouse v Backhouse[131] provides an interesting discussion of unconscionable bargaining when the agreement is between husband and wife. The judge considered the application of the doctrine to a property transaction that transferred the matrimonial home to the husband. Due to the court's jurisdiction to make ancillary relief provision in this case, Balcombe J did not have to decide the validity of the transaction, but he approached his assessment of what financial provision should be made on the basis that the transaction was not made (as it was an unconscionable bargain).[132] He considered the agreement to be unconscionable because, applying *Fry v Lane*,[133] the wife's share was sold at an undervalue and she

124 Ibid, 404.

125 *Cresswell v Potter* [1978] 1 WLR 255.

126 See Capper, above n 123.

127 Ibid.

128 *Nicols v Jessop* [1986] 1 NZLR 226.

129 See Capper, above n 123, referring to Sir Anthony Mason, in 'The Place of Equity and Equitable Doctrine in the Common Law World—an Australian Perspective' in D Waters (ed), *Equity, Fiduciaries and Trusts* (Carswell 1993) 410.

130 *Credit Lyonnais Bank Nederland NV v Burch* [2002] EWCA Civ 885.

131 *Backhouse v Backhouse* [1978] 1 All ER 1158.

132 Ibid, 252.

133 See *Fry v Lane*, above n 118.

did not receive independent legal advice. Whilst she was not 'poor and ignorant'[134] pursuant to *Fry v Lane*, she was not experienced or knowledgeable about property transactions, or about the conveyancing document in question. Interestingly, the fact that the parties in this case did not have equal bargaining power was highly relevant, and it was also recognised that the wife had experienced 'great emotional strain'[135] when signing the agreement because of the breakdown of her marriage. In this intimate context the court accounted for the fairness of the situation and did not allow an agreement to stand that deprived the wife of 'her only substantial asset'.[136] In spite of this, Pawlowski asserts that *Boustany v Piggott*[137] has more recently clarified that 'unequal bargaining power, or objectively unreasonable terms, will not in themselves provide a basis for equitable interference in the absence of unconscientious or extortionate abuse of power'.[138] This suggests that prenups might be considered to be unconscionable bargains only in narrow circumstances.

Application to Prenuptial Agreements

The concept of unconscionability is relevant to the discretionary enforcement of prenups in the UK. If *Backhouse* is applied, it could be argued that a prenup is an unconscionable bargain if the moneyed spouse is experienced in business and financial matters, and the non-moneyed spouse does not have this experience. However, other cases suggest that the behaviour of the moneyed spouse must also have been immoral.[139] Furthermore, there is no way of knowing what approach the court would adopt, as there are no cases that specifically consider the doctrine of unconscionable bargaining in the context of prenups. As a result, it is again convenient to consider the approach of the courts in US cases.

The law of unconscionability in the US differs from the law in the UK. In the US, a more general concept of unconscionability is incorporated into statute. Pursuant to the Second Restatement of Contracts:

> If a contract or term thereof is unconscionable at the time the contract is made a court may refuse to enforce the contract, or may enforce the remainder of the contract without the unconscionable term, or may so limit the application of any unconscionable term as to avoid any unconscionable result.[140]

This doctrine of unconscionability only applies to the process under which the agreement was created. It should be distinguished from the concept of unconscionability referred to in chapter three, which requires an assessment of the

134 Ibid.
135 See *Backhouse*, above n 131, 251.
136 Ibid, 244.
137 See *Boustany*, above n 122.
138 See Pawlowski, above n 60, 29.
139 See *Boustany*, above n 122.
140 See Restatement of Contracts, above n 34, §208.

agreement at the time of enforcement. *Morad v Morad*,[141] which concerned the enforceability of a separation agreement, defined unconscionability as follows:

> An unconscionable bargain is one which no person in his or her senses and not under delusion would make on the one hand, and no honest and fair person would accept on the other, the inequality being so strong and manifest as to shock the conscience and confound the judgment of any person of common sense.[142]

This is a high threshold, under which agreements must be shockingly unfair to be unconscionable. In the case *In Re Marriage of Bernard*,[143] the prenup was procedurally unconscionable because the terms were extremely one-sided. The wife testified that she felt she had no choice but to sign the agreement. She did not have the benefit of independent counsel[144] and the parties' bargaining positions were 'grossly imbalanced'.[145] However, as *Sailer v Sailer*[146] noted, the standard of unconscionability for prenups in the US is the same as the standard used in commercial law.[147] This commercial standard will often fail to recognise the more subtle problems of power that feature in intimate contracts like prenups. As a result, prenuptial issues less extreme than those in *Bernard* are unlikely to be taken into account by the court.

Difficulties with Applying Unconscionability to Prenuptial Agreements

From the perspective of the judiciary in the UK, it is likely to be difficult to persuade the court that a prenup is an unconscionable bargain unless there is evidence of explicit exploitation from the more powerful party. It is probable that even this approach would not compensate for cases where power disparities within a prenup are overlooked by undue influence. This is because in many cases it will be difficult to prove that the respondent has clearly acted in a morally reprehensible manner. As with duress and undue influence, this suggests that only evidence of blatant pressure would be deemed unconscionable by the court. On the other hand, a judicial attitude that reflects Lord Denning MR's proposition of an inequality of bargaining power doctrine could be beneficial in the prenuptial context. This would arguably give fairness a more influential role in the courtroom, which could facilitate recognition of more subtle instances of bargaining inequality. Yet this development might also fail to address many power issues attached to

[141] *Morad v Morad* 27 AD 3d 626 (New York 2006).

[142] Ibid, 628.

[143] *In Re Marriage of Bernard* 155 P 3d 171 (Washington 2007).

[144] Although she had received legal advice, the court felt that the wife's attorney had not advised her accurately.

[145] See *Bernard*, above n 143, [16].

[146] *Sailer v Sailer* 788 NW 2d 604 (North Dakota 2010).

[147] This statement was made in reference to s 6 of UPAA, which discusses the standard of unconscionability for prenups.

prenups, as the US case law suggests that a contract is unconscionable only in quite exceptional circumstances.

Conclusion

The purpose of this chapter has been to assess whether contract law can effectively recognise issues of power between parties to prenups. In order to do so, contract law principles must be able to recognise situations in which the autonomy of parties is compromised. This is important, because earlier chapters have explained that whilst enforcing prenups is not always problematic, sometimes the sacrifices made by non-moneyed spouses leave them in a difficult position on divorce. Party autonomy is also compromised when unequal bargaining power leads to the creation of an agreement that is much more favourable to one party at the expense of the other party.

However, these contractual imbalances are typical in commercial contract making. It is a feature of the marketplace that each party exploits any contractual advantage it may have for its own benefit. The boundaries of right and wrong conduct are set out by the doctrines discussed above: duress, undue influence and, in some cases, unconscionable bargaining. This chapter has considered the capacity of these doctrines to address more intimate power imbalances. However, it is also important to look to the theory underpinning the law of contract. The capability of contractual doctrines to address prenuptial power issues will often depend on their rationale, and on the principles that have influenced their development. Chapter five will explore contract theory, and whether an alternative contractual approach to prenups might be more appropriate.

5

Towards a Feminist Relational Contract Theory of Prenuptial Agreements

> [O]nce you say, there was no fraud, duress, coercion ... in the formation of the contract, then it's just a contract ... whether it is a bad bargain it is the bargain you made and you will be held to it because there [would] be chaos if people weren't held to their contracts. So you have to have either a very sloppy judge or an outrageous set of circumstances to get a prenup overturned.[1]

Introduction

As this book has argued, there are two significant problems with treating prenups like ordinary contracts. First, the balance of power between parties to these agreements is usually unequal, and thus may not represent the autonomy of both parties. Secondly, circumstances often change significantly from the time a couple enter into an agreement to the point at which they separate. There is no legislation that deals explicitly with these issues, and so if prenups have contractual force, the court reaches for existing contractual tools to find a solution. Nevertheless, chapter four demonstrated that these tools (namely the doctrines of duress, undue influence and unconscionability) fall short of addressing issues of power connected to prenups. Indeed, the relatively limited scope of these contractual doctrines means that equal power is often presumed in practice.

This chapter will explore why this is the case, beginning with an overview of theories that have shaped existing contractual doctrine. This will subsequently facilitate an understanding of the adequacies and inadequacies of contractual remedies for power disparities in intimate relationships. However, in highlighting the inadequacies of contract law, it is important not to rule out alternative contractual approaches more suited to prenups. The second section of the chapter will therefore present an explanation of relational contract theory, pioneered by Ian Macneil. This theory is arguably the antithesis of 'mainstream' contractual ways

[1] Practitioner 3.

of thinking, because instead of viewing relationships as contracts, contracts are viewed as relationships.[2] As a result, relational contract theory provides a means of deconstructing the theory behind existing doctrine by highlighting the importance of context, and thus can be developed to recognise and engage with the complex nature of prenups.

This development will be pursued in the third section of this chapter, which will argue that relational contract theory should be considered in line with feminist perspectives. One of the main reasons for this is that relational contract theory is primarily intended to resolve contextual problems in the commercial sphere. Although this does not render its application to prenups useless, commentators have advised caution when applying to intimate agreements a theory that has been created in a commercial context. As Scoular explains:

> Macneil's focus [on relational contract] would seem to provide a hospitable framework for feminists attempting to disrupt dominant norms of contract. While certainly offering a parallel description of contract law's inability to be context-specific, it should be noted that it also applies in a very different context … [W]e must be vigilant and not rush in to uncritically adopt into a long term intimate context norms which apply to long term commercial transactions. This is a pit into which significant and oft-quoted feminist work has already fallen.[3]

Nevertheless, an explicitly feminist perception of relational contract theory might be more appropriate when developing a suitable contractual approach for prenups, in addition to emphasising the particular context in which these agreements are made. Feminist perspectives provide a crucial insight into power imbalance[4] because, as Conaghan puts it, they 'highlight the gendered assumptions embedded in [legal and social] arrangements, assumptions too often rendered invisible'.[5] Indeed, the problem with theories included within what Conaghan refers to as 'traditional academia' is that they are objective and gender neutral, and are ill equipped to deal with the emotional intricacies of prenups. Therefore, this chapter will employ feminist perspectives on contract and autonomy to make *visible* the gender dimension of prenups obscured by orthodox contract theory. In doing so, feminism proffers a more profound understanding of the prenuptial power issues not addressed in practice.

The fourth section of this chapter will combine feminist and relational contract theory to form an alternative view of autonomy. This approach attaches significance to elements of the prenuptial relationship left out of traditional conceptions of these agreements, and therefore produces a different understanding and appreciation of how power operates between the parties.

[2] L Mulcahy, 'The Limitations of Love and Altruism—Feminist Perspectives on Contract Law' in L Mulcahy and S Wheeler (eds), *Feminist Perspectives on Contract Law* (Routledge 2005) 8.

[3] J Scoular, 'The Revival of Equitable Doctrine in Scots Law—a Space for Gender Concerns?' in S Scott-Hunt and H Lim (eds), *Feminist Perspectives on Equity and Trusts* (Routledge 2001) 126.

[4] See G Brod, 'Premarital Agreements and Gender Justice' (1994) 6 *Yale Journal of Law and Feminism* 229.

[5] J Conaghan, 'Reassessing the Feminist Theoretical Project in Law' (2000) 27(3) *Journal of Law and Society* 351, 359.

Perhaps the most difficult issue for which this chapter must account is what Hadfield has called the 'dilemma of choice'. She explains this as 'the conflict between promoting women's autonomy and freedom of choice on the one hand, and protecting women from the harmful consequences of choices made under conditions of inequality on the other'.[6] This dilemma resonates with the difficulties surrounding prenups, whereby protecting either spouse from the harsh consequences of an agreement could also mean limiting his or her agency to enter into a prenup in the first place. The majority of the court in *Radmacher*[7] was in favour of enforcing prenups because the outcome of these agreements is what the parties have chosen. But the court's conception of choice represents the dilemma described by Hadfield, as it arguably fails to encapsulate the context in which prenups are often signed, where the autonomy exercised by one of the parties is undermined by a disparity of power. In other words, the autonomy or free choice of the parties is presumed by the court. The following section explores some of the theory from which this view of autonomy has emerged, to highlight why perspectives influenced by relational and feminist theories of contract are more appropriate than traditional contractual perspectives when recognising the power dimension of prenups. The alternative view posited by relational and feminist theories enables power to be recognised in numerous contexts where disparities of power exist, but the particular context of prenups is the focus of this book. Prenups are uniquely problematic because the intimate nature of the agreement is exacerbated by the fact that it is made before the marriage, before the circumstances of the parties on relationship breakdown are known, and before the respective financial and non-financial contributions of the parties can be valued and accounted for in the redistribution of assets. For these reasons, existing contractual views of autonomy must be re-evaluated, to ascertain whether these particular problems can be addressed when prenups are given effect on divorce.

'The Theory is a Mess'[8]

Considering contract theory is a complicated task. There is no definitive theory of contract, but there is a plethora of perspectives, particularly regarding the degree to which the state ought to intervene in agreements. Thus Atiyah has said that whilst contract law works 'well enough' in practice, 'the theory is a mess'.[9] The lack of any definitive theory of contract is evident in the diversity of approaches and philosophies adopted by the judiciary. This is exemplified by the opposing views

[6] G Hadfield, 'The Dilemma of Choice: A Feminist Perspective on *The Limits of Freedom of Contract*' (1996) 33 *Osgoode Hall Law Journal* 337.

[7] *Radmacher v Granatino* [2010] UKSC 42.

[8] P Atiyah, *An Introduction to the Law of Contract* (5th edn, Clarendon Law Series 1995) 173.

[9] Ibid.

of Lord Denning and Lord Scarman, which were examined in chapter four. Lord Denning famously suggested a unifying contractual doctrine based on fairness, which would allow the court to vitiate unconscionable transactions.[10] However, Lord Scarman later asserted his opinion that judicial intervention on this basis was inappropriate.[11] According to Atiyah, the judiciary's divergence of approach has led to an *ad hoc* development of the law because, as he puts it, 'there is no such thing as a typical contract at all'.[12] From this perspective, there is no reason to exclude prenups from contractual regulation, because the distinct nature of these agreements does not make them special when every contract is unique.

In spite of this, many theorists have attempted to discern a unifying set of contractual principles. In an attempt to untangle the mess of theory to which Atiyah refers, contractarians frequently refer to two models: classical and neo-classical. The centrality of classical and neo-classical theories within modern contract law means that they represent a 'mainstream' school of thought, and the primary theoretical influences underpinning these models are considered below.

Classical Contract Theory

According to Mulcahy, the classical model, which gained prominence in the 1800s, was 'clearly designed to serve a free market or laissez-faire economy and to act as a framework within which the free play of competitive forces could operate'.[13] The focus of this model is on the liberty of the contracting parties to make agreements to their own advantage, which in turn would facilitate competition.[14] Thus, at the heart of this approach is the principle that parties have not only freedom to contract (that is, to decide whether or not to contract) but also freedom *of* contract.[15] This means that the terms of a contract are dictated by the parties and not the law. As a result, intervention by the court either to vary or to set aside an agreement is prima facie completely discordant with the freedom of contract principle. Contracts create obligations, and it is not up to the court to allow people to avoid these obligations, because this would undermine the sanctity of the agreement.

Classical contract theory is still highly influential on the operation of modern contract law. For instance, the concept of freedom of contract is, to a degree,[16] significant to the enforcement of prenups, as the court has highlighted the

[10] *Lloyds Bank Ltd v Bundy* [1975] QB 326.

[11] *National Westminster Bank plc v Morgan* [1985] 2 WLR 588.

[12] See Atiyah, above n 8.

[13] L Mulcahy, *Contract Law in Perspective* (5th edn, Routledge-Cavendish 2008) 28.

[14] For more on this, see C Smith, *Adam Smith's Political Philosophy: The Invisible Hand and Spontaneous Order* (Taylor and Francis 2005).

[15] S Smith, *Contract Theory* (OUP 2004) 59.

[16] Admittedly, freedom of contract within the context of prenups is limited, because parties do not have the freedom to oust the jurisdiction of the court to make financial provision on divorce.

importance of respecting the autonomy of the parties.[17] Indeed, the judiciary has made it absolutely clear that it is irrelevant whether or not the outcome of a pre-nup is different from what the court would have ordered on divorce.[18] Couples should have *freedom* to order their own affairs. Similarly, doctrines like duress and undue influence are limited (as chapter four has described) because of respect for freedom of contract, and so it is important to explore this feature of the classical model in greater detail.

Freedom of contract, and the idea that the state should not interfere in contractual obligations, engenders a number of presumptions about the relationship between the contracting parties. That is, the emphasis is on the separate and individual intentions of the parties, rather than on the connection between the parties. Parties are presumed to bargain at arm's length, an abstract concept that suggests the completely selfish pursuit of individual interests. Most pertinently, freedom of contract assumes that the parties have contracted freely and autonomously. For if it is recognised that the parties have not truly consented to an agreement, the principle of freedom of contract is undermined. Under the classical model, contracting parties are self-motivated, self-assertive and agree to self-imposed obligations.[19] Fairness is achieved by the parties and not the court, which is not perceived to be problematic because the bargaining power of the parties is presumed to be equal. Parties are held to freely-made agreements, no matter how onerous the terms.

Unsurprisingly, prioritising autonomy in this way often means that bargaining inequalities are overlooked. However, the presumption made by freedom of contract, that parties always agree on a level playing field, is misleading. In cases where there is not a level playing field, the concept of freedom of contract is meaningless because the freedom of one party is restricted. Herring explains that the individualistic characterisations of autonomy associated with traditional contract perspectives emphasise 'the values of independence and self-sufficiency, while it is inter-dependence and connection which are the values at the heart of many people's lives'.[20] Such erroneous assumptions about equality can mean that 'contracts simply reflect power, or lack of it'.[21]

On the other hand, contract law has developed to recognise that parties to a contract do not always bargain from positions of equal power. This goes some way towards explaining the judiciary's increased emphasis on contractual fairness, which is considered in the following section.

[17] See Charles J in *V v V* [2011] EWHC 3230 (Fam), who overturned an earlier county court decision that took a 'pre *Radmacher*' approach and did not attach sufficient weight to the parties' 'choice they made as a basis for their marriage' ([72]).

[18] See *Radmacher*, above n 7.

[19] A Donchin, 'Understanding autonomy relationally' (2001) 26 *Journal of Medicine and Philosophy* 365.

[20] J Herring, 'Relational autonomy and rape' in S Day-Sclater *et al* (eds) *Regulating Autonomy: Sex, Reproduction and Family* (Hart Publishing 2009) 55.

[21] See Mulcahy, above n 13.

Neo-classical Contract Theory

Neo-classical contract theory might be described as a more principled and fair version of its classical predecessor, because it allows for exceptions to freedom of contract, such as vitiating factors. Perhaps the greatest influence on this development of fairness within contract law is the law of equity, as Keeton and Sheridan have said that the improving virtues of common law may be emended to it.[22] Before the unification of judicature,[23] equity was a source of law separate from the common law. In the early nineteenth century, equity intervened where common law did not, in situations of power imbalance between parties to an agreement. An early example of this is the Court of Chancery's intervention in 'catching bargains'.[24] These were agreements made in a specific context, where an expectant heir had transferred his expectancy at considerable undervalue. Intervention in these special cases indicated that the Court of Chancery recognised the importance of the conscience of the defendant, of power imbalances and of not using power exploitatively. Though this nineteenth-century law was based on technicality, the principles of conscience and power imbalance underpinning it have been refined in modern equity[25] to apply in situations very different from the context of catching bargains and expectant heirs.

The Judicature Acts in 1873 and 1875 brought the administration of equity and common law together. Importantly, this does not mean these bodies of law were amalgamated.[26] But equitable rules made a more direct contribution to the regulation of justice in contract law and could, for example, give the court reason to intervene in exploitative transactions. According to Kay J, the court could intervene when

> [t]he circumstances of poverty and ignorance of the vendor, and absence of independent advice, throw upon the purchaser, when the transaction is impeached, the onus of proving, in Lord Selborne's words, that the purchase was 'fair, just and reasonable'.[27]

This way of thinking is directly applicable to the development of vitiating factors, and undue influence in particular.

The discretion afforded to the judiciary by equitable principle consequently meant there was a shift away from the classical model towards a combination of different approaches applicable to the issue of power.[28] The recognition that power is not always equal indicates a regard for the procedural justice of agreements (considered in more detail below), for as von Mehren has said, 'the very

[22] G Keeton and LA Sheridan, *Equity* (2nd edn Milton 1976) 1.
[23] Supreme Court of Judicature Act 1875.
[24] See Keeton and Sheridan, above n 23, 227.
[25] E Burn and G Virgo, *Maudsley and Burn's Trusts and Trustees* (7th edn OUP 2008) 4.
[26] Indeed, s 25 of the Judicature Act 1873 said that common law rules prevail when they conflict with rules of equity.
[27] *Fry v Lane* (1888) 40 Ch D 312 [322].
[28] See Mulcahy, *Contract Law in Perspective* above n 13.

concept of contract as autonomous ordering implies a concern for the process out of which contracts arise'.[29]

The law of duress and undue influence is the best example of the development of attitudes towards contractual enforcement, particularly in court. As chapter four explained, the idea that power imbalances should not be unjustly or fraudulently exploited to the detriment of another meant that contracts could be set aside in these situations. This became increasingly useful where the welfare of the consumer in opposition to powerful corporations was a concern, as consumers are rarely in the same bargaining position as businesses or vendors. The development of contractual vitiating factors is contract's way of safeguarding against such exploitation of the weak.[30]

In spite of this, Tillotson has noted that modern contract law is still underpinned by classical doctrine to a large extent.[31] There has been no 'grand scale reformulation of the law',[32] as he says that change has simply been in the form of adjustments to the classical model. Tillotson questions the appropriateness of this development, as traditional doctrine is arguably inappropriate within 'the very changed circumstances of the modern world' where power imbalance is common both socially and commercially.[33] As a result, the legacy of the classic freedom of contract ideal remains. Intervention by the court must be justified, because it limits freedom of contract. As Hudson has said, fairness is achieved in a way that is balanced with the need for certainty.[34] Thus, intervention into inequitable bargains must take place within the common law's concern that people should be held to what they have agreed.

According to Smith's theory of contract, 'consent' and 'wrongdoing' are two concepts that justify intervention by the court into agreements.[35] Conceptually, as chapter four demonstrated, wrongdoing is *part* of consent in the context of undue influence, because the claimant's consent is defective as a result of the wrongdoing or influence of the defendant.[36] Furthermore, the importance of these concepts is evident in the case law on prenups, as the judiciary has emphasised that agreements must be made freely, knowingly and honestly.[37] That is, consent arguably

[29] A von Mehren, 'A General View of Contract' in *International Encyclopedia of Comparative Law* vol 7 (Tübingen 1982) 64.

[30] This has been referred to as 'consumer-welfarism' by J Adams and R Brownsword, 'The Ideologies of Contract' (1987) 7 Legal Studies 205, 205.

[31] J Tillotson, *Contract Law in Perspective* (Cavendish 2004) 39.

[32] Ibid.

[33] Ibid.

[34] A Hudson, *Equity and Trusts* (2nd edn, Cavendish 2001) 5.

[35] See Smith, above n 15, 317.

[36] However, as Chen-Wishart has noted, the language of wrongdoing implies the need for bad conduct, even though it is not required for the court to find undue influence: M Chen-Wishart, 'Undue Influence: Beyond Impaired Consent and Wrongdoing towards a Relational Analysis' in A Burrows and Lord Rodger of Earlsferry (eds), *Mapping the Law: Essays in Memory of Peter Birks* (OUP 2006) 202.

[37] For example, this terminology was employed throughout the Court of Appeal and Supreme Court judgments of *Radmacher*, above n 7, and was also used in *V v V*, above n 17, [71].

depends on the parties' level of freedom and knowledge when entering an agreement. Similarly, the wrongdoing of one party is patent if that party has not been honest when entering an agreement, for example if in a prenup he or she has not fully disclosed his or her assets.

The 'consent' principle[38] is rooted in the notion that one should be bound by an obligation only if one has consented to that obligation. A contract is not a contract without an intention to agree from all parties. But what does it actually mean to consent to an obligation? This is a complex but important question, because without knowing the meaning of consent, one cannot trace a lack of it.[39] Trebilcock[40] and Smith[41] have recognised two polar opposite views of consent. One view is that unless someone is physically forced to sign a contract, that person's consent is forthcoming. The consent is made clear by the fact that the contract was entered into. The opposing view is that parties never fully consent when contracting, as every agreement is inevitably made in the context of external pressures and 'we have no choice but to enter contracts in order to live'.[42] Theorising consent in the context of prenups means finding a definition placed between these two extreme views. If parties to a prenup always consent, because they have the option not to sign the agreement, inequality of power is not accounted for at all. Equally, while there are always pressures attached to negotiating a prenup, this does not mean that the parties never consent. Therefore, to achieve a level of certainty, the court determines whether parties have displayed a *level* of consent that is insufficient to justify upholding an agreement. In the context of undue influence, for example, the court focuses on clear evidence of impaired consent or on illegitimate pressure (which renders the claimant's consent defective and relates to the wrongdoing principle considered below). As Chen-Wishart has said, this has the benefit of clarity, but it 'misses the target when simply superimposed on the subtle and complex dynamics of trusting relationships'.[43] Indeed, this approach can lead to a narrowly circumscribed view of autonomy, whereby the 'complex dynamics' that characterise the prenuptial relationship are overshadowed by a focus on the consent of the applicant (informed by legal advice and financial disclosure)[44] and the 'bad conduct'[45] of the respondent.

The second concept propounded by Smith is the 'wrongdoing principle'. This means that a contract may not be enforced if the rights acquired by that contract were obtained through wrongdoing, as it is a well-known maxim that one cannot

[38] Other theorists, like von Mehren, have called this the will theory; see above n 29.

[39] For more on the complexity of consent, see P Westen, *The Logic of Consent: The Diversity and Deceptiveness of Consent as a Defence to Criminal Conduct* (Ashgate 2004).

[40] M Trebilcock, *The Limits of Freedom of Contract* (Harvard University Press 1993) 79.

[41] See Smith, above n 15, 331.

[42] Ibid. See also R Hale, 'Coercion and Distribution in a Supposedly Non-coercive State' (1923) 38 *Political Science Quarterly* 470.

[43] See Chen-Wishart, above n 36, 203.

[44] Elements the Supreme Court considered to be relevant to the question of consent in *Radmacher*, above n 7.

[45] See Chen-Wishart, above n 36, 202.

profit from one's own wrongdoing.[46] Thus in certain circumstances, the court will intervene in an agreement if one party exploits its dominant negotiating position at the expense of the weaker party. However, the court's involvement is not justified by the fact that one party has significantly more bargaining power than the other. That party must also abuse its position, which usually involves coercing the weaker party to enter an agreement. Hence, the wrongdoing of one party will mean the consent of the other party was not freely given. From this perspective, intervention is justified on the basis of one party's wrongdoing, because the quality of the other party's consent has been tainted, or the agreement is extremely unfair.

The influence of wrongdoing and consent can be traced into the judicial treatment of prenups when making financial orders on divorce in the UK. For example, in *Radmacher v Granatino*, the Supreme Court said that it would consider whether one spouse has exploited or taken advantage of the other party during negotiations.[47] The consent principle is also clearly entrenched in the Supreme Court's notion of a valid and enforceable prenup, as it must have been freely and knowingly entered into by both parties.

Nevertheless, restricting contractual validity to criteria based on wrongdoing and consent could in theory limit the capacity of the court to take *substantive* fairness into account. Commentators typically divide considerations of fairness into two categories: procedural justice and substantive justice. An assessment of the procedural justice of an agreement focuses on the process by which the contract was created. On the other hand, *substantive* justice encompasses much wider considerations of fairness, as it looks to the substance of the contract. Procedural fairness is significant in contract law, as the illegitimate exercise of power over another will render an agreement voidable. Substantive fairness is also important (the Unfair Contract Terms Act 1977 is evidence of this),[48] but it is limited to situations where injustice is fairly obvious and significant. This is because, for the most part, substantive fairness does not sit comfortably with the freedom of contract ideal that parties are free to agree to whatever they choose. Policing contracts is more easily justified if it can be shown (under duress, for example) that the agreement was not made freely. Whilst this will often ensure that the actual agreement is substantively fair, the philosophy of classical contract law persists: that parties are free to make bad bargains. However, a major problem with the liberalist idea of freedom of contract is that it presupposes autonomy, and that negotiations have been at arm's length.[49] As a result, the practical operation of contract law effectively ignores many *in*equalities emerging from agreements, particularly because a problem with prenups is their intimate context. As Pohjonen suggests,

[46] See *Tinsley v Milligan* [1993] UKHL 3; *Gray v Thames Trains* [2009] 3 WLR 167.

[47] See *Radmacher*, above n 7, [71].

[48] This Act ensures that freedom of contract is not abused by preventing the enforcement of unfair contract terms in some circumstances. The statute applies to exemption clauses that attempt to avoid liability for breach of contract.

[49] S Pohjonen, 'Partnership in Love and Business' (2000) 8 *Feminist Legal Studies* 47.

contracts are created due to a lack of trust;[50] yet for most couples (it is hoped), when entering marriage, this is not the case at all. Thus behind contractual theories of consent, will and autonomy, a different cognitive context exists for prenups.

Indeed, as outlined in chapter one, some of the strongest influences on parties agreeing to prenups are psychological. Bix has summarised these problems as 'power imbalances, bounded rationality and coercive circumstances' that do not satisfy the requirements of existing doctrine.[51] The impact of these factors on parties' decision making is often significant, as the testimony of the attorneys in chapter three has shown. If parties have been affected by these problems then they have not truly consented. From this perspective, concepts of consent and freedom of contract are arguably elusive. That is, in reality elements of freedom and consent are often missing, yet these circumstances are ignored when they do not fit within the boundaries of accepted principle. This has effectively exacerbated what Hadfield refers to as the dilemma of choice.[52] The emphasis on enforcement stems from the perception that parties have chosen to be obligated, but 'choice' becomes a dilemma when it loses its meaning because it has been assumed.

Atiyah's assertion that contract theory is a mess is well-founded because there is no clear aim for contract.[53] The neo-classical mixture of classical and welfarist approaches means that it is unclear whether contract law should encourage free competition or fairly-made bargains.[54] Thus, although it is increasingly important to protect contracting parties who are vulnerable due to power inequalities, this protection is provided within the boundaries of classical contract. By simply extending the scope of the classical model, the law's view of autonomy is in many ways impersonal and abstract. The theory that intervention by the court is justified by lack of consent and wrongdoing also presents an oversimplified view of autonomy. Certainly, as this book argues, autonomy is multi-faceted, yet mainstream attitudes are incapable of realising this when they are consumed with a concern for contractual certainty. As McLean argues, the legal concept of consent (and similarly wrongdoing) shows adherence to a particular form of autonomy, but it should not be assumed that an individual's autonomy will be protected by these concepts in reality.[55] This is because traditional approaches to consent focus on the moment in which the agreement is made, which can obscure factors relevant to autonomy, such as the wider context and the relationship of the contracting parties. As Herring puts it, '[t]he notion of consent is too narrow in its time frame. In answer to the question "did the defendant consent?" the law only permits the answers "yes" or "no".'[56] Herring explains that the problem with this binary view of consent is there is no room for the *stories* of the parties to be heard.

50 Ibid.
51 B Bix, 'Domestic Agreements' (2007) 35 *Hofstra Law Review* 1753.
52 See Hadfield, above n 6.
53 See Atiyah, above n 8.
54 See Mulcahy, above n 13, 35.
55 S McLean, *Autonomy, Consent and the Law* (Routledge 2010) 4.
56 See Herring, above n 20, 65.

Most of all, this concept of consent ignores the long-term interests of the parties as being part of what Nedelsky views as the autonomous process, in that autonomy is something that develops over time rather than in the moment the agreement is signed.[57] This particular understanding of autonomy has led McLean to observe that '[l]ittle purpose is served by maintaining the pretence that the law either does or can uphold individual autonomy when it manifestly has an agenda that is only in part concerned ... with the concept'.[58]

The failure of mainstream doctrine to recognise issues of power relating to prenups demonstrates contract law's continued deference to the freedom of contract principle. However, an approach that historically emerged to encourage competition in the liberal marketplace[59] cannot realistically apply to prenups. Therefore, an alternative contractual approach is necessary, one that can recognise the problems with enforcing such agreements. In the next section, the merits of relational contract theory will be considered in more detail. It is hoped that this type of contextual approach will provide for an understanding of autonomy that is not presumed, and is thus more appropriate for prenups.

Relational Contract Theory

Relational contract theory has been developed primarily by Ian Macneil.[60] As is suggested by the terminology, relational contract theory focuses on the relationship between parties to a contract. This relationship, Macneil argues, is crucial to the understanding of many types of agreement. He places contractual activity on a spectrum, with 'discrete transactions' at one end and 'ongoing relations' at the other end.[61] According to Macneil, discrete transactions are devoid of any connection between the parties. An illustration of this is 'a purchase of a non-brand name gasoline in a strange town one does not expect to see again'.[62] This kind of transaction, where there is no contractual duration, repeated exchange or connection between the parties, is obviously not representative of many types of contracting. In spite of this, Macneil argues that the approach of classical and neo-classical contract law is to treat all transactions as discrete.

Conversely, relational contracts are characterised by their considerable duration. Macneil has said that in these transactions, parties may 'view the relation as an

[57] J Nedelsky, 'Reconceiving autonomy: Sources, thoughts and possibilities' (1989) 1 *Yale Journal of Law and Feminism* 7, 10.

[58] McLean, above n 55, 227.

[59] See Smith, above n 15.

[60] Other academics, such as Richard Austen-Baker, have developed alternative versions of relational contract law. However, this chapter will focus on Ian Macneil's relational contract theory, and the academic contributions to the relational contract debate refer to this particular theory.

[61] I Macneil, *Contract: Exchange Transactions and Relations* (2nd edn, Foundation Press 1978) 12.

[62] Ibid.

on-going integration of behaviour to grow and vary with events in a largely unforeseeable future'.[63] From this perspective, prenups epitomise relational contract theory. If Macneil's spectrum of contractual activity is measured in terms of connection between the contracting parties, prenups are situated at the opposite end of the spectrum from discrete transactions. In spite of this, orthodox classical and neo-classical ways of thinking are relevant to the courts' view of autonomy in the context of prenups.[64] Relational contract presents an alternative theory that recognises the shortcomings of this approach, whilst offering a new legal framework that acknowledges the reality of agreements made in an intimate context.

Critique of Mainstream Contract Theory

One of the most pertinent elements of relational contract theory is the emphasis it puts on context. Whilst mainstream contract scholars focus primarily on the transaction, which is informed by relational elements, relational theorists look first to the relationship between the parties *before* looking at the transaction. Relational contract theory argues that because classical and neo-classical theories focus on the bargains made in the agreement, they are not sensitive to the potential inequalities arising from intimate relationships.[65]

Macneil has further rationalised the difficulties with mainstream theory for long-term relationships in terms of 'presentiation',[66] a technical term for contracts that deal with future situations as if they exist in the present. Take the hypothetical example of Bob and Mary, who enter into a prenup in the present to bind a situation that may or may not happen in future—their divorce. In the present, Bob and Mary wish to keep their assets separate in the event of divorce, but do not know that Bob will later win the lottery, and that Mary will leave her job to care for their children. If this unknown future is bound by Bob and Mary's present agreement, presentiation has occurred. Macneil uses the concept of presentiation to explain the classical contract approach, whereby the contract is made at one point in time, and it is the conditions at that time that bind future circumstances. This is patently problematic for prenups, as issues of power and the consequences of changed circumstances are neither taken into account nor addressed. In effect, it is not even possible to take changed circumstances into account, because the future cannot be predicted when presentiation is employed. This is why the court's regulation of prenups goes beyond the boundaries of classical contract. Indeed, whilst Macneil explains that presentiation is a cause for concern in any long-term

[63] Ibid.

[64] For a discussion of the court's engagement with relational contract theory, see L Mulcahy, 'Telling Tales about Relational Contracts: How Do Judges Learn about the Lived World of Contracts' in D Campbell, L Mulcahy and S Wheeler (eds), *Changing Concepts of Contract: Essays in Honour of Ian Macneil* (Palgrave Macmillan 2013).

[65] R Leckey, 'Relational Contract and Other Models of Marriage' (2002) 40 *Osgoode Hall Law Journal* 1.

[66] I Macneil, 'Contracts: Adjustment of Long-Term Economic Relations under Classical, Neoclassical and Relational Contract Law' (1978) 72 *Northwestern University Law Review* 854.

agreement, prenups are particularly complex because of the many unforeseeable ways in which the marital relationship may develop.

Although the neo-classical system does not exercise 'rigorous presentiation' like classical theory, Macneil has said it is also 'ill-designed' to address issues with long-term agreements.[67] Neo-classical theory does recognise power imbalance in some situations, but Feinman argues that it is inadequate because it does not *begin* with 'relational exchange'.[68] What he means is that neo-classical contract theory may account for context because, for example, it is concerned with consumer welfare. But neo-classical theory also remains tied to classical contract theory, and so in many cases rough equality is assumed between parties even when the relationship is characterised by dependency or pressure, elements that are highlighted by relational contract theory. Put simply, relational contract theory not only proffers an approach which can account for changes in circumstance, but it is also concerned with the context of the contractual *relationship*. This approach can appreciate the complexities of prenups, and contrasts with the mainstream contractual view of autonomy, which is informed by the circumstances at the time the agreement is entered into instead of the circumstances after the agreement has been made.

From the mainstream contractual perspective, an individual's autonomy is not flawed if he or she subsequently comes to regret the original agreement, as long as the court considers that individual to have been autonomous when he or she signed the agreement. In other words, mainstream contract champions what Elizabeth and Robert Scott have termed *ex ante* autonomy,[69] which means that circumstances at the time the agreement is negotiated and signed are privileged, including the freedom to contract in the first place. Therefore *ex post* autonomy,[70] which includes intervening circumstances, is a secondary consideration. Scott and Scott contend that the marital relationship 'does not fit this model well',[71] as it corresponds with Macaulay's description of long-term continuing relations, which he claims are 'not always nice situations for those short of power'.[72] Macaulay asserts that, contrary to classical and neo-classical perceptions, parties to long-term (and in this context marital) agreements are often dependent on each other. Furthermore, an individual's freedom of choice might extend only as far as choosing one unpleasant option over another. But by recognising the limitations of the orthodox conception of autonomy and binding enforceability, relational contract theory can provide a foundation for contractual principle based on the reality of long-term contracting.

Before examining the relational approach further, it is important to note that the relational critique of orthodox theory is not that it ignores context: it is that

[67] Ibid.

[68] J Feinman, 'Relational Contract and Default Rules' (1993-1994) 3 *Southern California Interdisciplinary Law Journal* 43, 53.

[69] E Scott and R Scott, 'Marriage as Relational Contract' (1998) 84 *Virginia Law Review* 1225, 1248.

[70] Ibid.

[71] Ibid.

[72] S Macaulay, 'An Empirical View of Contract' (1985) 3 *Wisconsin Law Review* 465.

context is not prioritised. This is illustrated by the approach of the courts towards prenups, which provides a useful practical example of what Leckey refers to as an atomistic liberal view of autonomy.[73] In *Radmacher v Granatino*, the majority said that the parties' emotional state and the pressures they were under to agree may be taken into account.[74] But they also said that it would be 'paternalistic and patronising' to override the exercise of individual autonomy.[75] Autonomy is established simply by the fact that a choice has been made, unless the decision maker is under duress or undue influence. The issue, therefore, is not that context is ignored; it is whether *enough* context is taken into account by the law when 'fixing the rights and obligations of the parties'.[76] However, when adopting a relational view, considering sociological factors does not mean that the court must limit enforcement of the agreement. This is because context is part of this alternative view of autonomy according to relational contract law, which recognises the human side of contracting instead of assuming that people are rational choosing machines.[77]

Relational Contract Theory and Prenuptial Agreements

The critique of contract law that has been presented so far arguably makes it seem as though contractual principles are not suited to prenups. In particular, if orthodox doctrine treats all transactions as discrete (whereby the ongoing relationship between the parties is disregarded), the complexities of the relationship between parties to a prenup cannot be accounted for. Presently, as earlier chapters have explained, the judiciary frequently go beyond mainstream contractual principles when scrutinising a prenup challenged by one of the spouses on divorce. However, these principles are increasingly influential, as the courts become more reluctant to set agreements aside out of respect for autonomy,[78] and so it must be determined whether contract law from a relational contract perspective can appreciate the problematic aspects of prenups.

A relational approach to any transaction requires a contextual response. Although context and relational theory are inextricably linked, Leckey has distinguished each concept.[79] He explains that relational theory focuses on the relationship of the parties and, within this framework, context is taken into account if it is relevant to the parties' relationship. On the other hand, a contextual approach considers the entire context of a situation, and so is more holistic. This book is limited to a discussion of relational theory, because without limiting context to

[73] R Leckey, *Contextual Subjects: Family, State and Relational Theory* (University of Toronto Press 2008) 102.

[74] See *Radmacher*, above n 7, [72].

[75] Ibid.

[76] H Beale, 'Relational Values in English Contract Law' in Campbell *et al* (eds), above n 64, 116.

[77] See Leckey, above n 73, 106.

[78] Specifically, since *Radmacher*, above n 7.

[79] See Leckey, above n 65.

the actual relationship of parties to prenups, separating the relevant from the irrelevant could be difficult.

As a relational perspective is contextual in nature, however, the emotions and pressures of the parties entering prenups are taken into account. But this does not mean that these agreements will be set aside simply because negotiations have taken place in an emotional context, for, as Mulcahy puts it, relational contract theory is not a 'mush of altruism'.[80] Macneil's emphasis on cooperation between parties does not make his theory unrealistic, sentimental or overly simplistic. It does not diffuse the importance of contractual obligations either. The answer to problems with prenups from the perspective of relational contract theory is not complete condemnation and non-enforcement. Indeed, Leckey argues that the non-enforcement position ironically endorses the existing operation of contract law.[81] Believing that the only alternative to implementing inequitable agreements is to set them aside suggests mainstream contract theory is the only way contracts may be enforced. Alternatively, relational contract theory presents another way of enforcing contracts that is sensitive to power imbalances.

Pursuant to relational contract theory, the obligations created by an agreement do not emanate solely from the time the agreement was signed; they arise as the relationship evolves.[82] In theory, this is well suited to intimate contracts like prenups, where different understandings about terms or changing circumstances can dramatically alter the outcome of an agreement. In spite of the obvious attraction of relational contract theory in this context, this theory has been developed by Macneil in the arena of commercial contracting. Wightman has therefore advised caution when applying this theory to more intimate agreements.[83] One reason for this is that presentiation presents particular difficulties when the parties are in an intimate relationship. This is because commercial relationships are often built on particular contractual and commercial norms; therefore responses to future incidents are more foreseeable. However, as the circumstances of each intimate relationship are different, there is no normative framework to rely on. An illustration of this difference is provided by Ellman:

> [T]here is a fundamental difference between marriage and commercial relations that renders relational contract concepts inadequate to resolve marital disputes. In the commercial arrangements on which relational contract literature focuses, the parties' relationship, no matter how long term or informal, is a means towards an understood end: making money. Conflicts can be evaluated in light of that external purpose. But in marriage it is the relationship itself that is the goal and purpose.[84]

For this reason, Ellman does not think relational contract provides appropriate solutions for intimate agreements. Wightman, on the other hand, believes that

[80] See Mulcahy in Mulcahy and Wheeler (eds), above n 2.

[81] See Leckey, above n 73, 114.

[82] J Wightman, 'Intimate Relationships, Relational Contract Theory and the Reach of Contract' (2000) 8 *Feminist Legal Studies* 93.

[83] Ibid.

[84] I Ellman, 'The Theory of Alimony' (1989) 77 *California Law Review* 1.

relational theory has potential in an intimate context, as long as the key differences between commercial and intimate relationships are assessed.

As a result, Wightman's development of relational contract theory for application to intimate relationships is especially helpful when thinking about prenups. Referring to express agreements, such as prenups or cohabitation contracts,[85] he explains that imbalances of power could lead to 'tacit understandings' between the parties, which are much more influential in an intimate context than in a commercial one. That is, factors like economic dependency might not be used as explicit bargaining tools, but the imbalance these factors cause, coupled with an awareness of an imbalance, could inhibit the negotiation of some issues.

If relational contract theory can recognise such tacit understandings and power imbalances, it is not presuming autonomy, it is ensuring autonomy. By recognising the difficulties with autonomy, relational contract theory is also recognising the dilemma of choice referred to above. Although this theory accounts for the tension between agency and unequal power, whether it can assist in resolving this tension will be explored later in this chapter. Yet it is significant that the relational contract perspective can at least highlight these issues.

Furthermore, though Wightman's thesis applies to partially express agreements and is not concerned with prenups, his conclusions about incomplete agreements could be used to formulate an alternative view of autonomy that does not take into account only circumstances at the time of the agreement. In other words, even though prenups are express contracts, it is possible that the parties entering these agreements might later share alternative understandings about property division. The empirical study in this book indicates that many people believe and are assured that their agreement will not be enforced due to future uncertainty.[86] From this perspective, a prenup resembles a floating charge, which does not crystallise until future circumstances are known. In this way, it is also similar to informal understandings or incomplete agreements between intimate parties about issues like financial support. Unfortunately, the legal regulation of what Wightman refers to as 'tacit understanding' is quite uncertain, and so it is difficult to envisage how shared intentions that are not made explicit in a prenup might be relied upon in court. The judiciary, as Wightman notes, is looking for something more, which can be interpreted as a bargain. But to require an enforceable bargain inevitably requires some kind of express agreement, like a prenuptial or postnuptial agreement, which in turn requires presentiation. As such, Wightman has explored the possibility of a 'non-bargain conception of contract which would transform such agreements into enforceable contracts'.[87]

[85] Aside from this example, Wightman's analysis of relational contract theory is not intended to apply to prenups, though it is still relevant to the arguments in this book.

[86] See also A Barlow and J Smithson, 'Is modern marriage a bargain? Exploring perceptions of prenuptial agreements in England and Wales' (2012) 24(3) *Child and Family Law Quarterly* 304.

[87] See Wightman, above n 82.

Though he does not consider it in the context of prenups, it is conceivable that Wightman's theory would be relevant if the circumstances and intentions of the parties changed during the marriage. Currently contract law does not recognise the changed intentions of the parties, but pursuant to Wightman's non-bargain theory, the evolving autonomy of parties can be taken into account without distortions caused by viewing the relationship as a bargain. His solution is to regard the relationship between parties as being interdependent. Both parties have an understanding of financial support on which they both rely, and this exchange of support or benefit does not require any bargaining to be enforced. Though this theory is similar to promissory estoppel, it requires reliance from both sides on the understanding between them. Indeed, Wightman rejects promissory estoppel as a way of making changing intentions in an intimate context enforceable, because 'a trace of self-interest remains in the requirement that the promisee must have relied or changed their position'.[88] As noted above, self-interest is arguably not a primary motivator in an intimate context. However, applying 'non-bargain reciprocity' means that 'because it underpins an evolving agreement, it is not found in isolated acts of reliance in response to particular promises (express or implied), but is pervasive in the parties' relationship with one another'.[89] In this way, it is conceivable that the reality of parties' intentions, which inevitably evolve as their circumstances change, may be taken into account at the time a prenup is enforced. Thus relational contract is potentially applicable to prenups because it emphasises 'what is implicit but not expressly spelt out'.[90]

The law of presumed undue influence is an example of how relational contract theory is relevant within current contractual doctrine because it *does* have regard to the nature of the relationship between parties. However, as chapter four demonstrated, even the doctrine of presumed undue influence does not adequately account for disparities of power between parties to prenups. This is because, though the parties' relationship is taken into account, the transaction is difficult to set aside unless the pressure exerted was quite exceptional. In effect, presumed undue influence remains underpinned by the orthodox notion of autonomy. Respecting this notion of autonomy requires a limitation of all vitiating factors. This example demonstrates what relational contract theory does that the mainstream theory informing current doctrine does not. The same limitations are not imposed by relational contract because it is context (and not a strict libertarian notion of autonomy) that underpins this theory. Therefore, it is conceivable that when developing a relational contract approach for prenups, the meaning of 'fairness' could refer to much more than regulation of procedural matters and of more extreme injustices. In theory, substantive elements of fairness would be influential, and could recognise more nuanced power imbalances between couples. Ideas of

[88] Ibid.

[89] Examples of this way of thinking in practice are noted by Wightman as being present in US implied contract cases like *In Re Estate of Steffes* 290 NW 2d 697 (Wisconsin 1980).

[90] See Wightman, above n 82, 104.

equality would also be substantive rather than formulaic, and a greater level of scrutiny of agreements would be justified in certain circumstances using a relational approach. Although these ideas as to what a relational approach would look like are admittedly speculative at this stage, the operation of this theory will be explored in greater detail later in this chapter and in chapter six.

When developing relational contract within intimate relationships, Wightman observed some difficulties with the approach. Most notably, he argues that the idea of cooperation in commercial contracts has 'radically different implications'[91] in comparison with intimate agreements. He explains that 'commercial parties are not … in business to benefit the other',[92] whilst parties entering prenups are arguably motivated by concerns other than self-interest. An awareness of these distinctions is important when developing a theory specifically for prenups. At the same time, relational contract theory is undoubtedly more capable than mainstream theory in recognising issues associated with prenups. Yet it does not specifically address the gender dimension attached to such agreements. Therefore, the next section of this chapter will explore feminist concerns with classical and neoclassical contract theory. This is because feminist critique is well established in the context of intimate power imbalance, autonomy and consent.

Feminist Perspectives on Prenuptial Agreements

Relational contract can be applied to prenups, particularly when employing Wightman's analysis. The contextual perspective it provides can recognise issues of power, and also asserts a more complex view of autonomy. However, a specifically *feminist* assessment is also necessary to ensure that disparity of power is a central rather than residual consideration, and in particular so that the gender dimension attached to prenups is recognised. As interviewees in New York have indicated, the person asking for the agreement (and incidentally the person with wealth to protect) is typically the man. This is supported by Lady Hale, who emphasised in *Radmacher v Granatino* that although the wealthy party in that case was female, there is a gender dimension to prenups because the circumstances of *Radmacher* are not usual.[93]

In practice, however, the gender dimension is relegated by the court in favour of a gender-neutral view of prenups.[94] Yet this perspective means that issues of power are missing from the court's analysis; issues to which a feminist perspective would attach significance. As Conaghan puts it, gender is 'too often rendered

[91] Ibid, 113.
[92] Ibid, 116.
[93] See *Radmacher*, above n 7 [137].
[94] Incidents of gender neutrality in the court's approach are set out in further detail in the next section.

invisible' in the courtroom, yet feminism can make gender *visible* by demonstrating how '"gender-neutral" laws can impact upon men and women differentially'.[95] Conaghan goes on to argue that in many ways the law *constructs* gender, for example through the image of the 'deserving' homemaker. And so conventionally, the legal subject is imagined as un-gendered, but feminist perspectives can expose it as being constructed on ideological, gendered perceptions of society.[96] In other words, a feminist lens enables structural problems underpinning prenups to be recognised. As chapter two demonstrated, historically, divorce law based on separate, strict equality reinforced *in*equality within the family,[97] because, as Smart explains, the law purported to help dependants (ie the non-moneyed spouse responsible for labour in the home) by extracting money from husbands, whilst 'lending massive ideological support to the structures of dependency within the family'.[98] This goes some way towards explaining why, traditionally, the moneyed spouse is usually male and, further, why a prenup is more likely to affect the wife detrimentally if circumstances have changed.[99] Yet as Fredman puts it, in spite of structural constraints, neo-liberal perspectives tend to emphasise women's freedom of choice, instead of acknowledging the impact social systems have on these 'freedoms'.[100]

Although the gender element is not the only explanation for power imbalances between parties to a prenup,[101] it should not be overlooked, as Gilligan argues that '[i]mplicitly adopting the male life as the norm [means trying] ... to fashion women out of a masculine cloth'.[102] Clearly, therefore, making assumptions about autonomy and power without taking into account differences in gender, wealth and circumstance is potentially problematic and unjust. Feminist perspectives are valuable in this context because they can recognise imbalances of power in intimate relationships, and highlight inadequacies in the law's ability to address such imbalances.[103]

There is no definitive feminist critique of contract law, rather there are many different perspectives. As Belcher puts it, '[t]o offer a *feminist* perspective on any theory is a complex task because there are, of course, many types of feminism'.[104]

95 See Conaghan, above n 5, 359.
96 Ibid, 361.
97 See, eg, C Smart, *The Ties That Bind: Law, Marriage and the Reproduction of Patriarchal Relations* (Routledge 1984) 230, where the structural inequalities on which the law is based are examined: 'Family law perpetuates an inadequate system of private economic support for women and children whilst constituting an obstacle to the development of a more adequate public system of support and benefit...'
98 Ibid.
99 See also Brod, above n 4.
100 S Fredman, *Women and the Law* (Clarendon Press 1998) 288–90.
101 Class dimension and wealth are also relevant, but there is insufficient room in this book to consider a Marxist analysis.
102 C Gilligan, *In a Different Voice: Psychological Theory and Women's Development* (Harvard University Press 1982) 6.
103 See Conaghan, above n 5.
104 A Belcher, 'A Feminist Perspective on Contract Theories from Law and Economics' (2000) 8 *Feminist Legal Studies* 29.

Whilst these perspectives all assess the impact of developments in contract theory on women, some are more optimistic than others, and some are more useful than others. Similarly, there is no definitive feminist perspective on prenups. An appropriate perspective in this context not only must recognise power imbalances, but also consider autonomy in a way that recognises the reality faced by parties who have entered such agreements. This may be achievable when using a feminist perspective, because, as Hanna has said, it demands that the law aims to *protect* autonomy and simultaneously *promote* gender equality.[105]

Feminist Responses to Issues with Power and Autonomy in Contract

In the UK, the judiciary's attitude towards prenups could be aligned with liberal feminist views of formal equality. Formal equality emphasises autonomy for both men and women through equal treatment,[106] and mirrors the gender-neutral attitude of Lord Phillips, when he said that individual autonomy should be respected, in *Radmacher v Granatino*.[107] It is assumed that parties will act rationally and that granting complete autonomy will mean people can be completely autonomous. On this view, there should be no unnecessary interference in men and women's ability to enter fully binding prenups. Even before *Radmacher* reached the Supreme Court, where it was held that prenups should have decisive weight, Wilson LJ stated the following in the Court of Appeal judgment for that case:

> No doubt in its application to each case the law must guard against the possible infection of a contract by one party's exploitation of the susceptibility of the other. But, as a general assumption, *the premise is patronising, in particular to women*; and I would prefer the starting-point to be for both parties to be required to accept the consequences of whatever they have freely and knowingly agreed.[108]

On the face of it, treating women and men equally in this way makes sense. But formal equality becomes less persuasive when considering what it means for the concept of autonomy. In reality, disadvantaged parties might not achieve such equality and autonomy due to the circumstances in which they find themselves. Thus proponents of substantive equality argue that formal equality does not do anything to change the traditional contractual, non-contextual view of autonomy. Individualism is emphasised rather than the social relationships of the people involved.[109] As Fredman explains, 'the courts remain distinctly uncomfortable with the handling of groups',[110] but adopting an individualistic approach misses the wider gendered

105 C Hanna, 'Rethinking Consent in a Big Love Way' (2010) 17 *Michigan Journal of Law and Gender* 111.

106 J Bourne and C Derry, *Women and Law* (Old Bailey Press 2004) 25.

107 See *Radmacher*, above n 7, [78].

108 *Radmacher v Granatino* [2009] EWCA Civ 649, [127] (emphasis added).

109 See Bourne and Derry, above n 106.

110 See Fredman, above n 100, 290.

issues affecting prenups. Furthermore, in an intimate context couples entering such agreements often do not behave individualistically or rationally when making decisions. In short, emphasising *only* individuality and imposing formal equality for all does not work in the context of prenups.[111] Therefore, although the formal versus substantive equality debate is dated, it helps illustrate current problems in practice, which fail to account for prenuptial power imbalances, particularly if they are subtle enough to escape protection by contractual vitiating factors.

Another dated but relevant feminist perspective is that the law of contract (like most branches of law) is a male construct,[112] which positions women as subjects of male oppression. This idea emerged from Carole Pateman's book *The Sexual Contract*, where she asserts that the rules of contract give men rights over women and perpetuate patriarchal norms within society.[113] Within the original social contract, Pateman argues that men are free actors but women are simply subjects, because patriarchy means that only the autonomy of men is recognised. She goes on to say that because actual agreements 'mirror the original [social] contract', women have been excluded from the creation and development of contractual theory.[114]

Rather than focusing on the master/subject dichotomy of Pateman's work, it is her warning that gender should not be made invisible in the law's regulation of contract that is significant to this book.[115] In a similar vein to Pateman, other commentators have argued that contract law is fundamentally tainted by masculine bias, and believe the classical norms of contract law must be reconstructed.[116] For instance, Tidwell and Linzer argue that the classical view of contract law is associated with norms of 'individual autonomy, hard bargaining and self-reliance … and of the Marlboro Man and the Winning of the West'.[117] Similarly, Lorraine Code criticises our cultural perceptions of autonomy as idealised by the '[a]utonomous man … a self-realizing individual who directs his efforts towards maximising his personal gains'.[118] These are not typical traits of prenuptial contracting because prenups are unsuited to emotionally detached ideas of bargaining.

[111] See Alison Jaggar, who criticises this focus on individualism for suggesting that 'logically if not empirically, human beings could exist outside a social context': A Jaggar, *Feminist Politics and Human Nature* (Rowman & Allanheld 1983) 29.

[112] D Threedy, 'Feminists and Contract Doctrine' (1999) 32 *Indiana Law Review* 1247.

[113] C Pateman, *The Sexual Contract* (Stanford University Press 1988).

[114] Ibid, 7.

[115] See also MJ Frug, 'Re-Reading Contracts: A Feminist Analysis of a Contracts Casebook' (1985) 34 *The American University Law Review* 1065.

[116] D Cornell, 'The Philosophy of the Limit: Systems Theory and Feminist Legal Reform' in D Cornell *et al* (eds), *Deconstruction and the Possibility of Justice* (Routledge 1992) 68. At the same time, Sally Wheeler has noted that when contractual rules were being developed during the classical era, women did have a role in commerce. However, their social status as wives (and therefore agents of their husbands) made these women invisible in the courtroom: S Wheeler, 'Going Shopping' in Mulcahy and Wheeler (eds), above n 2, 21.

[117] P Tidwell and P Linzer, 'The Flesh-Colored Band Aid—Contracts, Feminism, Dialogue and Norms' (1991) 28 *Houston Law Review* 791.

[118] L Code, 'Second Persons' in *What Can She Know? Feminist Theory and the Construction of Knowledge* (Cornell University Press 1991) 78.

According to Belcher, even though neo-classical theory contains 'feminine language' in line with principles other than freedom of contract (like fairness and cooperation), it is also affected by 'the persistence and centrality' of masculine traits.[119] That is, the expectation for parties to 'seek individual advantage'[120] is emphasised over and above elements relevant to the relationship of the parties, like mutual cooperation. However, it is important to note that this 'masculine' view of prenuptial contracting does not mean prenups are *necessarily* male-centred. As Collier explains, men are not a homogeneous group, but by treating men as subjects of masculinity, men are constituted as rational and autonomous in the same way the law is. With this in mind, a feminist perspective on the law underpinning contract places critical attention on the *assumptions* about the way people negotiate and enter into intimate agreements, and can therefore recognise disparities of power that are concealed when these assumptions are made.[121] Indeed, the rigidity of classical and neo-classical rules encourages the court to consider autonomy neutrally, but makes the realities of power and intimacy more difficult to address by dehumanising the parties involved.[122] For many feminists, the only appropriate way to refashion this formulaic type of autonomy is to focus on the experience of women.[123] In doing so, a more nuanced concept of autonomy is created, which acknowledges the voices of individuals who do not hold the majority of power in a relationship.[124]

Therefore, recognising that there is a gender dimension to prenups is important: first, because the male party often has more wealth and more power; and, secondly, because women are more likely to sacrifice career opportunities to undertake homemaking and parenting roles, and will likely be disadvantaged by an agreement that has not provided for this.[125] Then again, just because there are situations where women have less power when an agreement is signed, and less autonomy to protect their interests once circumstances have changed, does not mean women are vulnerable or have less power because they are weak in the face of inevitable male dominance. A theory that protects women *qua* women (and therefore as oppressed) fails to recognise the different contexts in which power imbalance occurs.

[119] See Belcher, above n 104, 35.

[120] Ibid, 36.

[121] R Collier, 'Feminist Legal Studies and the Subject(s) of Men: Questions of Text, Terrain and Context in the Politics of Family Law and Gender' in A Diduck and K O'Donovan, *Feminist Perspectives on Family Law* (Routledge-Cavendish 2006) 253, 240.

[122] See R Auchmuty, 'The Rhetoric of Equality and the Problem of Heterosexuality' in Mulcahy and Wheeler (eds), above n 2, 51.

[123] See Brod, above n 4.

[124] C Mackenzie and N Stoljar, 'Autonomy Refigured' in C Mackenzie and N Stoljar (eds), *Relational Autonomy: Feminist Perspectives on Autonomy, Agency, and the Social Self* (OUP 2000) 9.

[125] For detailed accounts of structural inequalities within marriage, such as the sexual division of labour and the lack of economic value attached to work in the home, see R Siegel, 'Why Equal Protection No Longer Protects: The Evolving Forms of Status-Enforcing State Action' (1997) 49 *Stanford Law Review* 1111; and N Fraser, 'After the family wage: Gender Equity and the Welfare State' (1994) 22(4) *Political Theory* 591.

In practice, however, the judiciary has struggled to appreciate this when considering bargaining inequalities between men and women. For example, in *Barclays Bank plc v O'Brien*,[126] Scott LJ (as he then was) recognised that there may be inequality of bargaining power between husband and wife in the context of surety transactions (which were discussed in chapter four). But his response to this problem was to discuss equity's 'special tenderness' towards women. Wheeler and Shaw believe this view encourages women to be 'delivered to the tutelage of the state, a situation of paternalist protection which many women simply find insulting and unacceptable'.[127] Auchmuty also questions why there should be a special tenderness for women, 'as if women were the difficulty'.[128] Similarly, Cretney does not believe that recognising issues of power along gender lines necessarily means assuming that all married women are vulnerable.[129] Scott LJ's assessment of the problem is based on the factual conclusion that wives need protection simply because they are wives, and so the wider context of power imbalances between parties to intimate agreements is ignored. Unfortunately, the alternative view of the judiciary seems to be not to recognise any gender dimension at all. Lord Scarman has said that inequality of bargaining power is not relevant to questions of undue influence; the law is based on the more rigorous tests of fact explained earlier in this chapter.

According to Kingdom, feminist concerns should not call for a protection of all women because they are female (or wives, as Scott LJ suggested).[130] A more worthwhile use of feminism is instead to focus any concerns on the interests of people who are affected by power imbalance. The context of any situation must be assessed in a way that recognises gender without creating gendered stereotypes, and where both men and women have the power to truly make autonomous decisions because the context of agreements is recognised above formality.[131]

Rather than concluding that the law cannot recognise feminist concerns because it is patriarchal and phallocentric, a richer, more recent argument criticises contract law for viewing obligations between intimate contracting parties in commercial terms. From this perspective, Kingdom argues that unequal bargaining power between women and men is obscured because the contractual ideal of formal equality is 'detached from real social circumstances'.[132] An abstract view of contractual obligation that is based on commerce has also been criticised by Biggs and MacKenzie, who have noted that obligations often primarily exist through informal social relationships that are affected by gender.[133] When the true context of

[126] *Barclays Bank plc v O'Brien* [1993] UKHL 6.

[127] S Wheeler and J Shaw (eds), *Contract Law: Cases, Materials and Commentary* (OUP 1994) 540.

[128] See Auchmuty, above n 122.

[129] S Cretney, 'The Little Woman and the Big Bad Bank' (1992) 108 *LQR* 534.

[130] E Kingdom, 'Cohabitation Contracts and the Democratization of Personal Relations' (2000) 8(1) *Feminist Legal Studies* 5.

[131] See R Auchmuty, 'When Equality is not Equity: Homosexual Inclusion in Undue Influence Law' (2003) 11(2) *Feminist Legal Studies* 169.

[132] Kingdom, above n 130, 6.

[133] H Biggs and R MacKenzie, 'Gendered Readings of Obligations: Social Lore or Strict Legal Forms?' (2000) 8(1) *Feminist Legal Studies* 1.

obligations is not recognised, contract law risks reproducing economic inequality.[134] In other words, inequality is *strengthened* by contractual obligation when it is not taken into account. This is patent in the prenuptial case, where the wealthier (and contractually more powerful) party makes an agreement that will exclude the other party from his or her wealth. The result of this is that contract law also potentially perpetuates inequalities in relationships, as Olsen says contracts often 'formalize domination as much as they express the will of the parties' in commerce.[135]

Responding to this critique is extremely difficult, as some commentators feel that women cannot be autonomous when the meaning of autonomy in the law of contract is so flawed. Thus when applied to prenups, the only solution seems to be to limit their enforcement. For instance, Younger has suggested that such agreements should have 'advisory status' only,[136] as the potential for injustice due to unforeseen circumstances is in her opinion too great. Yet for the enforcement of prenups, 'advisory status' would dilute the weight attached to these agreements in *Radmacher v Granatino*, which in turn would lead to a retreat to the court's approach in earlier case law. However, the positive judicial attitude towards enforcement would arguably mean prenuptial inequalities would be reproduced anyway, as autonomy is not properly interrogated in the courtroom before or after *Radmacher*.[137] According to Trebilcock, another solution encourages 'special' protection of women, but in his mind, suggesting that women are less rational because they are more susceptible to romantic infatuation, or because they are 'hormonal', is infantilising and 'reinforce[s] gender stereotypes'.[138] This accords with Chodorow's earlier assertion that sex differences do 'not mean that women have "weaker" ego boundaries than men or are more prone to psychosis'.[139] Such generalisations about the way women think should be avoided, particularly in light of Eisenberg's psychological study of the cognition of prenuptial contracting, which concludes that both parties may be affected by 'rational ignorance' and false optimism.[140]

Using Feminism to Re-evaluate Prenuptial Autonomy

A feminist perspective is important, because it highlights the need for context whilst capturing the 'realities of human interdependence'.[141] Being able to consider

134 See Brod, above n 4.

135 F Olsen, 'The Family and the Market: A Study of Ideology and Legal Reform' (1983) 96 *Harvard Law Review* 1497.

136 J Younger, 'Lovers' Contracts in the Courts: Forsaking the Minimum Decencies' (2007) 13 *William and Mary Journal of Women and the Law* 349.

137 As such, Younger's suggestion that the enforcement of prenups should heed minimum decencies (like independent legal advice) is preferred.

138 M Trebilcock and R Keshvani, 'The Role of Private Ordering in Family Law: A Law and Economics Perspective' (1991) 41 *University of Toronto Law Journal* 533.

139 N Chodorow, The Reproduction of Mothering: Psychoanalysis and the Sociology of Gender (University of California Press 1978) 167.

140 M Eisenberg, 'The Limits of Cognition and the Limits of Contract' (1995) 47 *Stanford Law Review* 211.

141 E Jackson and S Day-Sclater, 'Introduction' in Day-Sclater *et al* (eds), above n 20, 5.

autonomy and relationships in the context of gender also proffers a relational view on prenups. In this way, feminism makes relational contract theory more effective when applied to prenuptial autonomy. Relational autonomy has been fleshed out by feminists in different scenarios, such as rape and surrogacy.[142] This approach is particularly useful given that Macneil's work is routinely applied in a commercial context, and therefore is not always easily translated to the area of prenups. As Priaulx explains, a relational approach

> highlights those moments where the law has lost its moral compass in attempting to understand human decision making through a narrow (economic) lens based upon values which fail to fit the context—culminating in determinations of reasonableness that twist or exclude other ways of seeing ... A relational perspective challenges such narrow approaches to humanity: renders visible the broad spectrum of concerns that motivate human decision making; makes understandable what law sees as contradiction and can explain those instances where individuals are caught between yes/no, black/white and choice/no choice.[143]

When employing a relational autonomy-based analysis to the concept of consent, Herring uses the law on rape as an example of how current law fails to appreciate the wider social and cultural context in which, in the case of rape, sexual penetration takes place.[144] In particular, Herring says the use of consent in sexual offences is not understood in terms of the parties' relationship and the interactions between the parties prior to the event. Consent to sex is treated by law as an isolated incident, detached from the wider context of the situation, and similarly autonomy in contract law is confined to the bargaining process. In contrast, a relational approach exposes how 'thin' this notion of autonomy really is, and instead asserts that '[t]o be autonomous is not to be isolated and free of responsibility, but to be in a network of relationships, with their dependent responsibilities'.[145] Herring further argues that the perspective of relational autonomy provides a strong argument that prenups should not be enforced, because it reveals the particular problems associated with contracting before marriage about an unknown future:

> While contracts might work well when dealing with mechanical production, intimate lives are messy and unpredictable. The sacrifices called for can be unforeseen and obligations without limit ... To seek to tie these down at the start of the relationship in some form of 'once and for all' summation of their claims against each other ignores the realities of intimate relationships.[146]

In spite of this, relational autonomy does not necessarily mean that an individual's autonomy to enter into a prenup should be taken away. As Mackenzie and Stoljar explain, 'none of the major feminist critiques justifies repudiating the concept

[142] See J Herring, *Relational Autonomy and Family Law* (Springer 2014); Mackenzie and Stoljar (eds), above n 124.

[143] N Priaulx, *The Harm Paradox: Tort law and the unwanted child in an era of choice* (Routledge 2007) 170, cited in R Harding, 'Legal constructions of dementia: discourses of autonomy at the margins of capacity' (2012) 34 *Journal of Social Welfare and Family Law* 425.

[144] See Herring, above n 20, 53.

[145] Ibid, 68.

[146] Herring, above n 142, 37.

[of autonomy] altogether',[147] and so there is hope that if the exercise of autonomy in the context of prenups can be refigured, or conceived differently, these agreements can be given effect in a way that appreciates the power imbalances between the parties. But articulating what this version of autonomy would mean for prenups in practice is not straightforward, as Harding argues that although relational autonomy provides a useful critique of 'masculine autonomy', it does not properly explain what it means to place an individual decision in relational context.[148] As a result, there is a gap between this feminist interrogation of autonomy in theory and in practice, because the remit of relational autonomy is considered to be too vague.[149] Whether this theory can be excavated properly, so that it may apply in practice, will be explored in chapter six. At the very least, relational autonomy from a feminist perspective is a useful basis for demanding a more sophisticated way of thinking about 'the social dimensions of agency'[150] and autonomy. Put simply, this approach can re-evaluate power and autonomy without making generalisations about women or men, and without advocating non-enforcement of prenups.

The following section combines elements of feminism and relational contract theory to consider prenups in a way that appreciates women's experience and the reality of how power is exercised between the parties. Intersecting these two approaches facilitates the influence of *explicitly* contractual perspectives and *explicitly* gendered perspectives. Relational contract theory focuses on contract law and has been applied to various types of long-term agreements, such as employment contracts,[151] whilst feminist perspectives based on relational autonomy do not have a particular focus on contract and are concerned with decision making in general, yet highlight gendered power imbalances in a way that relational contract theory does not.[152]

Feminist Relational Contract Theory[153]

Whilst relational contract theory and feminist theory are both useful perspectives to adopt when addressing issues with prenups, it is clear that both theories have limitations. The strength of relational contract theory is that it recognises the problems associated with contract making in long-term situations (like marriage)

[147] Mackenzie and Stoljar, 'Autonomy Refigured' in C Mackenzie and N Stoljar (eds), above n 12, 3.

[148] Harding, above n 143.

[149] That is, it is unclear what a wider context encapsulates, though this will be developed further using relational contract theory, which arguably has more boundaries regarding relevant context.

[150] Jackson and Day-Sclater, above n 141.

[151] H Collins, 'The Contract of Employment in 3D' in Campbell *et al* (eds), above n 64.

[152] See Nedelsky, above n 57, 36.

[153] To my knowledge, the term 'feminist relational contract theory' has not been used before. This term refers to the integration of elements of feminist theory and relational contract theory to re-evaluate autonomy and power in intimate agreements (particularly prenups).

where circumstances often change in a way that cannot be predicted. Nedelsky explains that this theory appreciates that parties to agreements may be simultaneously self-interested and inter-dependent, as these characteristics are not mutually exclusive.[154] Thus relational contract theory engenders a much richer conception of autonomy in the particular context of contract law. However, it does not *explicitly* address the gendered power dimension that empirical research has demonstrated often occurs when entering prenups.

Many feminist critiques differ from the relational contract theory approach, particularly because the former direct 'critical fire at a version of contract law that [is] essentially classical'.[155] Feminist critiques of contract are typically based on the conception of contract as commerce; but if contract law is based only on norms associated with commerce, like self-interest and autonomy, then there is no room for utilising contract in a way that recognises the 'relationality'[156] of agreements. Therefore, as Kingdom argues, the weakness of a feminist critique that focuses entirely on orthodox theory is that '[o]nce the premisses of classical contract law are loosened … this feminist critique … is similarly challenged'.[157] However, these limitations are arguably overcome by 'feminist relational contract theory' (FRCT), proffering a combined approach that can recognise both relational and feminist concerns.

The marriage of feminism and relational contract theory is a happy one. Indeed, Brown has referred to relational contract theory as 'a present … for feminism'.[158] Wightman explains the attraction of the two theories as being caused by a shared message: first, that contract law should appreciate parties' changing understandings; and, secondly, that contract law should not be concerned only with 'wealth maximisation'.[159] Dalton has considered this approach of combined feminist and contractual perspectives in relation to cohabitation contracts.[160] In her opinion, 'the treatment of contracts … usually pays little attention to questions of power and fairness',[161] and even vitiating factors such as duress and undue influence are limited because they depend on recognised situations that deviate from the presumption that the parties contract equally. But as Dalton acknowledges, equal power is far from standard for intimate transactions, and so traditional contractual approaches preclude a 'richer examination' of these contexts.[162] Ultimately, however, Dalton's deconstruction of contract can be interpreted positively, because by recognising that doctrinal contract law 'recasts our concerns

[154] J Nedelsky, Law's Relations: A Relational Theory of Self, Autonomy and Law (OUP 2011) 151.

[155] See Wightman, above n 82, 105.

[156] This term is employed by Kingdom, above n 130, 6.

[157] Ibid.

[158] B Brown, 'Contracting Out/Contracting In: Some Feminist Considerations' in A Bottomley (ed), *Feminist Perspectives on the Foundational Subjects of Law* (Cavendish Publishing 1996) 14.

[159] See Wightman, above n 82.

[160] C Dalton, 'An Essay in the Deconstruction of Contract Doctrine' (1985) 94(5) *The Yale Law Journal* 997.

[161] Ibid, 1107.

[162] Ibid, 1108.

in a way that distances us from our lived experience of them',[163] we are taking a step towards building a notion of contract law that *can* go beyond the limitations of doctrinal approaches. For cohabitation contracts this means learning from the shortcomings of traditional contract and asking questions such as '[t]o what extent do [these relationships] reflect the shared expectations of their participants, and to what extent the imposition of terms by one party on another?'[164] Indeed, studying the limitations of duress and undue influence reveals situations where power inequalities are not addressed. In the context of prenups, learning from the limitations of these doctrines means developing a theory that can recognise the power disparities common in the prenuptial context.

The perspectives explored in this chapter suggest that an alternative theoretical perspective for prenups must begin with the relationship between the parties; and to achieve this, autonomy must be viewed differently. In addition, a different approach to prenuptial power should focus on empowerment rather than protection of parties, to emphasise that those who are marginalised by power are not weak and vulnerable.[165] These are the aims of FRCT, which will be tested to consider whether the theory could lead to the formulation of a new concept of autonomy that could work in practice. The following sections will proceed to outline Guggenheimer's work as a starting point for FRCT, as it proffers a feminist perspective that considers how prenups can be enforced without ignoring difficulties with power and autonomy.[166] When this has been examined in more detail, chapter six will proceed to clarify the potential applications of FRCT in practice.

The 'Feminomics' of Prenuptial Agreements—Guggenheimer's Approach

In her article, 'A Modest Proposal: The Feminomics of Drafting Premarital Agreements', Guggenheimer attempts to counteract what she refers to as the 'feminomics'[167] of prenups, which describes the situation where the husband uses such an agreement to consciously reap financial gain, or to ring-fence assets to the detriment of the wife. To address this gendered power dimension or 'feminomic' consequence of prenups, Guggenheimer advocates significant change in the form of 'a concomitant transformation in bargaining dynamics'.[168] To achieve this she has suggested that provisions in the agreement are 'woman-centred', because this encourages the participation of both parties. Guggenheimer argues that adjustment of the drafting process could give women the opportunity to participate in the process of prenups without being affected by issues of power. As a result, her

[163] Ibid.

[164] Ibid, 1109.

[165] See Hadfield, above n 6.

[166] L Guggenheimer, 'A Modest Proposal: The Feminomics of Drafting Premarital Agreements' (1996) 17 *Women's Rights Law Reporter* 147.

[167] Defined by Guggenheimer as 'the economic consequences of gender', ibid, 148.

[168] Guggenheimer, above n 166, 205.

proposals focus on empowering women to contract 'thoughtfully and successfully'. Indeed, Guggenheimer believes that emphasising women's inferior bargaining power instead of their 'autonomous right to structure their relations as they see fit' is infantilising.[169]

In practice, a woman-centred approach simply means that an agreement should guarantee financial well-being if parties divorce, and should subvert gender and institutional roles that tend to disadvantage the party with less power. Guggenheimer bases much of her argument on these institutional roles, whereby the male breadwinner is empowered and the female homemaker is not. Her explanation of these roles is based in part on feminist difference theory.[170] In contrast to liberal feminism, which holds the deep-seated belief that women and men are equal, difference theory acknowledges the differences between men and women. It says that these differences should be embraced and accommodated by society.[171]

In the context of prenups, Guggenheimer asserts that women view such agreements differently from men, because they have greater preference for cooperation, value marriage more, are more willing to reward their partner under the terms of the agreement, are more committed to the relationship and have a greater propensity for sacrifice. Guggenheimer also believes in gendered theories of development: that because boys and girls are *socialised* to behave in certain ways, when they are adults, women are 'less likely than men to privilege abstract rights over concrete relationships and are more attentive to values of care, connection and context'.[172] Put simply, Guggenheimer asserts that men and women are socialised into performing certain gendered roles, and this affects their experience of marriage and prenups. This particular element of Guggenheimer's thesis may be perceived as essentialist. Although less likely, it is of course possible that some men will be socialised in the way Guggenheimer says women are, and that some women will reject traditional gender roles.[173] However, Heyes suggests that we should 'examine how generalizations are used; not … reject the use of generality altogether, but … ask what is enabled and what is excluded in the context in question'.[174] By recognising the differences between men and women, Guggenheimer can emphasise the nuances of particular power disparities that would otherwise be obscured, such as her assertion that men can 'hold the relationship hostage' when it is valued more by women and 'milk it for more sacrifices than it is worth'.[175]

[169] Ibid, 155.

[170] See Gilligan, above n 102.

[171] See M Minow, 'The Dilemma of Difference' in D Adams (ed), *Philosophical Problems in the Law* (Wadsworth 2000); C Mackinnon, 'Difference and Dominance: On Sex Discrimination' in K Weisberg (ed), *Feminist Legal Theory: Foundations* (Temple University Press 1993).

[172] Guggenheimer, above n 166, 192. For an overview of the strengths and criticisms of this theoretical approach, see D Rhode, 'Feminist Critical Theories' (1990) 42 *Stanford Law Review* 614.

[173] See B Hooks, 'Understanding Patriarchy', available at <http://imaginenoborders.org/pdf/zines/UnderstandingPatriarchy.pdf>.

[174] CJ Heyes, 'Anti-Essentialism in Practice: Carol Gilligan and Feminist Philosophy' (1997) 12(3) *Hypatia* 142, 149.

[175] Ibid.

Consequently, she says, women's different perception of agreements and relationships gives men more leverage to attain terms that are beneficial to them. Again, this is not to say that men and women are inherently programmed to experience prenups in certain ways, but it does appreciate the social and structural context in which such agreements are made.

Guggenheimer's perspective is helpful in developing an alternative approach to prenups, because her exposure of a gendered power imbalance is an important step towards ensuring the inclusion and participation of both parties in such an agreement. Guggenheimer also considers the gendered power imbalance in connection with which party has the greater income. For example, she argues that 'the male partner invariably has more power to make decisions for the couple. This power is authorised and legitimised by the man's greater earnings.'[176] Furthermore, she says that where bargaining power follows economic power, those in a weaker financial position are systematically disadvantaged. Research corroborates her assertion that, as a result of these structural inequalities, women are usually in a worse position when drafting prenups.[177] As Pateman has put it:

> [M]ore mothers than ever before are now workers, but women generally are still paid less than men so that their economic dependence remains, albeit less severe than in the past. Nor has the sexual division of labour in private life been greatly affected by women's participation in the public workplace ...[178]

Recognising these socio-economic differences and the sexual division of labour facilitates an understanding of the gender dimension of prenups.

The strength of this reasoning is that it can also be applied in cases where the *man* does not perform traditional gendered roles and has less economic power. This is demonstrated in application to a case recalled by an interviewee from the study in New York:

> In one particular case ... the non-moneyed party was a man. There was an insistence that support be waived ... and [the moneyed party] would not agree otherwise. [The moneyed party] would not move on it. [She] would not agree that future interests acquired in a business are marital [assets] ... So he would never be a partner in the business, he wouldn't have a share in the business. But, during the marriage, he would be home taking care of the children ... [T]he money that she's deriving, that he's helping her to derive by contributing in other non-economic ways, he wouldn't have a share in.[179]

The attorney who described this case believed the agreement would be upheld. This demonstrates that power imbalances can disadvantage the male party too, depending on his role in the marriage. Thus although Guggenheimer's perspective purports to be women-centred, it can be applied to any party who does not fulfil

[176] Guggenheimer, above n 167, 200.

[177] See Brod, above n 4; B Atwood, 'Ten Years Later: Lingering Concerns about the Uniform Premarital Agreement Act' (1993) 19(2) *Journal of Legislation* 127.

[178] C Pateman, 'Equality, difference, subordination' in G Bock and S James (eds), *Beyond Equality and Difference: Citizenship, Feminist Politics and Female Subjectivity* (Routledge 1992) 28.

[179] Practitioner 12.

traditionally gendered roles and is in a weaker economic position. She advocates that the voices of both parties to a prenup must be heard. Therefore, in the context of the above example, the non-traditional male voice that was described should be empowered to participate on a more level playing field with the dominant party, and chapter six will examine how this is possible in practice.

Guggenheimer's explanation of power imbalance applies to both men and women in other ways. For example, she argues that people 'ultimately accept contracts antithetical to all their interests—except their interest in marriage generally' because the 'desire for the marriage relationship may be traded off against the desire for a favourable premarital agreement'.[180] First, this indicates that, in practice, prenups are different from separation agreements because, as Guggenheimer says, the latter lack the important element of relationship—the relationship has broken down. Secondly, this argument acknowledges that leverage is dictated not only by wealth. This theory accords with the responses in practice of attorneys interviewed for this book: 'Sometimes the wife wants the marriage more than the husband, sometimes the husband wants the marriage more than the wife, so it gives you negotiation powers; who is willing to walk away from the marriage.'[181] Consequently, one aspect of negotiating, according to practitioners, is being able to walk away from the wedding.[182] On the other hand, interviewees said it is not likely to give a client more power than the leverage attained from being the moneyed spouse. Thus when connecting theory and practice in chapter six, it will be important to determine other ways in which power imbalances caused by disparity of income can be addressed.

The first way in which Guggenheimer's approach can address issues of power is to encourage autonomy in a way that existing law does not. As Guggenheimer puts it, 'Real life people are involved and they bring their personalities, individual talents and skills, and emotional insecurities or strengths to the drafting endeavour. The bargaining dynamics will influence and direct the outcome of the agreement.'[183]

If these bargaining dynamics stifle the autonomy of one of the parties, then Guggenheimer's theory, when considered in a practical context, could be valuable. For instance, she says that '[t]he greater the disparity of income between a couple [whereby the wife is the non-moneyed spouse], the more likely the woman will respect and acquiesce the man's power to make decisions'.[184] The potential effect of this is 'economic alienation', where the non-moneyed spouse is excluded from financial aspects of the relationship and becomes increasingly dissatisfied. To address this in practice, Guggenheimer says that '[w]omen need to be involved in creating the range of drafting options' for prenups.[185] This assertion helps reduce

[180] Guggenheimer, above n 166, 189.

[181] Practitioner 13.

[182] Ibid.

[183] Guggenheimer, above n 166, 187.

[184] Ibid, 201. FRCT would assert that this is also applicable in situations where the wife is the moneyed spouse.

[185] Guggenheimer, above n 166, 204. These drafting options are considered further in ch 6.

economic alienation and also demonstrates a resistance to having less power during prenuptial negotiations. After all, '[b]eing the weaker bargaining partner—and accepting it—is self-enforcing',[186] according to Guggenheimer.

The gendered power dimension attached to prenups is also addressed by Guggenheimer's theory. She explains why such agreements should incorporate provisions that encourage neither shared income nor a complete pooling of assets:

> [W]omen [remain] saddled with the bulk of home and childcare work, and their ability to structure their own free time becomes greatly constrained … [T]here is some evidence to suggest that absolute separation of money and interests or the failure to deal with a wife's aspirations to be employed may doom a marriage to dissolution, and that complete pooling may also in fact harm a woman's bargaining power within the unit. This suggests that the best goal for a prenuptial agreement is some separation of income, some pooling of assets and some 'non-monetary' provisions dealing with couple management decisions.[187]

This demonstrates that bargaining power decreases when the non-moneyed spouse's assets are completely separated from or completely pooled with those of the moneyed partner. When assets are separated, the non-moneyed spouse is alienated financially; and when assets are pooled, the non-moneyed spouse has less control over the pot because he or she has less economic power within the relationship. Thus agreements that facilitate either extreme weaken the non-moneyed spouse's position, because it becomes contractually guaranteed. Spouses should be encouraged not to act according to their own self-interest, but instead to be equally empowered to guarantee mutual financial benefits on divorce by agreement. From this perspective, it seems that empowerment means individuals refusing to accept (unquestioningly) what the other party wants, and refusing to give into terms that will disadvantage them.

Distinguishing Guggenheimer's Approach from Feminist Relational Contract Theory

A significant distinction between FRCT and Guggenheimer's perspective is that Guggenheimer does not believe that prenups should be treated differently from other common contracts, even those made in commerce. Her reasoning is that agreements involve long-term relationships, where the evolution of that relationship and future circumstances are unknown.[188] However, by assimilating prenups with commercial contracts, Guggenheimer is overlooking the fact that the relationship between the parties in these two contexts is fundamentally different. Conversely, FRCT is informed by the context of the relationship.

[186] Ibid, 202.

[187] Ibid, 200.

[188] Guggenheimer uses the example of a 'professional partnership agreement with a dissolution clause', ibid, 155.

Another contextual issue with Guggenheimer's approach is that she focuses only on the drafting process of prenups, as she believes that problems with these agreements on marital dissolution are not caused by their enforcement: it is the actual agreement being enforced that is problematic. Guggenheimer also argues that addressing issues of fairness and unequal power at the time of enforcement only ensures justice on an ad hoc basis. Therefore, she does not support vitiation based on the fact the agreement is 'unfair' when enforced. On the other hand, FRCT recognises that a prenup spans a marital relationship, and the obligations under that agreement do not crystallise until that relationship breaks down. Before that point of crystallisation, as this book has repeatedly emphasised, circumstances typically change. But Guggenheimer's focus on the drafting process of prenups skews autonomy, so that it is fixed to the point at which the agreement is signed. Even if both parties have the opportunity to bargain fairly according to Guggenheimer's proposals, they might not have been truly autonomous if the potential for future changes had not been properly considered. Furthermore, building on Macneil and Wightman's analysis earlier in this chapter, it is possible that as the relationship progresses, tacit understandings between the parties about the effect of their prenup may change and new understandings may emerge. The possibility of this in theory recognises that autonomy changes over time, and in a relational context the nature of agreements can change with the relationship between the parties.

As a result of these differences, Guggenheimer's approach and FRCT also consider the gender dimension of prenups differently. This book has consistently stated that there are many cases where the woman is on the short end of the prenup, but this is not only at the negotiation stage. Change in circumstances may be gendered too, particularly in cases where the couple decide that the wife should sacrifice her career to care for the home and family. The current liberal attitude of the law treats everyone in the same way, regardless of their different circumstances. Yet FRCT proposes an alternative approach to avoid the harsh consequences of the current one. To begin with it applies Wightman's theory of 'non-bargain reciprocity',[189] which removes the bargaining element of the agreement. Prenuptial agreements are not necessarily viewed as instruments of self-interest, but instead the interdependence between the parties is taken into account. Acts of reliance are recognised during the relationship as evidence that the parties' initial intentions have changed. These acts of reliance (which could conceivably include career sacrifices, significant financial changes or other unforeseeable events that were not considered in the original prenup) could then be taken into account when the agreement is enforced. From this perspective, a prenup is not centred on bargaining but on the intentions shared by the parties. By shifting the focus away from bargaining and self-interest, the party who might otherwise have had less bargaining power may not be exploited by his or her partner.

[189] See Wightman, above n 82.

Conclusion

Applying Guggenheimer's theory to the drafting process of prenups could conceivably help to address issues of power imbalance connected to such agreements. For example, her strategy of empowerment (whereby couples draft mutually advantageous agreements) merits further consideration in practice.[190] However, Guggenheimer's approach does not fit with the aims of FRCT in a few respects: she considers only the drafting process of agreements, and she does not believe that prenups should be distinguished from other long-term agreements.

Patently, a limitation of Guggenheimer's approach when juxtaposed with FRCT is that the context of the relationship between parties entering prenups cannot be fully accounted for, unless the enforcement process of such agreements is considered. Indeed, criticisms of contract law considered in this chapter highlight the importance of context when considering party autonomy. Feminist and relational contract perspectives show that a contextual approach may be facilitated by focusing on the relationship of the parties involved *as a whole*, to gauge the realities of power and autonomy in a given situation. This leads to a re-evaluation of autonomy that recognises power imbalance, and represents a shift away from the individualised focus on property allocation typical to prenuptial contracting.

The feminist relational contract perspective has been outlined in some detail in this chapter, which raises Feinman's question: 'What do we do with the theory?'[191] A major obstacle to the utility of relational, contextual perspectives like FRCT is that they are not perceived to work in practice. As Eisenberg explains, there cannot be a law of relational contracts, because

> there is no significant difference between contracts as a class and relational contracts, [therefore] relational contracts must be governed by the general principles of contract law, whatever those should be. Of course, certain categories of contracts present special kinds of problems. These problems, however, derive not from the fact that the contracts in these categories are relational, but from more specific attributes … [R]elational contracts … are not a special category of contract, because all or virtually all contracts are relational.[192]

In counteracting this argument, it is important to emphasise that FRCT does not need to create a separate body of law to work in practice. Indeed, rather than attempting an overhaul of general contract law, the purpose of FRCT is to build

[190] It arguably leads to a way of circumventing the dilemma of choice referred to by Hadfield, above n 6.

[191] See Beale, above n 76, 116, referring to J Feinman, 'The Reception of Ian Macneil's Work on Contract in the USA' in D Campbell (ed), *The Relational Theory of Contract: Selected works of Ian Macneil* (Sweet & Maxwell 2001) 63.

[192] M Eisenberg, 'Why there is no law of relational contracts' (2000) 94 *Northwestern University Law Review* 805.

on pre-existing relational elements in contract law, so that when prenups are considered by the court, the relational context is a priority. As Beale has said, contract law has significant relational elements.[193] Therefore, it is conceivable that contract law also has the capacity to observe the aims of FRCT. Chapter six will consider how FRCT may be implemented in practice and, in particular, will explore whether the meaning of autonomy in light of this theory can be reflected in the courtroom.

193 See Beale, above n 76.

6

Prenuptial Agreements and the Presumption of Free Choice—Connecting Theory and Practice

Though there is no definitive answer to the question of what autonomy means, the concept is often blended with a singular caricature of individual autonomy.[1] Mackenzie and Stoljar explain this caricature as representing the 'self-sufficient ... rational maximising chooser of libertarian theory'.[2] It is this kind of autonomy that people who have entered prenups are presumed by the court to have (unless, for example, duress can be established). It is also this kind of autonomy that the UK Supreme Court says should be respected.[3]

The theory posited in this book, which is labelled 'feminist relational contract theory' (FRCT), rejects this 'paradigm view' of individualistic autonomy—that people make free and detached decisions when entering into prenups.[4] Instead, FRCT places these decisions in context and recognises that individuals do not enter into prenups in a vacuum. When interrogated, autonomy in reality means more than rational decision making, and choices made by parties in the prenuptial context are influenced by the pressures, emotions and dependencies of the relationship. As a result, FRCT engenders a contextual concept of autonomy necessary to recognise the reality of power imbalances between parties to a prenup. Key to this meaning of autonomy is the inability to provide properly for future circumstances that are not known at the drafting stage of these agreements. For this reason, the nature of parties' rights, obligations and intentions under a prenup could be described as 'floating', in that they change as circumstances change, and their effect is not really known until the time of enforcement.

A view of autonomy informed by FRCT also facilitates a subjective inquiry into the individual pressures experienced by the parties. When considering the practical outcome of a concept of autonomy informed by this theory, the drafting and enforcement processes of prenups are explored in accordance with the findings of

[1] C Mackenzie and N Stoljar, 'Autonomy Refigured' in C Mackenzie and N Stoljar (eds), *Relational Autonomy: Feminist Perspectives on Autonomy, Agency and the Social Self* (OUP 2000) 3.

[2] Ibid.

[3] *Radmacher v Granatino* [2010] UKSC 42.

[4] S Dodds, 'Choice and Control in Feminist Bioethics' in Mackenzie and Stoljar (eds), above n 1, 213.

the New York study and the doctrinal examination of contract law: first, different approaches to prenups before enforcement are examined; and, secondly, ways in which prenups could be given effect in accordance with FRCT are proposed.

Guggenheimer's approach is significant to this analysis, but primarily in relation to the drafting stage of these agreements.[5] As FRCT aims to produce a concept of autonomy that is exercised over the course of the entire agreement, it is also important to consider the enforcement process. In addition to considering practical methods of implementing a new approach to autonomy, the third section of this chapter will consider current jurisprudence, to demonstrate how a new approach would differ from the court's current approach to autonomy. The clearest way of doing this is to revisit *Radmacher v Granatino* in light of FRCT, to test this theory against the facts of an actual case.

Applying Feminist Relational Contract Theory to Prenuptial Agreements Before Enforcement

This section examines a range of practical methods to address issues with power and autonomy during the drafting process of prenups, and tests the effectiveness of these approaches using FRCT. The outcome of this evaluation facilitates a preliminary analysis as to the steps to be taken to implement a concept of autonomy compatible with the aims of FRCT.

Independent Legal Advice

The New York study written up in this book demonstrated that in practice, power imbalances are primarily addressed when prenups are negotiated. For this reason, independent legal advice was viewed by attorneys interviewed in the study as being the most effective way of facilitating party autonomy. Though respondents said that independent advice does not prevent their clients from making 'bad' decisions, it *can* prevent clients from making a bad deal and knowing it is a bad deal.[6] Competent legal advice will help individuals entering prenups to consider potential changes during the marriage. Thus independent legal advice should require more than simply ensuring each party is technically represented by different lawyers. Individuals also need to be made aware of the rights and protection being relinquished as a result of an agreement.

Put simply, a key advantage of independent legal advice is that the parties are made aware of consequences that may not be obvious at the time they enter an

[5] L Guggenheimer, 'A Modest Proposal: The Feminomics of Drafting Premarital Agreements' (1996) 17 *Women's Rights Law Reporter* 147.

[6] Practitioner 17.

agreement. This has particular significance for the gendered power dimension of prenups, as a woman who sacrifices her career for the sake of the family (but has not contracted to do so) may be made aware by her lawyer of the magnitude of the risk she is taking.[7] However, the reason alternative theoretical perspectives were explored in chapter five is that independent legal advice does not guarantee autonomy or a relationship of balanced power in the context of prenups, as the study presented in chapter three indicates that parties will not always listen to legal advice. Furthermore, future change in circumstances for couples cannot always be provided for by a prenup, even when lawyers can help their clients make rational decisions. But as earlier chapters have demonstrated, proof of independent legal advice is usually sufficient to satisfy the court that both parties have been autonomous, even when they have not been. Therefore, independent legal advice is not only potentially an unreliable indicator of autonomy, it may also mask power imbalance if the court treats the presence of such advice as being determinative, which, according to case law, often occurs.[8] This is not really compatible with FRCT, which advocates an approach that considers context beyond whether independent legal advice has been sought. Indeed, the problem with enforcing prenups, once certain 'tick box' conditions like this are satisfied, is summarised by Fehlberg and Smyth:

> Independent legal advice will not ensure that issues of power imbalance due to, for example, undue influence or unconscionable dealing are overcome, but the fact that independent advice has been given may nevertheless suffice to make the agreement enforceable.[9]

Chapter four has also demonstrated that the doctrines of duress and undue influence will recognise issues with power and autonomy only in extreme, narrowly circumscribed circumstances. In theory, however, solutions influenced by a feminist relational contract perspective are less restrictive. One way of adopting this perspective in practice is to re-evaluate vitiating factors in a way that widens their scope, which would mean that the more subtle power imbalances affecting autonomy as described in earlier chapters could be taken into account. The law on duress and undue influence will be considered later in this chapter, as although these vitiating factors are relevant when the agreement is being made, it is how they are taken into account at the time of enforcement that is relevant. However, consideration of the drafting process of prenups is also important, to explore whether there are other methods compatible with the relational view of autonomy produced by FRCT when an agreement is created. At first glance, the proposals made by the American Law Institute seem to incorporate a contextually sensitive view of autonomy, and so the next section will explore this work further.

[7] S Thompson, 'Levelling the Prenuptial Playing Field: Is Independent Legal Advice the Answer?' (2011) 4 *International Family Law* 327.

[8] For example, even though the parties were not independently advised in *Radmacher*, above n 3, the Court considered the couple's legal advice to be sufficient.

[9] B Fehlberg and B Smyth, 'Binding Prenuptial Agreements in Australia: The First Year' in L Mulcahy and S Wheeler (eds), *Feminist Perspectives on Contract Law* (Routledge 2005) 130.

The American Law Institute

The proposals made by the American Law Institute (ALI) in relation to marital property agreements[10] share a sentiment similar to that expressed in FRCT.[11] As Bix has said, the approach urged by the ALI is both respectful of party choice and sensitive to problems relating to bounded rationality.[12] From this perspective, the ALI want to achieve the same outcomes as FRCT: empowerment, true autonomy and recognition of power issues in context. Thus it is important to consider these proposals in more detail.[13]

When an agreement is entered into, the ALI has recognised that the following procedural requirements ought to be observed:

- the agreement is entered into at least 30 days before marriage;
- parties are advised to obtain independent legal counsel and should have a reasonable opportunity to do so;
- the agreement should be in plain language, explaining the nature of the rights being altered (particularly for agreements where one party did not have independent legal counsel); and
- the party waiving rights should at least have approximate knowledge of the other party's assets and income.[14]

According to the ALI, the purpose of these guidelines is that, if they are followed, it would be more likely an agreement would be made without duress and with informed consent, and a presumption of enforcement on this basis would therefore be more forceful.

Though many similar recommendations have been issued which focus on issues like advice, disclosure and 'cooling-off' periods, the ALI recommendations are interesting because they explicitly consider the problem of bounded rationality.[15] Bounded rationality affects the parties' ability to think clearly about protecting themselves financially on divorce in the early stages of a relationship, which stages are often marked by altruism and commitment.[16] This concern is synonymous with relational contract theory's concern regarding lack of presentiation—that it is difficult to make a rational and autonomous decision at present, when it will not

[10] ALI, *Principles of the Law of Family Dissolution: Analysis and Recommendations* (LexisNexis 2002).

[11] The ALI Principles are applicable to US states, the law of which was described in ch 3. The ALI Principles are not mandatory in the US, though states may elect to incorporate them into their legislation.

[12] B Bix, 'The ALI Principles and Agreements: Seeking a Balance between Status and Contract' in R Wilson (ed), *Reconceiving the Family: Critique on the American Law Institute's Principles of the Law of Family Dissolution* (Cambridge University Press 2006) 408.

[13] The guidelines relevant to the enforcement of marital agreements will be considered in the second section of this chapter.

[14] See ALI, above n 10, s 7.04(3), 960.

[15] For this reason the ALI proposals are considered in this section, instead of other reform proposals produced by bodies such as the Law Commission of England and Wales.

[16] See Bix, above n 12.

come into effect until the future.[17] Nevertheless, in spite of the ALI's intentions, its proposed guidelines arguably do not do anything to re-evaluate the notion of autonomy. They make generalised presumptions about consent, and this does not demonstrate the same concern for context engendered by a feminist relational contract perspective. Rather, FRCT incorporates relational contract's criticism of presentiation,[18] that '[p]rimarily through manipulations of the notion of consent, traditional contract theory create[s] a legal structure which in theory attempt[s] to presentiate not just part of the relation between contracting parties, but virtually all of it'.[19] By presuming consent according to guidelines like those suggested by the ALI, an inability to presentiate effectively (that is, properly provide for future change in circumstances) may not be recognised.

On the other hand, Bix believes the 'cognitive defects' of bounded rationality should not be overstated during the drafting process.[20] This is because a waiver of rights under a prenup is not tangential: it is the sole purpose of the agreement. Bix argues that because of this, even though people might not be able to think clearly about divorcing, their thinking is at least plainly directed to the issue of divorce.[21] Though this may not make presentiation any easier, focusing on how people can circumvent the effect of bounded rationality is arguably more productive. The following section examines methods of empowerment for parties to prenups by considering the approach of Guggenheimer and FRCT in a practical context. When juxtaposed with the ALI's proposals, Guggenheimer's theory reveals the inadequacy of the ALI's purely law-focused view, in that an alternative approach to prenups must respond to more than legal issues so that gendered issues of power can be recognised.

Applying Guggenheimer's Theory in Practice

The compatibility of Guggenheimer's theoretical approach with FRCT was considered in chapter five, but it is also important to consider her proposed solution to the 'feminomics' (or economic consequences of gender) of prenups in practice.[22]

Guggenheimer's theoretical approach to addressing issues of power and autonomy in the context of prenups is to change parties' bargaining dynamics by incorporating woman-centred provisions into these agreements. This could be beneficial in practice if, as Guggenheimer has suggested, woman-centred provisions lead to marital assets being shared but not completely pooled. Recent anecdotal evidence published by the *Guardian* suggests that where there is disparity of

[17] I Macneil, 'Restatement (Second) of Contracts and Presentiation' (1974) 60(4) *Virginia Law Review* 589.

[18] Refer to ch 5 for a more detailed explanation of the impact 'presentiation' has on long-term contracts, such as marital property agreements.

[19] Macneil, above n 17, 592.

[20] See Bix, above n 12.

[21] Ibid.

[22] See Guggenheimer, above n 5.

income between couples, a complete pooling or separation of assets can lead to control issues and resentment.[23] However, this article also indicated that different couples prefer to deal with their assets in different ways, which is why they enter into prenups. From this perspective, woman-centred provisions that restrict this flexibility cannot be justified. On the other hand, a practical benefit of Guggenheimer's woman-centred solution is that it could encourage a more general attitude of empowerment among parties entering prenups, which could make procedural safeguards like disclosure, cooling-off periods and independent legal advice much more effective. The more determined both spouses are to participate during the drafting process, the more likely their lawyers will be able to assist in formulating an agreement that is mutually beneficial to both parties. Unfortunately, while these considerations during the drafting process may improve matters, they do not directly deal with change in circumstances during the marriage. Feminist relational contract theory asserts that these changes should also be taken into account, for the purpose of a relational view of autonomy is that it develops with the relationship.

A case example from the New York study highlights the practical consequences of an agreement that does not account for changes in circumstance:

> My client's husband was worth about 60 million dollars when they got married, [and] is worth about $100 million today … She was a lawyer, a partner in a major New York law firm, and their agreement provided … that she would contribute 15% of her earnings to the expenses of their household, their living expenses throughout the marriage. And of course, 3 or 4 years into the marriage she stopped working. And here we are 15 years later, and he's found another woman, his third wife, she should have known better … second marriages are the triumph of optimism over experience! … But in any event, he's left her for another woman and she's going to get … about $15 million.[24]

Although $15 million is a significant amount of money by most standards, this anecdote is a pertinent illustration of how party autonomy can change over time. The wife's access to the husband's fortune before marriage might have been viewed by both parties as a windfall, but as sacrifices were made by the wife over time, access to this same fortune is instead something to which the wife would most likely have felt entitled. The intentions of the parties regarding financial provision also changed when the wife stopped working,[25] but this was not reflected in the agreement when it was first concluded. Feminist relational contract theory thus asserts that the autonomy of the non-moneyed spouse should be considered, but not prioritised over consideration for the autonomy of the moneyed spouse.

[23] O Gordon, 'What's mine is mine: 10 couples on how they arrange their finances', *Guardian* (London, 2 March 2013), available at <http://www.guardian.co.uk/money/2013/mar/02/whats-mine-is-mine-couples-cash?INTCMP=SRCH>.

[24] Practitioner 2.

[25] This is because a change in career is a significant change in the economic dynamic of the relationship.

In practice, therefore, Guggenheimer proposed two ways of addressing the issue of change in circumstances, which are in keeping with the aims of FRCT posited by this book. One suggestion is to incorporate sunset clauses. These are clauses that extinguish an agreement, or compel renegotiation after the occurrence of an event or time period specified in the original agreement. According to findings from the New York study, there is evidence that these clauses may promote 'walk out', encourage people to re-evaluate their marriage (when they might not otherwise) or simply replicate bargaining inequalities that might have occurred during the drafting process. However, Guggenheimer has helpfully suggested an alternative method of incorporating these clauses, whereby they are phased in over time. For example, rather than an agreement being concluded abruptly, provision for the non-moneyed spouse could be increased gradually over several years so that separation of assets would decrease over time.[26] This 'phase out' approach could overcome many of the disadvantages of sunset clauses observed by interviewees in New York.

The other suggestion made by Guggenheimer is regular renegotiation of the agreement.[27] This kind of periodic review recognises that what individuals view as appropriate financial provision on divorce invariably changes during marriage. A regular annual review not only empowers couples and encourages them to exercise a type of autonomy more synonymous with FRCT, it also simply allows people to change their minds. Agreements also remain more relevant to parties' circumstances, because they can be amended if 'important assumptions underlying the contract cease to operate, such as if the wife quits her job, or provides more domestic and hosting services for her husband that she anticipated, or gives birth to and mothers their children'.[28] In short, the reality of marriage and prenups is recognised, which is that the autonomy of the parties and the outcome of the agreement are 'floating' and susceptible to change until the time of enforcement.

Whilst it is conceivable that this approach could address issues with prenups in practice, there are limitations to Guggenheimer's proposed solutions when FRCT is used to interrogate her approach further.

Moving Forward—Altering Guggenheimer's Approach and Applying Feminist Relational Contract Theory in Practice (Before Enforcement)

Before re-evaluating Guggenheimer's approach in accordance with the theoretical aims of this book, it is necessary first to clarify what these aims are. As explained in chapter five, FRCT is influenced by Wightman's argument that the bargaining process of agreements is not as important as the intentions shared by the parties

26 See Guggenheimer, above n 5, 184.

27 Ibid.

28 Ibid.

over the course of the relationship.[29] These intentions are susceptible to change over time, and may be implied by acts of reliance, such as career sacrifice or some unforeseeable event. In effect, FRCT asserts that these shared intentions should be recognised in the context of prenups, so that party autonomy may be considered more realistically by the court.

Implementing this approach in practice might be difficult. One way would be for the court to consider whether there was any evidence that the parties had an understanding of financial support different from the prenup, and that they consequently relied on this changed understanding. This scenario shares some similarities with the operation of common intention constructive trusts. For example, in cases where property is in a couple's joint names but quantification of each parties' beneficial interests is an issue, their conduct and changing intentions may be taken into account by the court.[30] The effect of this on prenups at the time of enforcement is examined later in this chapter, but prior to enforcement, the non-bargain theory could be accounted for in practice if the couple review the original agreement in light of changed circumstances or understandings of economic support on divorce.

Although this approach is synonymous with Guggenheimer's proposal that agreements are regularly reviewed by the parties, the problem with requiring an explicit agreement is that, inadvertently, the element of bargaining (and the issues of power connected to bargaining) is still a lingering issue. For example, Guggenheimer's proposal requires both parties to cooperate in modifying the agreement, which may not always be possible. Indeed, she has conceded that her approach will not be effective unless '[an] overall change in drafting norms [is] effected, shifting away from focus[ing] exclusively on competing interests and claiming needs and moving towards a vision of private ordering that is governed by conjoining interests and distributional needs'.[31] However, such change may not be possible unless an approach that does not emphasise bargaining is properly facilitated. On the other hand, regular and open conversations about marital finances may encourage parties to exercise autonomy, especially as it changes over time. Even so, it could be argued that changing intentions and circumstances are more easily dealt with by the court on enforcement. This ensures that parties who did not have the opportunity to express autonomy in light of different circumstances are not overlooked.

A non-bargain theory emphasises the relational element of FRCT, but the feminist aspect is important too. It is particularly sensitive to the fact that career sacrifices or other changes in circumstance may affect women more if a prenup has not provided for these changes. This makes sense in practice, as an interviewee from the New York study recalled a case where the wife did not receive a sufficient award under the agreement to live near the area in which her children were educated.[32]

[29] J Wightman, 'Intimate Relationships, Relational Contract Theory and the Reach of Contract' (2000) 8 *Feminist Legal Studies* 93.

[30] *Stack v Dowden* [2007] UKHL 17; *Jones v Kernott* [2011] UKSC 53.

[31] See Guggenheimer, above n 5, 205.

[32] Practitioner 12.

However, if the court had adopted a feminist approach in this case, it might have been decided differently. Feminist relational contract theory recognises the potentially harsh consequences for parties who have not had the opportunity to express autonomy in the prenuptial context. Furthermore, creating a space in which the voices of both parties are heard ultimately allows men in non-traditional roles to be heard. This is particularly important when considering the following quotation from a participant in the New York study:

> I think it's interesting when you have the male who is the non-moneyed party and the views people take when it's he not she … [I]f it's a guy, if it doesn't work out in 10 years he can get up and get a job. If you said that and it was the woman who is the less moneyed fiancé, it would be … an offensive comment and so … I think it's even harder to negotiate for that person, that male in that position than the female because there is just this general acceptance of you know … the woman in that role, the non-moneyed role, and what the expectations are than if it's the man that is. I find it much more difficult to negotiate in that position.[33]

In practice, this demonstrates that the non-traditional male voice is also marginalised by the gender dimension attached to prenups. Feminist relational contract theory exposes this difficulty. But it also goes further than Guggenheimer's approach, as it prioritises a relational, non-bargain theory over traditional contractual views. To emphasise this distinction, prenups should encourage terms that are not 'woman-centred' but rather 'relationship-centred'.

In some ways, relationship-centred provisions would be similar to what Guggenheimer has proposed, as they would focus on outcomes that could benefit both parties, such as guarantees of fair standards of financial well-being for the family on divorce. However, when building on Guggenheimer's approach, terms would also indicate that the *relationship* rather than the moneyed spouse is at the centre of the agreement, and would provide for relationship-generated disadvantage. This would help prevent an agreement having a harsh outcome on divorce. Furthermore, a relationship-centred approach to autonomy would be different from Guggenheimer's theory in practice, as the court would be encouraged not to restrict its assessment of autonomy to the initial bargaining process of the prenup.

If altered slightly using FRCT, Guggenheimer's ideas are influential when considering how to facilitate a concept of autonomy in practice that addresses the intentions of both parties rather than the party with more bargaining power. Ultimately she proposes a new attitude towards the drafting process of prenups, which makes mutual benefit (and thus mutual empowerment) a chief concern of the parties. To safeguard this process in practice, she also advocates provisions based on independent legal advice, timing and disclosure. Although these proposals have been made by various other reform bodies, Guggenheimer's work is different because her recommended safeguards are intended to support a fundamental and theoretical change in approach for prenups. Using FRCT to change the emphasis of her proposals to be relationship-centred, the beginnings of a framework can be traced that could facilitate a more realistic view of autonomy in practice.

[33] Ibid.

In spite of this, the point of an integrated relational approach in FRCT is that agreements are considered in their entirety, and so it is crucial that the *process* of enforcement for prenups is re-evaluated according to this theory. Furthermore, this approach focuses on how the parties themselves and their lawyers may act according to an alternative form of autonomy. Importantly, however, this does not necessarily change the law's perception of autonomy. Therefore, the following section will consider enforcement *and* will focus on how the court may address power imbalance more effectively.

Applying Feminist Relational Contract Theory to Prenuptial Agreements at the Time of Enforcement

Even if the drafting process is modified, there are still cases where parties do not have equal power or opportunity to exercise their autonomy when making prenups. This has to be addressed on divorce. The difficulty lies in determining how the law can recognise power imbalance in practice, without being unfair to those who have relied on an agreement and without undermining the enforceability of prenups in general. As considered in earlier chapters, other theories dealing with these issues have suggested that non-enforcement is the best solution. This makes sense if autonomy is only associated with a liberal, atomistic model, allowing the more powerful party to act according to his or her own self-interest. But as this book asserts, the point of FRCT is to promote the exercise of *relational* autonomy, and non-enforcement prevents this as the possibility of an enforceable prenup compatible with FRCT is removed. As a result, this section applies this theory to the enforcement of agreements in an attempt to ameliorate power imbalances.

Adapting Vitiating Factors According to Feminist Relational Contract Theory

As demonstrated in chapter four, a significant issue with the enforcement of prenups in practice is that contractual vitiating factors are too narrowly construed to account for power imbalances and autonomy issues between parties to these agreements. However, as McLean asserts, if power imbalance is endemic but is not addressed by the court, then the court must perceive autonomy differently.[34] To re-model the orthodox view of autonomy, vitiating factors must also be re-evaluated. Feminist relational contract theory can assist in encouraging this alternative view, and so it will be used to interrogate the scope of duress and undue influence.

[34] S McLean, *Autonomy, Consent and the Law* (Routledge 2010) 23.

Duress

The doctrine of duress applies to prenups as it would apply to any contract, focusing on the consent of the parties and on the possibility of wrongdoing from either party. Gan explains that the problem with this is that 'what seems to the court as a consensual agreement is actually the result of a combination of social constraints and economic pressures exploited by the more powerful party'.[35] According to Gan, the court does not consider power relations between parties, or background circumstances like economic dependency. When theorising how the court could change its approach towards contracts, particularly in intimate situations, she extends feminist scholarship on consent to the concept of consent in contract law. She also considers the operation of duress law when agreements are enforced in practice. Thus, her work fits within a feminist relational contract approach, and should be applied to prenups.

According to Gan, feminist insights into consent in the rape context are valuable in the contract context too. Using these feminist insights, she attempts to enrich the law of duress. Chapter four of this book concluded that the doctrine of duress has limited ability to recognise power imbalance and lack of autonomy, because it only considers extreme situations where the parties had no reasonable alternative. Duress is also narrow in focus because it considers individual threats but, as Gan puts it, 'systemic economic constraints remain outside its scope'.[36] She compares this with MacKinnon's claim that criminal law 'normalizes the violence men inflict on women',[37] because rapists are viewed as deviant perpetrators instead of being connected to a wider societal context. Put simply, the issue Gan has with these areas of law is that they are disconnected from context, and from the realities with which people deal. For contract law, these shortcomings could be because the law is desensitised to issues of power when they are so prevalent in intimate agreements. Yet unfortunately the result of this is that contract law 'legitimizes cases of more modest but still pervasive economic compulsion'.[38]

These issues have all been considered earlier in this book, but Gan's work is notable due to her presentation of duress from a feminist perspective in an attempt to address these issues. Without a feminist perspective, Gan explains that the law relies on binary thinking. This creates what she refers to as a 'consent/coercion dichotomy', which means parties are viewed either as being completely autonomous or as 'victim[s] of coercion succumbing to pressures'.[39] In contrast to this, the feminist viewpoint treats concepts like autonomy and consent as being 'complicated and nuanced'.[40] Feminism can recognise the reality of human behaviour,

[35] O Gan, 'Contractual Duress and Relations of Power' (2013) 36 *Harvard Journal of Law and Gender* 171.

[36] Ibid, 16.

[37] Ibid, citing C MacKinnon, *Toward a Feminist Theory of the State* (Harvard University Press 1989) 172.

[38] See Gan, above n 35, 17.

[39] Ibid, 31.

[40] Ibid.

which causes 'intermediate feelings' that are not consent *or* duress, like stress or subtle pressure when entering agreements. Applying these insights to duress law would mean that instead of a situation being assessed according to duress or no duress, it could be situated on a spectrum of varying degrees of pressure. This is because Gan asserts that '[c]onsent [and duress] should be viewed as a continuum ranging from voluntary and free consent to coercion and duress with many [grey] areas in between'.[41]

In practice this means that the court should thoroughly consider the circumstances in which a prenup is signed in each case. For example, rather than only noting that legal advice had been obtained by parties to an agreement, the court could probe how each party was advised and the parties' reasons for entering an agreement. Widening the scope of duress would also mean the court could consider different kinds of pressure when assessing whether the 'aggrieved party' had the option to reject the prenup and walk away from the marriage. Currently the court's binary approach prevents a remedy for duress where one party is pregnant, or is presented with an agreement after wedding plans have been finalised, because that party is still considered to have the reasonable alternative of not marrying. However, rather than one party being faced with giving in to an agreement on the partner's terms or not getting married at all, Gan asserts that he or she should have a third option, to negotiate an agreement that satisfies both parties.[42] If this third option is not taken into account, power inequalities will be ignored and therefore legitimised.

Gan's approach considers all circumstances, as her formulation of duress accounts for varying degrees of pressure, depending on how the consent of the parties was affected. Furthermore, her approach considers consent during the negotiation, signing and performance of the agreement. That is, Gan accounts for the relational element of agreements and assesses 'pre-bargaining' and 'post-bargaining occurrences', because consent is 'dynamic and changing'. Lastly, allowing for a richer conception of coercion would address the gender dimension of prenups, as women's more limited options in cases where they are the non-moneyed, homemaking or caregiving spouse can be taken into account.

Gan's theory shares a similar purpose with FRCT, because at first glance it changes the meaning of autonomy *and* addresses issues of power. But when connecting her theory with practice, it is unclear whether widening the scope of

[41] Ibid, 32.

[42] This also corresponds with Mahoney's perception of agency in the situation of domestic abuse. Mahoney asserts that if agency is separated from social context, the choice to stay with an abusive partner is viewed as acceptance of that abuse. But if a more complex understanding is employed, refusing exit can signify resistance to power imbalance rather than acquiescence: M Mahoney, 'Exit: Power and the idea of leaving in love, work, and the confirmation hearings' (1991) 65 *Southern California Law Review* 1284; M Mahoney, 'Victimization or Oppression? Women's Lives, Violence, and Agency' in M Fineman and R Mykitiuk (eds), *The Public Nature of Private Violence: The Discovery of Domestic Abuse* (Routledge 1994). When applying this theory of agency to prenups, if a party is disadvantaged by the terms of an agreement but does not cancel the wedding, that party has not definitively acquiesced to those terms.

duress law could actually achieve this. As chapter four demonstrated, of the vitiating factors applicable to prenups, duress is the most difficult to establish. The law on presumed undue influence already purports to apply to situations where pressure is more subtle than in duress cases, though it still falls short of adequately addressing prenuptial power issues. Furthermore, it difficult to imagine what the court would make of a formulation of duress that accounts for all cases of power imbalance falling between extreme pressure and proper consent. Indeed, anything short of a relational concept of autonomy is not really duress. The problem with Gan's theory, therefore, is that she explains how duress can recognise power imbalance, but does not provide any specific guidance as to how duress might address this imbalance.

On the other hand, modifying the law of duress could be a practical way of adopting a nuanced approach to autonomy and to the pressure that affects it. The ALI has suggested a less radical change than Gan to the law of duress, proposing that 'a party seeking to enforce an agreement must show that the other party's consent to it was informed and not obtained under duress'.[43] The purpose of this provision is 'explicitly [to enhance] the duress doctrine', to better deal with prenuptial power imbalances.[44] By shifting the burden of proof to the party seeking to enforce the agreement, 'the stronger party is cautioned against overreaching tactics'[45] that would make it difficult to show that his or her partner did not act under duress. The ALI also believes that this requirement deters the stronger party from exploiting bargaining disadvantages of the other party, such as a 'misunderstanding of what is at stake',[46] and provides an incentive for procedural safeguards (considered in the first part of this chapter) to be complied with.

The ALI is also in favour of developing prenuptial duress to replace the voluntariness requirement currently provided in the Uniform Premarital Agreement Act,[47] which purports to focus on whether an agreement has been freely entered into. Though there is no legislative requirement of 'voluntariness' in England, Wales and Northern Ireland, this term is employed in all of the recent case law as evidence of autonomy. However, the ALI says that while 'voluntariness' expresses a heightened sensitivity to pressure in the context of prenups, it does 'not help much in implementing' these concerns in practice.[48] Attempting to define a voluntary or 'meaningful choice' is problematic, because even in duress cases the party under pressure to agree still means to sign the contract. Therefore, voluntariness in practice really means an agreement free from duress, though there is 'no guidance in relocating

[43] ALI, above n 10, s 7.04, 960,

[44] Ibid, 963.

[45] Ibid.

[46] Ibid.

[47] Amendments to the UPAA in 2012 made by the UPMAA did not change or define the voluntariness requirement. Oldham believes this is the 'biggest disappointment' of this reform: T Oldham, 'Would Enactment of the Uniform Premarital and Marital Agreement Act in All Fifty States Change US Law Regarding Premarital Agreements?' (2012) 46 *Family Law Quarterly* 367.

[48] ALI, above n 10, 963.

the duress doctrine's boundaries',[49] according to the ALI. Thus, the ALI believes that prenuptial power issues would be addressed more directly by expanding the current duress defence than under current voluntariness requirements.

The problem with the ALI's reform of duress is that it is informed by an orthodox view of autonomy. Its suggestion to shift the burden of proof for duress does not facilitate a more contextual enquiry, which would be consistent with FRCT, when establishing that there is not duress. Thus duress is still limited by an inability properly to consider pressure in the context of the relationship. Furthermore, though it might appear to be a technical distinction, focusing on whether there is *not* duress is different from focusing on whether there *is* autonomy. This is because there may still be issues with power and autonomy, even if there has been no duress in the prenuptial context. On the other hand, FRCT aims to produce an approach that recognises that autonomy changes and develops during the relationship, which can happen in cases where there has been no duress.

Re-constructing duress in a way that is consistent with FRCT is challenging in practice. It is a restrictive doctrine that does not afford much judicial discretion, so there are limitations as to the amount of context able to be taken into account. For this reason, it is more logical to consider the law of presumed undue influence from a feminist relational contract perspective, as the judge can take a wider range of pressures into account.

Presumed Undue Influence

The law of presumed undue influence is a better way of addressing prenuptial power imbalances, because, as chapter four explained, it can account for a wider range of circumstances than duress.[50] It is also more appropriate in connection with FRCT than the law on unconscionable bargains. This is because the law on unconscionable bargains focuses on explicit exploitation and the morally reprehensible behaviour of the stronger party, rather than focusing on the autonomy of the parties.[51]

To reiterate, presumed undue influence requires a relationship of trust and confidence between the parties, and the agreement must require explanation in a way that is not readily explicable by the relationship itself. Though couples entering into prenups are in a relationship of trust and confidence, it is difficult to show that their agreement calls for explanation in most situations of power imbalance. Parties seeking to rely on presumed undue influence must persuade the court that an agreement was not signed according to ordinary motives, and that the pressure

[49] Ibid.

[50] Actual undue influence is also inappropriate in connection with FRCT because, like duress, it is difficult to establish.

[51] But as Capper has explained, the law of unconscionable bargains in other common law jurisdictions is more similar to the doctrine of undue influence and does not require morally reprehensible conduct on the part of the defendant: D Capper, 'The Unconscionable Bargain in the Common Law World' (2010) 126 *LQR* 403.

to sign was abnormal. But unfortunately, prenups are characterised by power disparity, therefore in most cases the pressure applied will be considered normal.

However, if the law of presumed undue influence is considered from a feminist relational contract perspective, this is not necessarily the case. The difference between normal and abnormal pressure is currently measured by the court according to its prevalence, so that this equitable doctrine is applicable only in exceptional circumstances. On the other hand, an approach consistent with FRCT would distinguish between normal and abnormal pressure according to the experiences of individual couples. By taking individual relationship dynamics into account, power imbalances can be explained, because they do not fit within the context of what is 'normal' for that couple.

One way of applying this modified approach of presumed undue influence to prenups could be to consider developing the idea of a fiduciary relationship, as mentioned by attorneys in the New York study. This would mean that the party seeking to enforce the agreement would have to show that he or she did not have a distinct advantage over his or her partner. However, the judiciary in New York did not explain what it could mean to have a distinct advantage when negotiating a prenup. If this question was explored in line with FRCT, considering whether a distinct advantage had been retained by one party would first require the court to have regard to the relationship between the parties, and the reality of their autonomy (or lack of it). This approach would also allow the court to subject a prenup to a higher level of scrutiny. Furthermore, if these considerations were prioritised in cases of alleged presumed undue influence, a more realistic method of distinguishing between normal and abnormal pressure could be facilitated. This would mean that the reality of power imbalances would not be ignored and normalised by the court.

Though in this context FRCT may be advantageous, it does not allow for change in circumstances to be taken into account. By connecting the theory with the law on presumed undue influence, it can only really take undue pressure from the stronger party into account, rather than accounting for the parties' changing intentions during the marriage. As a result, additional solutions must be explored.

Taking a 'Second Look' at Prenuptial Agreements at the Time of Enforcement[52]

The court's ability to take a second look at prenups on divorce is considered by many to be an important way of ensuring fairness for parties at the time of enforcement. This is because the agreements can be re-evaluated in light of parties' circumstances at the time of separation, which are often different from what their situation was

[52] The approach is called 'second look' by Ellman: I Ellman, 'Marital Agreements and Private Autonomy in the United States' in J Scherpe (ed), *Marital Agreements and Private Autonomy in Comparative Perspective* (Hart Publishing 2012) 427.

before marriage. However, this book has demonstrated that in practice there is a tension between, first, ensuring fairness in this way and, secondly, limiting judicial intervention that imposes the court's sense of fairness. Feminist relational contract theory provides a useful method of analysis when evaluating the utility of a second-look approach during enforcement.

In chapter one, various recommendations for legislation on prenups in the UK were outlined, which generally incorporated provisions allowing changed circumstances to be taken into account. To reiterate, Resolution's suggestion was initially for agreements to be set aside if their effect was to cause 'significant injustice' to either party on divorce,[53] and its subsequent report suggested that this standard could alternatively be 'substantial hardship'.[54] Similarly, the Centre for Social Justice suggested that agreements should pass a threshold of 'significant injustice' to be set aside.[55] Ensuring that prenups meet a standard of fairness on divorce is also reflected in the case law, as the court will not enforce any such agreements that are unfair.[56] In the US, agreements regulated by the UPMAA and UPAA must not be unconscionable,[57] and this standard is also applicable in New York. The purpose of applying these standards of fairness when prenups are enforced is that the court is able to take a second look at the agreement. Therefore, if circumstances have changed during the marriage, and the effect of this change causes injustice or hardship, the court has discretion to set an agreement aside. In practice, however, as we have seen, this will happen only in exceptional circumstances. In particular, in New York, where agreements are routinely enforced, agreements are not held to be unconscionable unless the applicant suffers in a way that will shock the conscience of the court. Thus there is a concern that imposing standards in the UK that are similar to those applied in the US could lead to hardship, particularly for the non-moneyed spouse on divorce.

Furthermore, the unconscionability standard under the UPMAA and UPAA has been widely criticised by commentators in the US. For example, Atwood condemns unconscionability for being tantamount to a public welfare exception to the enforcement of prenups,[58] as it 'looks only to absolute need and ignores other modern justifications for spousal maintenance, such as reimbursement of a spouse for contributions to the other's earning power'.[59] There is also dissatisfaction with

[53] Resolution, *A more certain future—Recognition of pre-marital agreements in England and Wales* (2005).

[54] Resolution, *Family Agreements—Seeking certainty to reduce disputes: the recognition and enforcement of pre-nuptial and post-nuptial agreements in England and Wales* (2009).

[55] The Centre for Social Justice, *Every Family Matters: An in-depth review of family law in Britain* (2009).

[56] See *Radmacher*, above n 3, [72].

[57] The UPMAA was drafted in 2012, and the UPAA, which is the previous version of this legislation, was drafted in 1983. The New York study examined in this book was carried out before the UPMAA was drafted, although this Act did not change or define the unconscionability standard in the UPAA.

[58] See also Nasheri, who says that 'the only provision for "substantive fairness" [in the UPAA] is that section which requires courts to modify an agreement to the extent it causes one party to require public assistance': H Nasheri, 'Prenuptial Agreements in the United States: A Need for Closer Control?' (1998) 12 *International Journal of Law, Policy and the Family* 307.

[59] B Atwood, 'Ten Years Later: Lingering Concerns about the Uniform Premarital Agreement Act' (1993) 19(2) *Journal of Legislation* 127.

unconscionability in practice, as the New York study examined by this book demonstrates a general consensus among attorneys that this standard does not leave the court enough room to consider the substantive fairness of an agreement.

As a result of this criticism, the ALI has proposed that the court's scope to assess the substantive fairness of an agreement is widened. In particular, it has suggested that a prenup may be varied or set aside when it 'would work a substantial injustice'.[60] This is because the ALI has reasoned that even if parties enter agreements voluntarily and were fully informed, enforcement may still lead to a fairly significant degree of unfairness, though it will not necessarily reach the high standard of unconscionability. When assessing the meaning of 'substantial injustice' and whether or not it has occurred, the ALI has set out a number of tests. First, it is recommended that a judge would have discretion to consider whether there has been substantial injustice only if the party resisting enforcement can show that one or more of the following has occurred since the agreement was created:[61]

(a) more than a fixed number of years have passed, that number being set in a rule of statewide application;
(b) a child was born to, or adopted by, the parties, who at the time of execution had no children in common;
(c) there has been a change in circumstances that has a substantial impact on the parties or their children, but when they executed the agreement the parties probably did not anticipate either the change, or its impact.

Point (c) is of particular significance, as any unanticipated change in circumstances may be considered by the court, as long as the impact on the parties is 'substantial'. Once one of these situations is proved to have occurred, the judge must consider whether enforcing the prenup in question would lead to substantial injustice. As 'substantial injustice' is a vague term, the ALI set out the following guide to matters to be taken into account, so that the judge's discretion would be more principled:

(a) the magnitude of the disparity between the outcome under the agreement and the outcome under otherwise prevailing legal principles;
(b) for those marriages of limited duration in which it is practical to ascertain, the difference between the circumstances of the objecting party if the agreement is enforced, and that party's likely circumstances had the marriage never taken place;
(c) whether the purpose of the agreement was to benefit or protect the interests of third parties (such as children from a prior relationship), whether that purpose is still relevant, and whether the agreement's terms were reasonably designed to serve it;
(d) the impact of the agreement's enforcement upon the children of the parties.[62]

[60] See ALI, above n 10, s 7.05, 982.
[61] Ibid, s 7.05, 983.
[62] Ibid.

The ALI asserts that these provisions recognise the 'special difficulties' associated with prenups.[63] However, it is explained that greater scope to consider fairness and changed circumstances according to a standard of 'substantial injustice' does not require the court to examine all prenups on divorce. Rather, it is 'only a subset in which … difficulties are particularly likely'[64] that will attract attention.

The reasoning of these recommendations is explained further in accordance with what the ALI refers to as the 'bargain principle'. This principle 'assumes that the parties themselves are the best judges of their own self-interest',[65] but the ALI has said that this assumption disregards 'unrealistic optimism about marital success … the excessive discounting of future benefits, and the inclination to overweigh the importance of the immediate and certain consequences of agreement—the marriage—as against its contingent and future consequences'.[66]

These issues are all considered by the ALI, but its recommendations also retain 'considerable deference to contractual freedom'.[67] Therefore, any limitation of the bargain principle is justified by cognitive difficulties. On the other hand, continued emphasis of the bargain principle shows that mainstream contract theory is directly influential on the ALI proposals, even though they specifically address the issue of bargaining and cognitive difficulties connected to prenups. It appears that the primary constraint for the second-look approach is a concern that the court's discretion to impose its own sense of fairness would undermine what the parties had agreed. This concern is also evident in the UK. For example, in *Radmacher v Granatino*, although Mr Granatino's situation had changed significantly on divorce, the Supreme Court did not consider his premarital waiver of rights to Ms Radmacher's property to be unfair.[68] Furthermore, the Court did not consider that the intentions of the parties with regard to financial redistribution may have changed either, even though Mr Granatino left a lucrative career to pursue scientific research.

As a result, the tension between fairness and interference permeates the enforcement of prenups, and undermines recommendations that attempt to make these agreements substantively fair. An alternative second-look approach is advocated by Brod, who attempts to circumvent this tension by proposing a more objective standard of economic justice.[69] This involves calculating the worth of sacrificed educational, business or career opportunities, and varying the agreement to account for the economic disparity arising from these sacrifices. Not only does this account for economic disadvantage generated by the relationship that is not provided for by the prenup, but the gender dimension can also be addressed. This is because Brod's proposal applies in cases where women suffer from what

63 Ibid, 987.
64 Ibid.
65 Ibid, 984.
66 Ibid, 987.
67 Ibid, 985.
68 See *Radmacher*, above n 3.
69 G Brod, 'Premarital Agreements and Gender Justice' (1994) 6 *Yale Journal of Law and Feminism* 229.

Mackay refers to as the 'feminisation of poverty'.[70] For example, if women have made economic sacrifices to contribute to non-financial aspects of the relationship, the financial deprivation experienced 'is exacerbated by marriage breakdown'.[71] Fehlberg and Smyth also note that prenups 'risk further entrenchment of the well-documented economic disadvantages typically experienced by women on divorce and their dependent children'.[72] But using Brod's theory, if such disadvantage is not provided for in a prenup, her economic justice approach could resolve hardship faced by the non-moneyed spouse. An illustration of this in practice could be the Law Commission's recommendation that prenups should be enforced as long as the needs of the parties are provided for.[73]

Though there is merit in this theory of economic adjustment, it does not relate to an alternative perspective of autonomy as advocated by FRCT. The idea of a second-look approach that uses standards like unconscionability, significant injustice and unfairness is *also* problematic because it is not connected to party autonomy; it is connected to the courts' sense of justice. Perhaps it is because of this that 'fairness' is interpreted so narrowly in practice. As a result, in connection with FRCT, a second-look approach from the ALI or Brod's perspective is arguably not ideal, because it is unable to recognise the reality of party autonomy and power imbalances. Thus, the following section develops ideas of FRCT in connection with the enforcement of prenups.

Developing a 'Non-bargain' Approach for Prenuptial Agreements[74]

The first part of this chapter explained that FRCT can recognise parties' changing intentions as marriage develops, and can also reduce power disparity by removing the bargaining element of prenups. The most appropriate time to take stock of parties' expectation of financial provision is at the time a prenup is being given effect. This is because expectations and intentions fluctuate over time, particularly when there are unforeseeable changes during the marriage that affect couples' wealth or families. Accounting for change is possible according to FRCT, which is significant considering that many other theories prioritise mainstream autonomy and enforce an intention that may seem absurd in light of different circumstances once parties are getting divorced.

By viewing the autonomy of parties to a prenup as developing over time, however, the focus is on the parties' relationship instead of the bargaining process at the time the agreement was signed. In practice, changing intentions can be taken into

[70] A Mackay, 'Who Gets a Better Deal? Women and Prenuptial Agreements in Australia and the USA' (2003) 7 *University of Western Sydney Law Review* 109.

[71] Ibid.

[72] B Fehlberg and B Smyth, 'Pre-nuptial Agreements for Australia: Why Not?' (2000) 14 *Australian Journal of Family Law* 80.

[73] Law Commission, *Marital Property, Needs and Agreements* (Law Com No 343, 2014).

[74] As noted above, a non-bargain view of contract is attributed to Wightman, above n 29.

account by the court in two ways. First, if the parties have expressly reviewed their agreement during the marriage, this process may be considered. However, sunset clauses or review clauses might not be drafted into the agreement, and so the court should also be able to consider the implicit intentions of the parties. A framework for considering a couple's intentions could be influenced by the equitable concept of the common-intention constructive trust,[75] as applied in the Supreme Court case *Jones v Kernott*.[76] There, an unmarried couple's respective beneficial interests were inferred from their conduct during the relationship. Because of this, the Court could consider the change in circumstances that had taken place since the time the property in question was purchased. Importantly, it is not being suggested that applying a non-bargain theory leads to prenups being re-conceived as common-intention constructive trusts. Rather, a non-bargain theory promotes the *idea* that one party's conduct (for example, an unforeseen contribution or sacrifice) causes him or her to suffer detrimental reliance, perhaps because that party did not expect to be disadvantaged by his or her sacrifice or contribution.

The idea of fairness is still obviously relevant to this framework of non-bargaining and implied intent, but it is the relational autonomy of the parties (informed by their conduct) that would be the focus of the court. This would mean that the court could avoid criticism for imposing its own sense of fairness on divorce, and the intentions of the parties would still regulate property redistribution in accordance with the aims of a prenup. Furthermore, if the process of a non-bargain theory were principled enough, it is conceivable that individual circumstances could be catered for, and there would be a degree of certainty. Individuals would know that if there were a change in circumstances during the marriage to which the original prenup would not apply, their altered intentions could be taken into account. However, the situation is more complex in cases where one spouse has relied on the other's oral assurances that, for example, the prenup will be abandoned in future. Unless, at the time of enforcement, the parties agree that assurances were made, the court will have insufficient evidence of these intentions if they are not in writing, or are not substantiated by parties' actual conduct.[77]

It is important to note that an approach consistent with FRCT and aspects of non-bargain theory in practice would not promote estoppel claims. This is because, as explained in chapter five, estoppel requires the court to consider isolated acts of reliance and specific promises, instead of focusing first on the parties' relationship with each other.[78] However, non-bargain theory advocates an approach that considers conduct as evidence of party autonomy in the overall context of the

[75] Estoppel is not considered in this book because the remedy for proprietary estoppel is the minimum amount required to do justice. This might not reflect the parties' intentions as to how property should be divided.

[76] *Jones v Kernott*, above n 30.

[77] In *Cioffi-Petrakis v Petrakis* 960 NYS 2d 152 (App Div 2013), the prenup was set aside because the court found that the wife had been fraudulently induced to sign it by the husband, who assured her that the agreement would be destroyed if they had children. On divorce, he sought to rely on the prenup even though the marriage had indeed produced children, but the agreement was successfully challenged by the wife.

[78] See Wightman, above n 29.

relationship. Thus, when considering conduct that is relevant to this enquiry, a *Jones v Kernott*[79] approach could be followed. Lord Walker and Lady Hale cited Lord Diplock when explaining how intention should be deduced:[80]

> [T]he relevant intention of each party is the intention which was reasonably understood by the other party to be manifested by that party's words and conduct notwithstanding that he did not consciously formulate that intention in his own mind or even acted with some different intention which he did not communicate to the other party.[81]

The kind of conduct that would indicate parties' changed intentions in the context of a prenup cannot be set out prescriptively. The most obvious incidences would be where parties change their careers, income, or deal with assets differently from the way anticipated by the agreement. But the focus of this approach would not be on these incidents per se; it would be on how, for example, a career change had affected the parties' relationship with one another and their intentions regarding financial arrangements.

The 'non-bargain' approach could be developed through case law. Again, when considering how this theory may be applied in practice, the aim is not to change general contract law but to consider how the theory might lead the court to regard autonomy in a more relational way. In the US there are cases that suggest that a non-bargain approach could be effective in practice.[82] In Oregon, in *Baxter v Baxter*,[83] the court held that parties' mutual intentions had changed. The prenup specified that ownership of the parties' assets would remain separate. Though the parties kept their assets separate during the first 13 years of their marriage, during the latter part of the marriage the wife left her job to work unpaid in her husband's business, and paid off some of the business debt using her separate assets.[84] Accordingly, variation of the agreement was justified by the court. Another approach similar to this is enshrined in a New Mexico statute, which provides that a prenup may be varied or set aside if there has been 'a consistent and mutual course of conduct, which evidences an amendment to or revocation of the premarital agreement'.[85] Ellman has suggested that these specific provisions could be based on a principle that partial performance in some cases justifies modification of the original terms of the agreement.[86]

[79] See also *Stack v Dowden*, above n 30.

[80] See *Jones v Kernott*, above n 30, [51].

[81] *Gissing v Gissing* [1971] AC 886, 906 (Lord Diplock).

[82] In the US, Oldham has said that an agreement may be explicitly revoked if the parties do not act in accordance with its terms: T Oldham, *Divorce, Separation and the Distribution of Property* (Law Journal Press 1987) 407. This could happen if there has been a change in circumstances and the parties do not act according to the original prenup, because the terms of that agreement are no longer relevant.

[83] *Baxter v Baxter* 911 P 2d 343 (Oregon 1996).

[84] Other examples from the US where agreements were reconsidered by the court in light of the parties' conduct are: *In Re Marriage of Zimmerman* 714 P 2d 927 (Colorado 1986); *Liebelt v Liebelt* 870 P 2d 9 (Idaho 1994); *In Re Pillard* 448 NW 2d 714 (Iowa 1989); *Prather v Cox* 689 SW 2d 623 (Kentucky 1985); *Jensen v Jensen* 753 P 2d 342 (Nevada 1988); *In Re Marriage of Fox* 795 P 2d 1170 (Washington 1990); *In Re Marriage of Sanchez* 654 P 2d 702 (Washington 1982); *Krejci v Krejci* 29 Fam L Rep (BNA) 1405 (Wisconsin 2003); *Brandt v Brandt* 427 NW 2d 126 (Wisconsin 1982).

[85] NM Stat Ann § 40-3A-6 (2009), cited in Ellman, above n 52.

[86] If the conduct of the parties suggested that partial performance of the contract was acceptable to both parties.

On the other hand, he also says that this approach may be interpreted more broadly as recognising that often parties 'will end up conducting their lives differently than they contemplated at the time of an agreement years earlier—thus justifying a second look'.[87] There are currently few examples from the US in practice where conduct was explicitly considered in a way that illustrates the non-bargain approach towards prenups. Nevertheless, it is conceivable that this approach could be developed to apply in England, Wales and Northern Ireland in practice, so that the reality of parties' intentions over time can be considered when agreements are enforced.

Following this approach in practice would represent the aims of FRCT in numerous ways. The feminist concern that women are often disadvantaged by agreements is brought the fore in a non-bargain scenario, because the court can consider how the autonomy of the parties was affected by their particular situation. This also means that the reality of power imbalances between the parties can be taken into account. Furthermore, a non-bargain theory incorporates the relational contract concern that long-term agreements should not be regulated by a singular discrete exchange. Considering the long-term intentions of individuals alleviates this concern, and accounts for the wider relational context of agreements.

There is likely to be opposition to this approach, particularly from individuals in favour of stringently enforcing prenups, and who believe the original agreement should guarantee the financial provision it has specified. Another anticipated criticism of this theory is that it would engender uncertainty, encourage judicial intervention and promote litigation. However, this is not necessarily the case. The court will not have to scrutinise every prenup on divorce, because not every agreement will fail to anticipate significant changes if the approach to drafting agreements considered in the first part of this chapter is implemented. This approach could prioritise clauses that would encourage regular revision of the agreement during the marriage, so that explicit intentions could be considered by the court in addition to non-bargained implicit intentions. Either way, it is conceivable that judicial consideration of implicit intentions relevant to the effect of prenups could be made more principled (though not prescriptive) on a case-by-case basis. From this perspective, a more flexible and contextual approach does not really make enforcement of prenups more complex than it is already. It would not necessarily mean that fewer agreements would be enforced either—agreements would simply be enforced according to the couple's *real* intentions.

Re-visiting *Radmacher v Granatino*

To properly test the type of practical approach that could be taken to issues like power and autonomy in practice, this section will revisit the Supreme Court judgment in

[87] See Ellman, above n 52, 427.

Radmacher v Granatino. Therefore, the effect of an alternative perception of autonomy on the facts of *Radmacher* (consistent with FRCT) will be explored.

This is not the first time that a judgment has been evaluated in connection with feminist and relational perspectives. Academic work such as the *Feminist Judgments Project* shows that writing alternative judgments is a logical and effective way to speculate how theory may be applied in practice.[88] As Balkin has said, '[i]t is one thing to offer academic theories … it is quite another to have to … demonstrate that one's views … really are consistent with a successful and acceptable judicial performance'.[89] Thus, for this book, considering the compatibility of the majority and minority judgments in *Radmacher* with FRCT means that the strengths and weaknesses of this theory can be tested in practice.

The majority opinion of Lord Phillips and the dissenting opinion of Lady Hale will be explored separately in this section.[90] The approach of each to the position of prenups and to the particular facts of the case will be set out according to FRCT. When applying this theory to *Radmacher*, it is not being suggested that the judiciary's approach to prenups should be completely replaced by an approach representative of FRCT. Rather, the point of this theory in practice is to encourage the court to interrogate issues like autonomy and power in a more relational and gendered way.[91] The court should be sensitive to context and to the importance of cooperation in a situation where the parties are entering a long-term, intimate agreement as future husband and wife, not business partners.

Lady Hale's opinion will be considered first, because, although a minority view, her judgment demonstrates how an approach influenced by FRCT should apply in practice. This is not surprising given Lady Hale's involvement, since hearing *Radmacher*, in *Feminist Judgments*[92] (a project where 'missing' feminist judgments are provided in key cases), where she outlined three reasons as to why a feminist approach is important:

> First, it is remarkable how plausible [the feminist judgments] mostly are, not only as judicial writing but also as examples of how a different judgment might properly have been written in that case and at that time. Secondly, it makes such a difference how the story is told. Feminist judges will take different facts from the mass of detail to tell the story in a different way, to bring out the features which others discard, and to explain the features which others find difficult to understand. The third is context. Feminist judges will set the story in a different context which they understand but others may not.[93]

[88] R Hunter *et al* (eds), *Feminist Judgments: From Theory to Practice* (Hart Publishing 2010).

[89] J Balkin, *What Roe v Wade Should Have Said: The Nation's Top Legal Experts Rewrite America's Most Controversial Decision* (New York University Press 2005), cited in E Rackley, 'Why Feminist Legal Scholars Should Write Judgments: Reflections on the Feminist Judgments Project in England and Wales' (2012) 24 *Canadian Journal of Women and the Law* 389.

[90] Lord Mance also provided a short judgment in this case, but it is not considered here as he agreed with the majority decision and did not raise any further issues in connection with FRCT.

[91] Wightman provides an excellent explanation of how feminist and relational perspectives work best in practice: J Wightman, 'Baird Textile Holdings v Marks and Spencer Plc' in Hunter *et al* (eds), above n 88, 184.

[92] See Hunter *et al* (eds), above n 88.

[93] Ibid, v.

Features like plausibility and a different, more contextual perspective will be equally important when exploring an alternative approach to *Radmacher*. But, as will be demonstrated below, elements of Lady Hale's approach in this case are already compatible with both feminist theory and relational contract theory, as she clearly recognises the significance of gender, context and the relationship between the parties. Using FRCT to connect these elements of Lady Hale's opinion could provide a clearer idea of how relational autonomy can be ascertained for prenups in practice.

Lady Hale

Chapter one of this book explained that Lady Hale and Lord Phillips formulated the test for determining the weight to be attached to prenups differently. Lord Phillips' test, that prenups will be enforced unless unfair, represents the precedent set by the Supreme Court. But Lady Hale's approach, which considers the fairness of prenups *before* enforcement, puts context first. In her dissenting judgment, Lady Hale clearly considers the social and emotional context of such agreements. Most notably, she recognises that individual parties' perceptions of autonomy and power are often different from the type of autonomy presumed by the court:

> Some may regard people who are about to marry as in all respects fully autonomous beings; others may wonder whether people who are typically (though not invariably) in love can be expected to make rational choices in the same way that businessmen can. Some may regard the recognition of these factual differences as patronising or paternalistic; others may regard them as sensible and realistic.[94]

This observation reflects the fact that whilst autonomy and power may commonly affect the prenup process, these issues play out differently in every case. As Lady Hale has said, an individual case cannot set out a definitive solution to these issues. Thus the court needs to be flexible in its approach, to recognise that there is a wider context affecting the fairness of an agreement and the autonomy of the parties involved. Flexibility is also important when applying FRCT in practice, and so this part of Lady Hale's judgment indicates an approach consistent with this theory.

Another aspect of Lady Hale's judgment that is consistent with FRCT is her discussion of the gender dimension attached to prenups. This particular observation by Lady Hale has been noted several times in this book, and must also be highlighted here. Her recognition of a gender dimension significantly sets her opinion apart from the majority in *Radmacher*, which she has said is unsurprising given that she is the only female Supreme Court Justice. But taking gender into account is imperative when considering a case like *Radmacher* from the perspective of FRCT. Lady Hale has said that the court 'can all too easily lose sight of'[95] the gendered

[94] See *Radmacher*, above n 3, [135].

[95] Ibid, [137].

context of prenups. Arguably Lady Hale's recognition of gendered power imbalances is a significant reason why her approach is so different from that of the majority. Like the aims of FRCT, she is sensitive to the fact that the object of a prenup can be to 'deny the economically weaker spouse the provision to which she—it is usually although by no means invariably she—would otherwise by entitled'.[96] Her opinion thus reflects the interests and autonomy of both spouses, though it does not prioritise the interests of the wife or the non-moneyed spouse.

Lady Hale's approach to choice, for instance, indicates a more context-specific conception of autonomy than is evident in the majority opinion. In particular, she is sensitive to the relationship of the parties and that they are entering marriage, not a business partnership. This inevitably has some bearing on the choices couples make when entering a prenup and organising their finances during the relationship. As Lady Hale explains:

> Most spouses want their partners to be happy—partly, of course, because they love them and partly because it is not much fun living with a miserable person. So, choices are often made for the sake of the overall happiness of the family … one of [the parties] may give up a well-paid job that she hates for the sake of a less lucrative job that she loves; one may give up a dead-end job to embark upon a new course of study. These sorts of things happen all the time in a relationship. The couple will support one another while they are together. And it may generate a continued need for support once they are apart.[97]

This perspective is a sound example of relational contract theory in practice. By looking at the relationship instead of the agreement, it is clear that autonomy represents much more than an abstract and individual choice, and instead depends significantly on cooperation. Furthermore, the above extract highlights the choices that are made after the agreement is made. By taking these choices into account in addition to those made during the initial negotiating process, it is recognised that autonomy develops over the course of the relationship.

The final element of Lady Hale's opinion which can be used to reflect FRCT in practice is her discussion of conduct. In developing a non-bargain approach in the second part of this chapter, it was concluded that acknowledging the conduct of the parties in relation to their finances during the marriage could be an effective way of measuring how autonomy develops over time. This approach would also represent the 'floating' nature of prenups, in that the effect of these agreements is not known until enforcement, and so changing circumstances and intentions should be considered when interrogating issues of autonomy and power in reality. Lady Hale's opinion could be used to summarise how this approach might work in practice. For example, she considered that autonomy changes because the 'couple are bound together in more than a business relationship, so of course they modify their plans and often compromise their individual best interests to accommodate these new events'.[98] As a result, she said that the subsequent conduct of the parties

[96] Ibid.
[97] Ibid, [188].
[98] Ibid, [175].

must be a relevant circumstance when considering the weight to be attached to a prenup.[99] At the same time, 'if things have indeed turned out much as the parties expected and intended, it could well be fair to give effect to their agreement'.[100]

Importantly, Lady Hale said that consideration of conduct should be confined to how parties dealt with financial affairs, as an assessment of marital conduct could be problematic.[101] Indeed, couples' general behaviour during the marriage does not always provide the court with an accurate picture of what financial provision was intended. However, conduct that includes non-financial sacrifice could be considered in some situations if it contributed to the financial success of the couple. In addition, it might be argued that certain behaviour is relevant to the balance of power in a relationship, and so should be considered. Therefore, limiting the consideration of conduct in practice does not lead to a restrictive approach; it simply means avoiding assessments such as whether the wife had been a good housewife.[102] This consideration of conduct could be developed in accordance with a non-bargain approach to produce an assessment of autonomy that is consistent with FRCT, and which recognises the realities of autonomy and power discourse as the relationship develops. In future, it is proposed that considerations of conduct could be made in accordance with the approach put forward in section two of this chapter.

Lady Hale's consideration of gender, choice and conduct produced an outcome for Ms Radmacher and Mr Granatino that did not ignore the context of their relationship as a whole. In her consideration of fairness, Lady Hale examined the three strands of need, compensation and sharing (discussed in chapter two), and in particular whether the parties' conduct affected application of the sharing strand. The fact that Ms Radmacher had kept her assets separate from the marital funds indicated to Lady Hale that the sharing strand would not apply, as the concept of equal sharing clearly did not reflect the intentions of the parties according to the prenup. However, Lady Hale believed that need and compensation would be relevant, and said that Mr Granatino should receive an award sufficient to meet these elements, because his change in career was a mutual decision that may have been for the benefit of the family. Prior to this change, Mr Granatino had supported the family with his income. Thus the decision made by the couple that Mr Granatino would undertake a PhD could arguably indicate changed intentions regarding financial support. Accordingly, Lady Hale decided that the terms of the original agreement should be varied to allow Mr Granatino to occupy his English home for life.[103] This differed from the majority verdict, which limited Mr Granatino's occupation of the English home until the younger daughter reached the age of 22. The right to occupation granted by Lady Hale incorporates her analysis of issues like conduct

[99] Ibid, [179].
[100] Ibid, [177].
[101] Ibid, [180].
[102] Ibid. This example was used by Lady Hale.
[103] Ibid, [194].

and compensation, whilst the award made by the majority is only intended to reflect Mr Granatino's role as father (and not spouse).

Importantly, the award made by Lady Hale was much less than the trial judge had originally awarded Mr Granatino. At first instance[104] he received an award exceeding £5.5 million, which would allow him to purchase a home in London where his children could visit him, and would also provide him with an income of £100,000 per annum for life.[105] At trial, Baron J's reasoning was based on her assertion that the agreement was flawed due to lack of independent legal advice and other safeguards that had previously been set out in the government Green Paper, *Supporting Families*.[106] However, just as the majority appears to presume the autonomy of parties entering prenups, Baron J's approach equally assumes that parties have not been autonomous on the basis of uniform standards that do not require sufficient contextual analysis of the parties' situation. For instance, the empirically-based study examined in this book found that independent legal advice as a requirement does not ensure that parties have or have not been autonomous. Furthermore, the fact that Mr Granatino would receive less according to Lady Hale's assessment shows that a contextual approach does not consider the interests of the non-moneyed spouse to be any more important than those of the moneyed spouse.

Lord Phillips

A significant portion of Lord Phillips' judgment in *Radmacher v Granatino* considered the public policy objections to prenups, and said they were no longer justified because they restricted individual autonomy when entering these agreements. This is a stark illustration of McLean's assertion that, in practice, emphasis is on the right to autonomy instead of on how autonomy is *exercised*.[107] Indeed, once the public policy objections were swept away, Lord Phillips held that prenups should carry decisive weight when financial orders are made on divorce.

Furthermore, in contrast to Lady Hale's approach, Lord Phillips' reasoning as to how prenups should be enforced did not consider the context of the parties' relationship as a whole. He decided that

> the reason why the court should give weight to a nuptial agreement is that there should be respect for individual autonomy. The court should accord respect to the decision of a married couple as to the manner in which their financial affairs should be regulated.[108]

This reference to autonomy is limited to the time the prenup is signed. In addition, Lord Phillips does not interrogate what 'respect for individual autonomy' actually

[104] *NG v KR (Pre-nuptial Contract)* [2008] EWHC 1532 (Fam).
[105] Mr Granatino was also awarded £700,000 to pay off his debt.
[106] Home Office, *Supporting Families: A Consultation Document* (1998).
[107] See McLean, above n 34.
[108] See *Radmacher*, above n 3, [78].

means. When outlining factors that would detract from the weight to be attached to an agreement, Lord Phillips clearly states that the intentions of the parties are relevant, but when establishing intention he does not fully account for the context of the parties' relationship.

Lord Phillips is opposed to the prescriptive approach to autonomy employed by Baron J at first instance, which, as previously noted, depended on various safeguards like independent legal advice. However, his approach is arguably just as limited in its capacity for context. If, for example, the parties have been properly advised and have been provided with enough 'material' information, Lord Phillips said it will be assumed that the parties intended that the prenup would be effective. But this approach is quite narrow when juxtaposed with Lady Hale's assertion that the court should be sensitive to the wider context in which people make decisions. Indeed, parties may have enough information according to the court, but this does not necessarily mean they have been autonomous.

Lord Phillips *is* clearly aware of this, as he considers that parties entering prenups may experience bargaining inequalities. But his approach in recognising power issues does not appreciate the particular context of the relationship parties to such agreements are in. First, he says the court should consider whether any vitiating factors are present. The limitations of factors like duress and undue influence have already been explored in some detail in this book. Lord Phillips also said that the weight of an agreement may be reduced by 'unconscionable conduct such as undue pressure (falling short of duress) … and other unworthy conduct, such as exploitation of a dominant position to secure an unfair advantage'.[109] Though this may indicate an appreciation of power imbalance, Lord Phillips' approach falls short of a relational analysis. He considers factors such as whether the parties were entering a second marriage, and their age, instead of focusing on the specific relationship between them. Furthermore, Lord Phillips does not mention the gender dimension of prenups highlighted by Lady Hale.

A significant difference between Lord Phillips' and Lady Hale's opinions is that Lord Phillips' analysis of autonomy and power is limited to the time the agreement is signed, but Lady Hale considers the context of the whole relationship. This difference is illustrated by Lord Phillips' dictum on future change in circumstances that could lead to unfairness. He considered quite limited situations that would justify variation of the agreement, such as if one party is 'left in a predicament of real need, while the other enjoys a sufficiency or more',[110] or 'if the devotion of one partner to looking after the family and the home has left the other free to accumulate wealth'[111] but the latter partner will retain all he or she has earned. He said it is unlikely that the parties would intend these harsh outcomes. But these examples are quite limited in scope. In contrast, Lady Hale asserted that the parties' course of

[109] Ibid, [71].
[110] Ibid.
[111] Ibid, [81].

conduct could be evidence that the parties' autonomy had changed. The difference in approach is simply that Lord Phillips looks at the factual circumstances (like a situation of 'real need'),[112] while Lady Hale looks to the conduct, and therefore the autonomy and relationship, of the parties.

The effect of these approaches is evident in the outcome for Mr Granatino. Like Lady Hale, Lord Phillips used the three strands of fairness to guide his analysis. But unlike Lady Hale, he did not think that compensation was relevant to the facts of the case. In his opinion, Mr Granatino became a PhD student out of self-interest, though it is not clear why Lord Phillips made this assumption. However, treating this career change as being a decision made by Mr Granatino for his own benefit means that the autonomy of both parties in the wider context of the relationship is not taken into account. The majority approach, therefore, arguably takes a more restrictive approach to need and compensation than Lady Hale did in her dissent. From this perspective, the majority did not properly interrogate autonomy when the agreement was made and as the relationship of the parties developed. As a result, the 'floating nature' of the prenup was not recognised either, due to the narrow approach adopted to change in circumstances.

Radmacher v Granatino and Feminist Relational Contract Theory

This analysis of *Radmacher* indicates that the opinion of Lady Hale is clearly more consistent with FRCT than the opinion of Lord Phillips. However, it is the latter approach that is set in precedent. Lady Hale's judgment not only is made distinct by her feminist perspective; her consideration of context is also much clearer. As a result, when developing an approach for prenups that represents the aims of FRCT in practice, Lady Hale's reasoning is a sound starting point. For clarity, the salient points of her reasoning to carry forward are:

(a) the gender dimension of prenups is an important consideration (particularly when considering power imbalance); and
(b) conduct relevant to financial provision throughout the relationship can help provide a more contextual assessment of autonomy.

However, a practical approach could be developed further using FRCT, particularly when addressing issues of power and autonomy during the drafting process of prenups. When considering the particular facts of *Radmacher v Granatino*, it is clear that the terms were not relationship-centred. Indeed, for much of the drafting process Mr Granatino was completely excluded. Drafts of the agreement were prepared without his knowledge, and evidence was presented to the court that

[112] Ibid.

the notary was angry about this.[113] This lack of participation could explain why the agreement is so one-sided, and included a clause providing for the 'mutual waiver of claims for maintenance of any kind whatsoever following divorce'.[114] Ms Radmacher's father was also involved in the process, as he told his daughter she would be disinherited unless the agreement was entered into and met with his approval.

In the context of *Radmacher*, the relationship-centred approach to drafting that was outlined in the first part of this chapter is futile, because the agreement is being enforced. On the other hand, appreciating that these terms were *not* relationship-centred could encourage the court to recognise power imbalance in a way that is more contextual than the law of duress and undue influence.[115] As a result, though the majority and minority of the Court in *Radmacher* concluded that Mr Granatino understood the agreement he was entering into (particularly because of his business acumen), a relationship-centred approach would question his level of autonomy to a greater degree due to his lack of participation in the negotiation process. The involvement of Ms Radmacher's father would also lead to a more detailed assessment of the wife's autonomy, as that third-party pressure clearly influenced the agreement, but it was not really addressed by the Supreme Court. Even Lady Hale's more contextual analysis did not appear to pay much attention to the autonomy of Ms Radmacher. Arguably this is understandable, as Ms Radmacher was seeking to enforce the original agreement. However, when considering autonomy from a relational perspective, her conduct and decisions about the couple's finances are a relevant consideration when determining how changing circumstances might have affected the prenup.

Taking all circumstances into account, the outcome favoured by Lady Hale is still appropriate, even though FRCT would lead to a different approach. That is, Lady Hale did not fully interrogate the autonomy of the parties during the drafting process, but the couple's intentions during the marriage are still reflected in the award she would have made in favour of Mr Granatino. Using the combination of relationship-centred and non-bargain approaches advocated by FRCT, a different award might have been made to Mr Granatino had Ms Radmacher not continued to keep her assets separate from those of her husband, as this could be evidence that the couple's intentions were very different.[116]

[113] Ibid, [91].

[114] Ibid, [99].

[115] This would accord with the approaches of commentators like Gan, above n 35, and J Herring, *Relational Autonomy and Family Law* (Springer 2014), who employ a more complex analysis of autonomy and agency. In the prenup scenario, considering *why* parties chose to agree to particular terms reveals more about their autonomy than deciding whether parties did or did not choose to agree to those terms.

[116] Not enough is known about the couple's situation in *Radmacher* to assess whether a claim of presumed undue influence, as developed by FRCT in the second part of this chapter, could have been made. If a case of presumed undue influence had been made, FRCT could have been employed when discerning 'abnormal pressure'.

Conclusion

Though there are relational elements in Lady Hale's opinion, an explicitly relationship-centred analysis would be the most effective way of uncovering the true context of both parties' autonomy. Even if this does not produce an outcome different from that arrived at by Lady Hale, an approach that considers parties' actual autonomy is important when the court regards party autonomy to be the reason for enforcing prenups. The fact that the couple's autonomy was not fully interrogated in *Radmacher* and was instead assumed, due to factors like Mr Granatino's business experience, indicates that the Court had decided it was fair to conclude that Mr Granatino should be held to what he had agreed, even though he had clearly been excluded from the drafting process. Thus the Court's consideration of fairness is separate from its analysis of autonomy.

Put simply, if the court's approach is imagined as a set of scales, fairness and needs are on one side, which is in favour of the prenup being set aside or reconsidered. Balanced against this is autonomy, on the side that is in favour of enforcement, because, as case law has repeatedly stated, autonomy is *the* reason for giving effect to prenups. But a different perception of autonomy does not automatically lead to this conclusion, and could find instead that respect for autonomy[117] is a reason *not* to give effect to a prenup, because the parties' intentions are not represented in the terms of the agreement. Indeed, by *re-conceptualising* autonomy for prenups, many issues relating to power imbalance and changed circumstances could be resolved in practice. Feminist relational contract theory could assist, not by attempting to revolutionise practice, but by prompting an alternative approach to be considered in addition to the court's current approach to prenups.

[117] It is important to note this is distinguished from a lack of autonomy, ie that an agreement will be set aside if it is made under duress. Rather, it is suggested that the agreement does not represent the autonomy of the parties, once autonomy is re-conceived according to FRCT.

Conclusion

> When I got married to my present wife, we had each been married three times before, so we did a prenup. Ten years after we were married, we had a party, invited all our friends and burned the thing.[1]

This New York attorney's personal experience shows that prenups can be a very good idea. The prenup in this situation gave the couple the financial reassurance they needed when entering their third marriage, but 10 years later they realised they no longer felt the way they had done before the marriage, so they destroyed the agreement. As a lawyer with significant experience in this area, this interviewee was aware of the effect a prenup would have in spite of changing intentions and circumstances during the marriage, and he knew precisely how to legally invalidate the agreement. But as the research from New York found, not all prenups work out as well as in the above example. In many cases, parties enter into such agreements as financially independent individuals who intend to be, but often are not, financially independent in the event of divorce. Three notable examples taken from interviews with New York lawyers demonstrate the consequences of this in practice.

First is the wealthy actress who says she does not want or need to share in her husband's wealth, and who wants the terms of their prenup to reflect this:

> I had a famous actress about a month ago and she was marrying someone with a lot of money, and he wanted a prenuptial agreement. I had to explain to her that famous actresses don't make money forever. Famous actresses who are having children don't usually get movie roles offered to them … [S]he was also talking about giving up a lot of her career to be with this man … giving me the speech that a lot of women are saying to me. I don't need that money, I'll be fine … Everyone wants to feel independent and not act like they're dependent on someone else's money but … you may be making a lot of sacrifices, don't put yourself in the position when you have two, three children, not being able to support them. Or recognise that you could support them but in an entirely different lifestyle than you are going to enjoy during the marriage.[2]

On the face of it, it is not surprising that a famous actress would enter into a prenup. However, the above scenario is a stark reminder of how individual autonomy in the context of prenups is not exercised independently of familial pressures, and is instead dependent on relationships with others. This even applies to those who are very wealthy before the marriage.

1 Practitioner 11.
2 Practitioner 17.

The second example is similar to the first, in that it highlights the unforeseeable ways in which financial positions may change. As an interviewee explains in the following extract, the terms of a prenup often do not account for a spouse's future contributions and sacrifices when supporting a partner in furthering his or her career:

> [Y]our husband didn't have a great career but he decided he wanted to spend some time writing a novel. You were out working, earning money and making a high income supporting him. But he is home writing a novel and you had a prenup agreement that said because you are currently successful and you have got a high income, he can keep whatever he makes and you are going to keep whatever you make. Well he goes and sits in coffee shops and libraries and writes the new Harry Potter novel and … the marriage doesn't work out. In that situation you would say well when [the agreement was] made … it seemed very fair. Now years later you look at what happened, it may not be so fair because [you were] supporting him all those years while he was running out writing this novel.[3]

If there were no prenup in this situation, when making a financial provision order on divorce the judge would have discretion to compensate the spouse whose support of her partner enabled him to write 'the new Harry Potter novel'. But a prenup entered into before these events are known is unlikely to be set aside by the court for being unfair, since the husband in *Radmacher* experienced a significant change in his financial circumstances but this did not prevent the agreement in question from having decisive weight.

The third example to emerge from the New York study is of a woman who agrees to sign an agreement to prove to her husband that she is not marrying for money:

> She did not want to sign the prenup. He insisted and at the last minute he capitulated and said it was alright. It was almost like it was a test. And because she said she would do it, [he knew] 'ok you're not marrying me for my money.' I was sort of pleased for her because the terms of the agreement were egregious in my opinion. And by that I mean she was going to be put in the position of probably not working with children.[4]

In this scenario the attorney explained that the agreement would have prevented the wife from making any claim on her partner's assets in the event of divorce. Although the agreement was not finalised, the female party did agree to sign it under pressure from her future husband. Therefore, the prenup would have been effective if the husband had been serious about signing it, instead of trying to ascertain whether or not his fiancée was a 'gold digger'. An agreement entered into in this context is clearly affected by issues of power, but the courts in the UK and New York are reluctant to address the pressures and power imbalances affecting almost every prenup, if it would mean that these agreements would not have any effect on divorce.

[3] Practitioner 8.

[4] Practitioner 15.

In spite of this, the idea that power inequality undermines the legitimacy of prenups is clear, according to Bix, who asserts that entering into a marriage governed by an agreement that greatly favours one party at the expense of the other 'is worse than no marriage at all'.[5] The court has said it will not tolerate 'unfair exploitation of superior strength',[6] therefore intervention in a case of clear duress is not at issue: but the *degree* of power imbalance the court will not tolerate is. The UK Supreme Court Justices have suggested they will overlook power imbalance in some situations, because 'we must assume that each party is a grown-up and able to look after him- or herself'.[7] This is consistent with the approach in New York, as one attorney put it:

> Grownups should be held to their decisions. If I decide to stop working and let my husband support me, knowing I have an agreement that says that if he leaves me I get no alimony (financial support), well, then I should either not quit my job or I should renegotiate that agreement to account for the change in circumstances. And if he won't do that then I know something about him that I didn't know three weeks ago, and if I stay with him anyway, it is a nice concept of the law that I have made my bed to lie in.[8]

From this perspective, prenups are like any other contract, and provide a form of insurance against financial risk for people entering marriage with property they want to protect. However, marriage is so much more than catering for financial risk. As a result, contract law does not adequately resolve power in the intimate context of prenups, because it is based on a model that assumes, like the above interview extract, that when entering into such an agreement the parties are self-interested and intent on negotiating the best terms for themselves as individuals. This approach also means that contractual vitiating factors such as duress, undue influence and the law of unconscionable bargains do not recognise many situations of power imbalance. As chapter four found, the court would not necessarily find duress if one party was pregnant, or if the prenup was entered into on the eve of the wedding. Furthermore, even though it is less onerous to make a claim of undue influence (particularly presumed undue influence) than duress, it was concluded that it would not properly address issues with power either. The main issue is that the claimant must have been under abnormal pressure. As pressure and power imbalance is so common in the context of prenups, it is difficult to persuade the court that the circumstances are not normal in order to satisfy the requirements of vitiating factors. This means that in many cases, the court is desensitised to more subtle power imbalance.[9] For this reason, even though prenups must have

[5] B Bix, 'The ALI Principles and Agreements: Seeking a Balance between Status and Contract' in R Wilson (ed), *Reconceiving the Family: Critique on the American Law Institute's Principles of the Law of Family Dissolution* (Cambridge University Press 2006) 389.

[6] *Radmacher v Granatino* [2010] UKSC 42 [51].

[7] Ibid.

[8] Practitioner 3.

[9] The law of unconscionable bargains was also found to be inappropriate in the context of prenups because the respondent must have behaved in a morally reprehensible manner. Rather than focusing on the autonomy of both parties, this causes the court to focus on the behaviour of one party.

contractual validity to be effective, the law in the UK and US goes beyond contract law when examining such agreements on divorce.

In the UK, a prenup will be enforced unless it is unfair.[10] The Supreme Court has said that 'unfair' could mean pressure short of duress,[11] but that the situational monopolies that affect most agreements would be insufficient to meet this threshold. Instead, when ascertaining unfairness at the time the prenup is made, the courts have looked for evidence of financial disclosure and legal advice, although complete disclosure and independent legal advice are not mandatory.[12] At the time of enforcement, an agreement could also be considered 'unfair' if it did not comply with the needs and compensation strands of fairness[13] outlined in *Miller; McFarlane*, and examined in chapter two.[14] This approach focuses on questions of fairness whilst emphasising respect for autonomy. Crucially, however, it does not focus on whether or not both parties have in fact been autonomous, or whether the autonomy of one party has been compromised by the more subtle issues of power imbalance examined in this book.

In addition, the scope to vitiate prenups if unfair in the UK and unconscionable in New York[15] was criticised by experienced practitioners in the New York research. First, there was a general consensus that 'unconscionability' is not an appropriate standard in practice in New York because, as chapter three discussed, it allows many harsh outcomes caused by the enforcement of prenups to stand. Secondly, practitioners did not think that setting aside 'unfair'[16] prenups was appropriate either, generally contending that the judiciary should not be able to assert its perception of fairness (particularly because this may not accord with what the couple in question views as fair). Furthermore, when compared with empirical data from England, it transpired that both jurisdictions were keen to emphasise respect for autonomy.[17] However, the New York study found that in many instances, the court's limited desire to scrutinise prenups on divorce meant that it did not address many power imbalances and instances when autonomy was not exercised by both parties.

[10] See *Radmacher*, above n 6.

[11] Ibid, [71].

[12] Ibid, [114]–[117] (Lord Phillips).

[13] Ibid, [81], though the sharing strand is implicitly waived by prenup. Furthermore, the compensation strand is only invoked in 'rare and exceptional' cases: *SA v PA (Pre-marital Agreement: Compensation)* [2014] EWHC 392 (Fam) [36] (Mostyn J).

[14] *Miller v Miller; McFarlane v McFarlane* [2006] UKHL 24. This is the most significant indictor that prenups in England, Wales and Northern Ireland cannot oust the jurisdiction of the court to make financial provision orders on divorce. Only Parliament can limit this discretionary power, which is permitted by the MCA 1973.

[15] Domestic Relations Law §236 B 3(3).

[16] Although this research was carried out before the Supreme Court's statement of principle in *Radmacher*, above n 6, that agreements would be enforced unless unfair, interviewees' general reticence toward this standard of enforcement allows one to assume that they would not favour the current judicial approach towards prenups in the UK.

[17] E Hitchings, *Law Commission Report: A study of the views and approaches of family practitioners concerning marital property agreements* (2011).

Another finding from the New York research was that expert practitioners (such as the interviewees in the study) take steps during the drafting process to try to ameliorate bargaining inequalities, because they are aware that this may be the only means of addressing issues of power and autonomy.[18] However, this is not an ideal solution, because interviewees said their clients do not always act on their advice and changing circumstances cannot always be provided for. Furthermore, not everyone entering prenups will have access to expert lawyers who will dispense this kind of advice.

Lastly, the New York study illustrated an approach whereby it could be argued that the parties to an agreement are in a fiduciary relationship, which would justify greater scrutiny of the agreement by the court at the time of enforcement.[19] This argument was not fleshed out in subsequent case law. However, an approach like this, which examines the nature of the relationship, enables the way in which power and autonomy are exercised to be appreciated when giving effect to prenups. It also facilitates an alternative approach to autonomy that does not mean the court has to dismiss power inequalities so that the parties' autonomy can be respected. Rather, by examining the relationship between the parties and expressions of power in the context of prenups, autonomy can be better understood, because, as Nedelsky put it, 'relatedness is not, as our tradition teaches, the antithesis of autonomy, but a literal precondition of autonomy, and interdependence a constant component of autonomy'.[20] Therefore, if it is recognised that many individuals do not enter into prenups in an independent, self-interested and disconnected way, it is easier to recognise imbalances of power connected with such agreements.

As the stories taken from the research in New York have revealed, marriage and family life more often than not create dependency in a way that may not be anticipated by the terms of a prenup. So even if parties begin their marriage as financially independent individuals, this is frequently not the case at the end of the marriage. Whilst matters sometimes work out as planned in the prenup, this should not detract from the fact that commonly, particularly in longer marriages, things do change.

The dependencies that emerge during married life may also be gendered. This is apparent in all three of the above interview extracts, where each attorney emphasised the future career sacrifices to be made by the *wife* if children were born, which might not have been provided for in the prenup. As this book has explained, domestic work such as childcare is gendered, and so more women than men give up financial independence to fulfil these roles. In addition, the majority of respondents in the New York study identified gendered power issues when the

[18] This includes steps described in ch 3, such as incorporating terms into the agreement that require the agreement to be revised if circumstances change.

[19] The argument was made in *Matter of Greiff* 90 NY 2d 341 (New York 1998).

[20] J Nedelsky, 'Reconceiving Autonomy: Sources, Thoughts and Possibilities,' (1989) 1 *Yale Journal of Law and Feminism* 7, 12.

prenup is created, referring to the wife as the non-moneyed spouse 'because [she] almost always is'.[21] The problem with this is that, as attorneys explained, the non-moneyed party tends to have less leverage, especially if she has no particular desire for a prenup to be signed.

This shows how important it is to consider the context in which autonomy is exercised so that issues of power, including gendered power, can be recognised. Feminist relational contract theory encapsulates these considerations, because it focuses on the relationship of parties to prenups at the time the agreement is entered into *and* throughout the marriage. Before the marriage, an approach based on FRCT is concerned with the level of participation of both parties in the prenup. It is suggested that this could be achieved by incorporating review clauses into the agreement, and by ensuring independent and competent legal advice during the drafting process. As a result, both parties are encouraged to amend their agreement as circumstances change. Furthermore, independent advice can, to an extent, help the party with less bargaining power ensure that an agreement is in his or her interest. In short, a review of procedures during the drafting process of prenups means parties are encouraged to exercise autonomy on a more level playing field.

At the time of enforcement, FRCT is particularly useful. It enables issues with power, autonomy and gender to be taken into account during the entirety of the relationship, instead of focusing on the bargaining process at the time the prenup was signed. As chapter six concluded, a non-bargain method of implementing FRCT could be effective in practice. This would require an evaluation of agreements at the time of enforcement, which would specifically consider parties' intentions as they evolved during the marriage. Evidence of intention would require assessing parties' express or implied conduct, in a way similar to the court's approach in *Baxter v Baxter*.[22]

Most importantly, this approach recognises that, depending on the length of the marriage, there may be a significant period between when a prenup is created and the time it may take effect. During this time, a couple's needs, desires and autonomy will usually change. By accounting for this, FRCT rejects the mainstream contractual focus on discrete bargains and makes the enforcement of prenups more useful by ensuring they reflect parties' actual (rather than presumed or outdated) intentions. Issues of power are, in theory, avoided when parties' intentions are gleaned by the relationship, rather than only being informed by the bargain made when the prenup was created. In practice, however, the law of vitiating factors should also be evaluated in light of FRCT. Not only would this mean widening the scope of duress (as Gan has suggested),[23] but the law of presumed undue influence could also be made more contextual. That is, a relationship-centred approach could

[21] Practitioner 20.

[22] *Baxter v Baxter* 911 P 2d 343 (Oregon 1996). Lady Hale's dicta on conduct in *Radmacher* could also help formulate this approach. See *Radmacher*, above n 6, [179].

[23] O Gan, 'Contractual Duress and Relations of Power' (2013) 36 *Harvard Journal of Law and Gender* 171.

consider pressure that is abnormal in the particular context of the prenup in question. Addressing the impact of such agreements on gender inequality (and vice versa) would also be possible when employing a contextual approach, which considers the ways in which gendered power is manifested during the relationship. This would differ from the current approach, which categorises pressure as normal because it often occurs, and therefore as 'normal' to the prenuptial relationship. However, adopting a feminist relational contract perspective means considering the context of autonomy and intentions of the parties, therefore also assessing the actual effect of the pressure. Thus, one is not desensitised to prenuptial power imbalances and pressures that may affect the autonomy of the party with less power.

In conclusion, there is always inequality of power between parties entering prenups. One party will usually want an agreement more than the other. A prenup may not accurately reflect the wishes of both parties. More often than not, as this book has argued, such an agreement is created *because* there is inequality of bargaining power. One solution to this could be to not enforce prenups at all. But this would take power away from couples for whom it is important to decide who gets what before walking down the aisle. As a result, it is becoming increasingly difficult to challenge prenups on divorce, so that couples can be almost guaranteed that their prenup will be effective in the event of separation. In New York, it is extremely difficult to persuade the court that a prenup should be set aside because it is unconscionable, to the extent that one attorney in the empirical study commented that 'there have been in the past ten years litigated agreements that I thought were offensive that have been upheld'.[24] The law in the UK is also making it increasingly difficult to vitiate a prenup, and it is perhaps only a matter of time before such agreements become binding according to statute. But for now, the judiciary in the UK still has considerable discretionary power to give effect to prenups. Accordingly, it is able to consider power inequalities that would not be unconscionable according to New York standards, but which must be addressed to ensure the autonomy of both parties. And so, for better or worse, and despite all its uncertainties, the law on prenups pursuant to *Radmacher v Granatino* is the best starting point when addressing issues of power in theory and in practice. The discretion reserved for the judge to refuse to give effect to a prenup if unfair means there is scope for autonomy and power to be considered differently, for the context of the relationship to assume greater significance and for gendered power to be recognised (as it was by Lady Hale).

[24] Practitioner 12.

BIBLIOGRAPHY

Adams, D (ed), *Philosophical Problems in the Law* (Wadsworth 2000).

Adams, J and Brownsword, R, 'The Ideologies of Contract' (1987) 7 *Legal Studies* 205.

Atiyah, P, *An Introduction to the Law of Contract* (5th edn, Clarendon Law Series 1995).

Atwood, B, 'Ten Years Later: Lingering Concerns about the Uniform Premarital Agreement Act' (1993) 19(2) *Journal of Legislation* 127.

—— 'Marital Contracts and the Meaning of Marriage' (2012) 54 *Arizona Law Review* 11.

—— and Bix, B, 'A New Uniform Law for Premarital and Marital Agreements' (2012) 46 *Family Law Quarterly* 313.

Auchmuty, R, 'Law and the Power of Feminism: How Marriage Lost its Power to Oppress Women' (2012) 20(2) *Feminist Legal Studies* 71.

—— 'The Fiction of Equity' in Scott-Hunt, S and Lim, H (eds), *Feminist Perspectives on Equity and Trusts* (Cavendish Publishing 2001).

—— 'The Rhetoric of Equality and the Problem of Heterosexuality' in Mulcahy, L and Wheeler, S (eds), *Feminist Perspectives on Contract Law* (Routledge 2005).

—— 'The Married Women's Property Acts: Equality Was Not Enough' in Hunter, R (ed), *Rethinking Equality Projects in Law: Feminist Challenges* (Hart Publishing 2008).

—— 'When Equality is not Equity: Homosexual Inclusion in Undue Influence Law' (2003) 11(2) *Feminist Legal Studies* 169.

Baker, L and Emery, R, 'Why Every Relationship is Above Average: Perceptions and Expectations of Divorce at the Time of Marriage' (1993) 17(4) *Law and Human Behaviour* 439.

Balkin, J, *What Roe v Wade Should Have Said: The Nation's Top Legal Experts Rewrite America's Most Controversial Decision* (New York University Press 2005).

Bamforth, N, 'Unconscionability as a Vitiating Factor' [1995] *LMCLQ* 538.

Barlow, A and Smithson, J, 'Is modern marriage a bargain? Exploring perceptions of pre-nuptial agreements in England and Wales' (2012) 24(3) *Child and Family Law Quarterly* 304.

Bartlett, K and Kennedy, R (eds), *Feminist Legal Theory: Readings in Law and Gender* (Westview Press 1991).

Beale, H, 'Relational Values in English Contract Law' in D Campbell, L Mulcahy and S Wheeler (eds), *Changing Concepts of Contract: Essays in Honour of Ian Macneil* (Palgrave Macmillan 2013).

Beatson, J, *Anson's Law of Contract* (28th edn, OUP 2002).

—— and Friedman, D (eds), *Good faith and Fault in Contract Law* (Clarendon Press 1995).

Belcher, A, 'A Feminist Perspective on Contract Theories from Law and Economics' (2000) 8 *Feminist Legal Studies* 29.

Biggs, H and MacKenzie, R, 'Gendered Readings of Obligations: Social Lore or Strict Legal Forms?' (2000) 8(1) *Feminist Legal Studies* 1.

Birks, P and Nyuk Yin, C, 'On the Nature of Undue Influence' in Beatson, J and Friedman, D (eds), *Good Faith and Fault in Contract Law* (Clarendon Press 1995).

Bix, B, 'Bargaining in the Shadow of Love: The Enforcement of Premarital Agreements and How We Think About Marriage' (1998) 40 *William and Mary Law Review* 145.

—— 'Domestic Agreements' (2007) 35 *Hofstra Law Review* 1753.

—— 'Private Ordering and Family Law' (2010) 23 *Journal of the American Academy of Matrimonial Lawyers* 249.

—— 'The ALI Principles and Agreements: Seeking a Balance between Status and Contract' in Wilson, R (ed), *Reconceiving the Family: Critique on the American Law Institute's Principles of the Law of Family Dissolution* (Cambridge University Press 2006).

Bochel, E *et al* (eds), *Social Policy Review, 15: UK and International Perspectives* (The Policy Press 2003).

Bottomley, A (ed), *Feminist Perspectives on the Foundational Subjects of Law* (Cavendish Publishing 1996).

Bourne, J and Derry, C, *Women and Law* (Old Bailey Press 2004).

Bronstein, P, 'The pre-nuptial agreement in the United States of America' in Salter, D *et al*, *International Pre-Nuptial and Post-Nuptial Agreements* (Jordans 2011).

Brown, B, 'Contracting Out/Contracting In: Some Feminist Considerations' in Bottomley, A (ed), *Feminist Perspectives on the Foundational Subjects of Law* (Cavendish Publishing 1996).

Burn, E and Virgo, G, *Maudsley and Burn's Trusts and Trustees* (7th edn, OUP 2008).

Butruille-Cardew, C, 'Marital Property Agreements in France' in Salter, D *et al* (eds), *International Pre-Nuptial and Post-Nuptial Agreements* (Jordans 2011).

Brod, G, 'Premarital Agreements and Gender Justice' (1994) 6 *Yale Journal of Law and Feminism* 229.

Buckley, L, 'Matrimonial Property and Irish Law: A Case for Community?' (2002) 53 *Northern Ireland Law Quarterly* 39.

Campbell, D (ed), *The Relational Theory of Contract: Selected Works of Ian Macneil* (Sweet & Maxwell 2001).

—— *et al* (eds), *Changing Conceptions of Contract: Essays in Honour of Ian Macneil* (Palgrave MacMillan 2013).

Capper, D, 'The Place of Equity and Equitable Doctrine in the Common Law World—an Australian Perspective' in D Waters (ed), *Equity, Fiduciaries and Trusts* (Carswell 1993).

—— 'The Unconscionable Bargain in the Common Law World' (2010) 126 *LQR* 403.

Chen-Wishart, M, *Unconscionable Bargains* (Butterworths 1989).

—— 'Undue Influence: Beyond Impaired Consent and Wrongdoing towards a Relational Analysis' in Burrows, A and Lord Rodger of Earlsferry (eds), *Mapping the Law: Essays in Memory of Peter Birks* (OUP 2006).

Chodorow, N, *The Reproduction of Mothering: Psychoanalysis and the Sociology of Gender* (University of California Press 1978).

Cobbe, F, 'Criminals, Idiots, Women and Minors' in Hamilton, S (ed), *Criminals, Idiots, Women and Minors: Victorian Writing by Women on Women* (Boardview Press 1995).

Code, L, 'Second Persons' in *What Can She Know? Feminist Theory and the Construction of Knowledge* (Cornell University Press 1991) 78.

Cohen, N and Arieli, T, 'Field research in conflict environments: methodological challenges and snowball sampling' (2011) 48 *Journal of Peace Research* 423.

Collier, R, 'Feminist Legal Studies and the Subject(s) of Men: Questions of Text, Terrain and Context in the Politics of Family Law and Gender' in Diduck, A and O'Donovan, K (eds) *Feminist Perspectives on Family Law* (Routledge-Cavendish 2006).

Conaghan, J, 'Reassessing the Feminist Project in Law' (2000) 27(3) *Journal of Law and Society* 351.

Cooke, E, 'Matrimonial Property needs and agreements: the Law Commission's extended project' (2012) 34 *Journal of Social Welfare and Family Law* 509.
—— 'Pre-nups and beyond: what is the Law Commission up to now?' (2012) 42 *Family Law* 323.
—— 'The Law Commission's Consultation on Marital Property Agreements' in Scherpe, J (ed), *Marital Agreements and Private Autonomy in Comparative Perspective* (Hart Publishing 2012).
—— 'The Law Commission's report on matrimonial property, needs and agreements' (2014) 44(3) *Family Law*, 304.
—— '*White v White*: A New Yardstick for the Marriage Partnership' (2001) 13 *Child and Family Law Quarterly* 81.
Cornell, D, 'The Philosophy of the Limit: Systems Theory and Feminist Legal Reform' in Cornell, D *et al* (eds), *Deconstruction and the Possibility of Justice* (Routledge 1992).
—— *et al* (eds), *Deconstruction and the Possibility of Justice* (Routledge 1992).
Cotterrell, R, 'Power, Property and the Law of Trusts: A Partial Agenda for Critical Legal Scholarship' (1987) 14 *Journal of Law and Society* 77.
Cretney, S, 'Community of Property Imposed by Judicial Decision' (2003) 119 *LQR* 349.
—— *Family Law in the Twentieth Century* (OUP 2003).
—— 'The Family and the Law—Status or Contract?' (2003) 15 *Child and Family Law Quarterly* 403.
—— 'The Little Woman and the Big Bad Bank' (1992) 108 *LQR* 534.
Dalton, C, 'An Essay in the Deconstruction of Contract Doctrine' (1985) 94(5) *The Yale Law Journal* 997.
—— 'Deconstructing Contract Doctrine' in Bartlett, K and Kennedy, R (eds), *Feminist Legal Theory: Readings in Law and Gender* (Westview Press 1991).
Day-Sclater, S *et al* (eds), *Regulating Autonomy: Sex, Reproduction and Family* (Hart Publishing 2009).
Dicey, AV, *Lectures on the Relation between Law and Public Opinion in England during the Nineteenth Century* (2nd edn, Macmillan 1962).
Diduck, A, 'Dividing the Family Assets' in Sclater, S and Piper, C (eds), *Undercurrents of Divorce* (Ashgate 1999).
—— 'Fairness and Justice for All? The House of Lords in *White v White* [2000] 2 FLR 981' (2001) 9 *Feminist Legal Studies* 173.
—— *Law's Families* (Lexis Nexis Butterworths 2003).
—— and Kaganas, F, *Family Law, Gender and the State* (2nd edn, Hart Publishing 2006).
—— 'What is Family Law For?' (2011) 64 *Current Legal Problems* 287.
Dodds, S, 'Choice and Control in Feminist Bioethics' in Mackenzie, C and Stoljar, N (eds), *Relational Autonomy: Feminist Perspectives on Autonomy, Agency and the Social Self* (OUP 2000).
Donchin, A, 'Understanding autonomy relationally' (2001) 26 *Journal of Medicine and Philosophy* 365.
Duncan, S *et al*, 'Motherhood, paid work and partnering: values and theories' (2003) 17(2) *Work, Employment and Society* 309.
Eekelaar, J, 'Back to Basics and Forward Into the Unknown' (2001) 31(1) *Family Law* 30.
—— and Maclean, M, *Maintenance after Divorce* (Clarendon Press 1986).
—— '*Miller v Miller*: the Descent into Chaos' (2005) 35(11) *Family Law* 870.
—— 'Property and Financial Settlement on Divorce—Sharing and Compensating' (2006) 36(9) *Family Law* 754.

—— 'Then and Now—Family Law's Direction of Travel' (2013) 35(4) *Journal of Social Welfare and Family Law* 415.

Eisenberg, M, 'The Limits of Cognition and the Limits of Contract' (1995) 47(2) *Stanford Law Review* 211.

—— 'Why there is no law of relational contracts' (2000) 94 *Northwestern University Law Review* 805.

Ellman, I, 'Marital Agreements and Private Autonomy in the United States' in Scherpe, J (ed), *Marital Agreements and Private Autonomy in Comparative Perspective* (Hart Publishing 2012).

—— 'The Theory of Alimony' (1989) 77 *California Law Review* 1.

Erickson, AL, *Women and Property: In Early Modern England* (Routledge 1993).

Ertman, M, 'Commercializing Marriage: A Proposal for Valuing Women's Work through Premarital Security Agreements' (1998) 77 *Texas Law Review* 17.

Fehlberg, B,

—— and Smyth, B, 'Binding Prenuptial Agreements in Australia: The First Year' in Mulcahy, L and Wheeler, S (eds), *Feminist Perspectives on Contract Law* (Routledge 2005).

—— and —— 'Binding Pre-nuptial Agreements: Will They Help?' (1999) 53 *Family Matters* 55.

—— and —— 'Binding Prenuptial Agreements in Australia: The First Year' (2002) 16 *International Journal of Law, Policy and the Family* 127.

—— 'Money and Marriage: Sexually Transmitted Debt in England' (1997) 11 *International Journal of Law, Policy and the Family* 320.

—— and Smyth, B, 'Pre-nuptial Agreements for Australia: Why Not?' (2000) 14 *Australian Journal of Family Law* 80.

—— *Sexually Transmitted Debt: Surety Experience and English Law* (Clarendon Press 1997).

Feinman, J, 'Relational Contract and Default Rules' (1993-1994) 3 South Carolina Interdisciplinary Law Journal 43.

—— 'The Reception of Ian Macneil's Work on Contract in the USA' in Campbell, D (ed), *The Relational Theory of Contract: Selected works of Ian Macneil* (Sweet & Maxwell 2001).

Fineman, M and Mykitiuk, R, *The Public Nature of Private Violence: The Discovery of Domestic Abuse* (Routledge 1994).

Fraser, N, 'After the family wage: Gender Equity and the Welfare State' (1994) 22(4) *Political Theory* 591.

Fredman, S, *Women and the Law* (Clarendon Press 1998).

Freeman, J *et al*, 'Guarding the Triple Crown: Pre-Nuptial Agreements in Three Jurisdictions' (2008) 38 *Family Law* 239.

Frug, MJ, 'Re-Reading Contracts: A Feminist Analysis of a Contracts Casebook' (1985) 34 *The American University Law Review* 1065.

Gan, O, 'Contractual Duress and Relations of Power' (2013) 36 *Harvard Journal of Law and Gender* 171.

George, R, 'Family Finances and the Corporate Veil: *Prest v Petrodel*' (2013) 43(8) *Family Law* 991.

Gilligan, C, *In a Different Voice: Psychological Theory and Women's Development* (Harvard University Press 1982).

Glendon, MA, *The Transformation of Family Law: State, Law and Family in the United States and Western Europe* (The University of Chicago Press 1989).

Guggenheimer, L, 'A Modest Proposal: The Feminomics of Drafting Premarital Agreements' (1996) 17 *Women's Rights Law Reporter* 147.

Hadfield, G, 'The Dilemma of Choice: A Feminist Perspective on *The Limits of Freedom of Contract*' (1996) 33 *Osgoode Hall Law Journal* 337.

Hale, B, 'Equality and Autonomy in Family Law' (2011) 33 *Journal of Social Welfare and Family Law* 3.

—— *et al, The Family, Law and Society: Cases and Materials* (OUP 2008).

Hale, R, 'Coercion and Distribution in a Supposedly Non-coercive State' (1923) 38 *Political Science Quarterly* 470.

Hanna, C, 'Rethinking Consent in a Big Love Way' (2010) 17 *Michigan Journal of Law and Gender* 111.

Harding, R, 'Legal constructions of dementia: discourses of autonomy at the margins of capacity' (2012) 34 *Journal of Social Welfare and Family Law* 425.

Harper, M and Frankle, B, 'An English Practitioner's View on Pre-Nuptial, Post-Nuptial and Separation Agreements' in Scherpe, J (ed), *Marital Property Agreements and Private Autonomy in Comparative Perspective* (Hart Publishing 2012).

Herring, J, 'Relational Autonomy and Rape' in Day-Sclater, S *et al* (eds), *Regulating Autonomy: Sex, Reproduction and Family* (Hart Publishing 2009).

—— *Relational Autonomy and Family Law* (Springer 2014).

—— 'Why Financial Orders on Divorce should be Unfair' (2005) 19 *International Journal of Law, Policy and the Family* 218.

—— Harris, P and George, R, 'Ante-nuptial agreements; Fairness, Equality and Presumptions' (2011) 127 *LQR* 335.

Heyes, C, 'Anti-Essentialism in Practice: Carol Gilligan and Feminist Philosophy' (1997) 12(3) *Hypatia* 142.

Holcombe, L, *Wives and Property: Reform of the Married Women's Property Law in Nineteenth Century England* (University of Toronto Press 1982).

Hudson, A, *Equity and Trusts* (2nd edn, Cavendish 2001).

Hunter, R *et al* (eds), *Feminist Judgments: From Theory to Practice* (Hart Publishing 2010).

Ingham, M, *Now we are thirty: Women of the breakthrough generation* (Eyre Methuen 1981).

Jackson, E and Sclater, S, 'Introduction' in Sclater, S *et al* (eds), *Regulating Autonomy: Sex, Reproduction and Family* (Hart Publishing 2009).

Jaggar, A, *Feminist Politics and Human Nature* (Rowman & Allanheld 1983).

Johnson, B, 'Examining the validity structure of qualitative research' (1997) 118 *Education* 282.

Kahn-Freund, O, 'Inconsistencies and Injustices in the Law of Husband and Wife' (1952) 15 *MLR* 133.

Keeton, G and Sheridan, LA, *Equity* (2nd edn Milton 1976).

Kingdom, E, 'Cohabitation Contracts and the Democratization of Personal Relations' (2000) 8(1) *Feminist Legal Studies* 5.

Krause, H, 'Comparative Family Law' in Reimann, M and Zimmermann, R (eds), *Oxford Handbook on Comparative Law* (OUP 2006).

Leckey, R, *Contextual Subjects: Family, State and Relational Theory* (University of Toronto Press 2008).

—— 'Relational Contract and Other Models of Marriage' (2002) 40 *Osgoode Hall Law Journal* 1.

Lee, B, *Divorce Law Reform in England* (Peter Owen 1974).

Leech, S, '"With All My Worldly Goods I Thee Endow"? The Status of Pre-Nuptial Agreements in England and Wales' (2000) 34 *Family Law Quarterly* 193.

Lowe, N, 'Marital Property Agreements' in Boele-Woelki, K *et al* (eds), *Principles of European Family Law Regarding Property Relations Between Spouses* (Intersentia 2013).

Macaulay, S, 'An Empirical View of Contract' (1985) 3 *Wisconsin Law Review* 465.
Mackay, A, 'Who Gets a Better Deal? Women and Prenuptial Agreements in Australia and the USA' (2003) 7 *University of Western Sydney Law Review* 109.
Mackenzie, C and Stoljar, N, 'Autonomy Refigured' in Mackenzie, C and Stoljar, N (eds), *Relational Autonomy: Feminist Perspectives on Autonomy, Agency and the Social Self* (OUP 2000).
—— and —— (eds), *Relational Autonomy: Feminist Perspectives on Autonomy, Agency and the Social Self* (OUP 2000).
MacKinnon, C, 'Difference and Dominance: On Sex Discrimination' in Weisberg, K (ed), *Feminist Legal Theory: Foundations* (Temple University Press 1993).
MacKinnon, C, *Toward a Feminist Theory of the State* (Harvard University Press 1989)
Macneil, I, *Contract: Exchange Transactions and Relations* (2nd edn, Foundation Press, 1978).
—— 'Contracts: Adjustment of Long-Term Economic Relations Under Classical, Neoclassical and Relational Contract Law' (1978) 72 *Northwestern University Law Review* 854.
—— 'Restatement (Second) of Contracts and Presentiation' (1974) 60(4) *Virginia Law Review* 589.
Mahoney, M, 'Exit: Power and the idea of leaving in love, work, and the confirmation hearings' (1991) 65 *Southern California Law Review* 1284.
—— 'Victimization or Oppression? Women's Lives, Violence, and Agency' in Fineman, M and Mykitiuk, R (eds), *The Public Nature of Private Violence: The Discovery of Domestic Abuse* (Routledge 1994).
McKendrick, E, *Contract Law* (8th edn, Palgrave Macmillan 2009).
McLean, S, *Autonomy, Consent and the Law* (Routledge 2010).
McLellan, D, 'Contract Marriage—The Way Forward or Dead End?' (1996) 23 *Journal of Law and Society* 234.
Meehan, A, 'Analyse This: Radmacher v Granatino' (2009) 39(9) *Family Law* 816.
Miles, J, 'Marital Agreements and Private Autonomy in England and Wales' in Scherpe, J (ed), *Marital Agreements and Private Autonomy in Comparative Perspective* (Hart Publishing 2012).
Milligan, P, 'Pre-Nuptials Beware' (1999) 29 *Family Law* 483.
Minow, M, 'The Dilemma of Difference' in Adams, D (ed), *Philosophical Problems in the Law* (Wadsworth 2000).
Morley, J, 'Enforceable Prenuptial Agreements: Their Time Has Come' (2006) 36(9) *Family Law* 768.
Mulcahy, L, 'The Limitations of Love and Altruism—Feminist Perspectives on Contract Law' in Mulcahy, L and Wheeler, S (eds), *Feminist Perspectives on Contract Law* (Routledge 2005).
—— *Contract Law in Perspective* (5th edn, Routledge-Cavendish 2008).
—— 'Telling Tales about Relational Contracts: How Do Judges Learn about the Lived World of Contracts' in Campbell, D, Mulcahy, L and Wheeler, S (eds), *Changing Concepts of Contract: Essays in Honour of Ian Macneil* (Palgrave Macmillan 2013).
—— and Wheeler, S (eds), *Feminist Perspectives on Contract Law* (Routledge 2005).
Murray, A, 'Are our Higher Courts Prejudiced against the Role of the Married Woman? The Need for Reform' (2013) 43(1) *Family Law* 66.
Nasheri, H, 'Prenuptial Agreements in the United States: A Need for Closer Control?' (1998) 12 *International Journal of Law, Policy and the Family* 307.
Nathan Thal, S, 'The Inequality of Bargaining Power Doctrine: The Problem of Defining Contractual Unfairness' (1988) 8 *OJLS* 17.

Nedelsky, J, *Law's Relations: A Relational Theory of Self, Autonomy and Law* (OUP 2011).

—— 'Reconceiving Autonomy: Sources, Thoughts and Possibilities' (1989) 1 *Yale Journal of Law and Feminism* 7.

Nievod, A, 'Undue Influence in Contract and Probate Law' (1993) 10(1) *Cultic Studies Journal* 1.

Norrie, K, 'Marital Agreements and Private Autonomy in Scotland' in Scherpe, J (ed), *Marital Agreements and Private Autonomy in Comparative Perspective* (Hart Publishing 2012).

Okin, SM, 'Patriarchy and Married Women's Property in England: Questions on some Current Views' (1983) 17 *Eighteenth-Century Studies* 121.

Oldham, T, *Divorce, Separation and the Distribution of Property* (Law Journal Press 1987).

—— 'Would Enactment of the Uniform Premarital and Marital Agreement Act in All Fifty States Change US Law Regarding Premarital Agreements?' (2012) 46 *Family Law Quarterly* 367.

Olsen, F, 'The Family and the Market: A Study of Ideology and Legal Reform' (1983) 96 *Harvard Law Review* 1497.

Pateman, C, *The Sexual Contract* (Stanford University Press 1988).

—— 'Equality, difference, subordination' in Bock, G and James, S (eds), *Beyond Equality and Difference: Citizenship, Feminist Politics and Female Subjectivity* (Routledge 1992).

Pawlowski, M, *Undue Influence and the Family Home* (Cavendish Publishing 2002).

Phillips, J, 'Protecting those in a disadvantageous negotiating position: unconscionable bargains as a unifying doctrine' (2010) 45 *Wake Forest Law Review* 837.

Pohjonen, S, 'Partnership in Love and Business' (2000) 8 *Feminist Legal Studies* 47.

Priaulx, N, *The Harm Paradox: Tort law and the unwanted child in an era of choice* (Routledge 2007).

Price, D, 'Pension sharing on divorce: the future for women' in Bochel, C *et al* (eds), *Social Policy Review, 15: UK and International Perspectives* (The Policy Press 2003).

Probert, R, 'The controversy of equality and the Matrimonial Causes Act 1923' (1999) 11(1) *Child and Family Law Quarterly* 33.

Rackley, E, 'Why Feminist Legal Scholars Should Write Judgments: Reflections on the Feminist Judgments Project in England and Wales' (2012) 24 *Canadian Journal of Women and the Law* 389.

Regan, M, *Alone Together: Law and the Meanings of Marriage* (OUP 1999).

Reimann, M and Reinhard, Z (eds), *Oxford Handbook on Comparative Law* (OUP 2006).

Reiter, B and Swan, J (eds), *Studies in Contract Law* (Butterworths 1980).

Rhode, D, 'Feminist Critical Theories' (1990) 42 *Stanford Law Review* 614.

Salter, D *et al* (eds), *International Pre-Nuptial and Post-Nuptial Agreements* (Jordan Publishing 2011).

Schechter, S, *New York Family Law* (2nd edn, Delmar Cengage Learning 2006).

Scherpe, J, 'Introduction' in Scherpe, J (ed), *Marital Agreements and Private Autonomy in Comparative Perspective* (Hart Publishing 2012).

—— (ed), *Marital Agreements and Private Autonomy in Comparative Perspective* (Hart Publishing 2012).

—— and Piper, C (eds), *Undercurrents of Divorce* (Ashgate 1999).

Scott, E and Scott, R, 'Marriage as Relational Contract' (1998) 84 *Virginia Law Review* 1225.

Scott-Hunt, S and Lim, L (eds), *Feminist Perspectives on Equity and Trusts* (Cavendish Publishing 2001).

Scoular, J, 'The Revival of Equitable Doctrine in Scots Law—a Space for Gender Concerns?' in Scott-Hunt, S and Lim, H (eds), *Feminist Perspectives on Equity and Trusts* (Routledge 2001).

Shanley, M, *Feminism, Marriage and the Law in Victorian England* (Princeton University Press 1993).
Sharot, T *et al*, 'How unrealistic optimism is maintained in the face of reality' (2011) 14 *Nature Neuroscience* 1475.
Shortall, S, *Women and Farming, Property and Power* (Macmillan 1999).
Siegel, R, 'Why Equal Protection No Longer Protects: The Evolving Forms of Status-Enforcing State Action' (1997) 49 *Stanford Law Review* 1111.
Singer, P, 'Sexual Discrimination in Ancillary Relief' (2001) 31(2) *Family Law* 115.
Singer, S, 'Charman v Charman (No 4) [2007] 1 FLR 1246' (2008) 30 *Journal of Social Welfare and Family Law* 155.
Smart, C, *The Ties That Bind: Law, Marriage and the Reproduction of Patriarchal Relations* (Routledge 1984).
Smith, C, *Adam Smith's Political Philosophy: The Invisible Hand and Spontaneous Order* (Taylor and Francis 2005).
Smith, S, *Contract Theory* (OUP 2004).
Stetson, D, *A Woman's Issue: Politics of Family Law Reform in England* (Greenwood Press 1982).
Summerskill, E, *A Woman's World* (Heinemann 1967).
Symes, P, 'Indissolubility and the clean break' (1985) 48(1) *MLR* 44.
Taylor, M, 'On the Conditions of Women as Affected by the Law' (1862) 10 *The English Woman's Journal* 124.
Thompson, S, 'Levelling the Prenuptial Playing Field: Is Independent Legal Advice the Answer?' (2011) 4 *International Family Law* 327.
—— '*Radmacher v Granatino* [2010] UKSC 42' (2011) 33(1) *Journal of Social Welfare and Family Law* 61.
—— 'Review of International Pre-Nuptial and Post-Nuptial Agreements (eds) David Salter, Charlotte Butruille-Cardew and Stephen Grant' (2011) 23 *Child and Family Law Quarterly* 423.
Threedy, D, 'Feminists and Contract Doctrine' (1999) 32 *Indiana Law Review* 1247.
Tidwell, P and Linzer, P, 'The Flesh-Colored Band Aid—Contracts, Feminism, Dialogue and Norms' (1991) 28 *Houston Law Review* 791.
Tillotson, J, *Contract Law in Perspective* (Cavendish 2004).
Trebilcock, M, 'An Economic Approach to the Doctrine of Unconscionability' in Reiter, B and Swan, J (eds), *Studies in Contract Law* (Butterworths 1980).
—— 'The Doctrine of Inequality of Bargaining Power: Post-Benthamite Economics in the House of Lords' (1976) 26 *University of Toronto Law Journal* 359.
—— *The Limits of Freedom of Contract* (Harvard University Press 1993).
—— and Keshvani, R, 'The Role of Private Ordering in Family Law: A Law and Economics Perspective' (1991) 41 *University of Toronto Law Journal* 533.
Treitel, G, *The Law of Contract* (7th edn, Stevens & Sons 1987).
von Mehren, A, 'A General View of Contracts' in *International Encyclopedia of Comparative Law* vol 7 (Tübingen 1982).
Waddams, S, 'Unconscionability in Contracts' (1976) 39 *MLR* 369.
Ward, P, *Divorce in Ireland: Who Should Bear the Cost?* (Cork University Press 1993).
Weisberg, K, *Feminist Legal Theory: Foundations* (Temple University Press 1993).
Westen, P, *The Logic of Consent: The Diversity and Deceptiveness of Consent as a Defence to Criminal Conduct* (Ashgate 2004).

Wheeler, S, 'Going Shopping' in Mulcahy, L and Wheeler, S (eds), *Feminist Perspectives on Contract Law* (Routledge 2005).
—— and Shaw, J (eds), *Contract Law: Cases, Materials and Commentary* (OUP 1994).
Wightman, J, 'Baird Textile Holdings v Marks and Spencer Plc' in Hunter, R *et al* (eds), *Feminist Judgments: From Theory to Practice* (Hart Publishing 2010).
—— 'Intimate Relationships, Relational Contract Theory and the Reach of Contract' (2000) 8 *Feminist Legal Studies* 93.
Williams, G, 'The Legal Unity of Husband and Wife' (1947) 10 *MLR* 16.
Wilson, N, 'Ancillary Relief Reform: Response of the Judges of the Family Division to the Government Proposals (made by way of submission to the Lord Chancellor's Ancillary Relief Advisory Group)' (1999) 29(3) *Family Law* 159.
Wilson, G, 'An Australian Perspective on International Pre-Nuptial Agreements' in Salter, D *et al* (eds), *International Pre-Nuptial and Post-Nuptial Agreements* (Jordan Publishing 2011).
Wilson, R (ed), *Reconceiving the Family: Critique on the American Law Institute's Principles of the Law of Family Dissolution* (Cambridge University Press 2006).
Younger, J, 'Lovers' Contracts in the Courts: Forsaking the Minimum Decencies' (2007) 13 *William and Mary Journal of Women and the Law* 349.
Zweig, F, *Women's Life and Labour* (Gollancz 1952).

Command Papers and Parliamentary Reports

Finer, M, *Report of the Committee on One Parent Families* (HMSO Cmd 5629, 1974).
Home Office, *Supporting Families: A Consultation Document* (Green Paper, 1998).
Morton, F, *Report of the Royal Commission on Marriage and Divorce 1951–1955* (Cmd 9678, 1956).
The Centre for Social Justice, *Every Family Matters: An in-depth review of family law in Britain* (2009).

Law Commission Reports

Law Commission, *Family Law: First Report on Family Property—A New Approach* (Law Com No 52, 1973).
Law Commission, *Marital Property Agreements* (Law Com No 198, 2011).
Law Commission, *Matrimonial Property, Needs and Agreements* (Law Com No 343, 2014).
Law Commission, *Matrimonial Property, Needs and Agreements: A Supplementary Consultation Paper* (Law Com No 208, 2012).
Law Commission, *Proposal for the Abolition of the Matrimonial Remedy of Restitution* (Law Com No 23, 1969)
Law Commission, *Reform of the Grounds of Divorce—The Field of Choice* (Law Com No 6, 1966).
Law Commission, *The Financial Consequences of Divorce: the Basic Policy* (Law Com No 103, 1980).

Online Articles

Grossman, J, 'Prenuptial Agreements: The Iowa Supreme Court takes a Strong Pro-Enforcement Stance' (*FindLaw's Writ*, 6 January 2009), available at <http://writ.lp.findlaw.com/grossman/20090106.html>, last accessed 12 February 2015.

Hirsch, P, 'Bodichon, Barbara Leigh Smith (1827–1891)', *Oxford Dictionary of National Biography* (OUP 2004), available at <http://www.oxforddnb.com/view/article/2755>, last accessed 12 February 2015.

Hooks, B, 'Understanding Patriarchy' available at <http://imaginenoborders.org/pdf/zines/UnderstandingPatriarchy.pdf>, last accessed 12 February 2015.

James, B, 'Unintended Consequences of Family Justice Reform' (Family Law Week, 27 June 2014), available at <http://www.familylawweek.co.uk/site.aspx?i=ed130634>, last accessed 12 February 2015.

O'Connor, S, 'Regional housing price disparities increased following the economic downturn' (Office of National Statistics, 28 May 2014), available at <http://www.ons.gov.uk/ons/rel/hpi/house-price-index/march-2014/sty-regional-house-prices.html>, last accessed 12 February 2015.

Poladian, C, 'Billionaires' homes around the world: New York City houses 103 of the richest people on the planet', *International Business Times* (1 October 2014), available at <http://www.ibtimes.com/pulse/billionaires-homes-around-world-new-york-city-houses-103-richest-people-planet-1697132>, last accessed 12 February 2015.

Reynolds, KD, 'Norton , Caroline Elizabeth Sarah [other married name Caroline Elizabeth Sarah Stirling Maxwell, Lady Stirling Maxwell] (1808–1877)', *Oxford Dictionary of National Biography* (OUP 2004), available at <oxforddnb.com/view/article/20339, last accessed 12 February 2015.

Standler, R, 'Voluntary Consent in Prenuptial Contracts in the USA' (27 September 2009), available at <http://www.rbs2.com/dcontract3.pdf>, last accessed 12 February 2015.

Online Newspaper Articles

Allen, N, 'Tiger Woods' wife will get $100 million in divorce', *Telegraph* (London, 2 July 2010), available at <http://www.telegraph.co.uk/sport/golf/tigerwoods/7869437/Tiger-Woods-wife-will-get-100-million-in-divorce.html>, last accessed 12 February 2015.

Bingham, J, 'Prenup plans could empty "till death do us part" vow of all meaning, Bishop', *Telegraph* (London, 17 February 2014), available at <http://www.telegraph.co.uk/news/religion/10642082/Prenup-plans-could-empty-till-death-do-us-part-vow-of-all-meaning-Bishop.html>, last accessed 12 February 2015.

Britten, N, '£48 million for my ex-wife is grotesque and I'm going to fight it, says magnate', *Telegraph* (London, 4 August 2006), available at <http://www.telegraph.co.uk/news/1525533/48million-for-my-ex-wife-is-grotesque-and-Im-going-to-fight-it-says-magnate.html>, last accessed 12 February 2015.

Davies, C, 'Three-year wife's £5 million divorce "a meal ticket for life"', *Telegraph* (London, 31 January 2006), available at <http://www.telegraph.co.uk/news/uknews/1509263/Three-year-wifes-5m-divorce-a-meal-ticket-for-life.html>, last accessed 12 February 2015.

Gentry, C, 'Why prenuptial agreements may be a smart option for women', *Guardian* (London, 1 September 2009), available at <http://www.theguardian.com/lifeandstyle/2009/sep/01/prenuptial-agreements-women>, last accessed 12 February 2015.

Gillan, A, 'Divorcee gets day in court to claim share of £45 million fortune', *Guardian* (London, 20 December 2007), available at <http://www.theguardian.com/uk/2007/dec/20/uknews4.mainsection1>, last accessed 12 February 2015.

Gordon, G, 'What's mine is mine: 10 couples on how they arrange their finances', *Guardian* (London, 2 March 2013), available at <http://www.guardian.co.uk/money/2013/mar/02/whats-mine-is-mine-couples-cash?INTCMP=SRCH>, last accessed 12 February 2015.

Myers, R, 'Prenups Undermine Marriage', *Guardian* (London, 23 March 2010), available at <http://www.guardian.co.uk/commentisfree/2010/mar/23/prenuptual-agreements-supreme-court>, last accessed 12 February 2015.

Pierce, A, 'John Cleese in £12 million divorce settlement', *Telegraph* (London, 18 August 2009), available at <http://www.telegraph.co.uk/news/celebritynews/6043628/John-Cleese-in-12-million-divorce-settlement.html>, last accessed 12 February 2015.

Rowan, D, 'Til dosh do us part', *The Sunday Times* (London, 9 October 2005), available at <http://www.ejfi.org/family/family-25.htm>, last accessed 12 February 2015.

Saner, E, 'The myth of the kept woman', *Guardian* (London, 19 September 2009), available at <http://www.theguardian.com/lifeandstyle/2009/sep/19/divorce-settlements-law-deech>, last accessed 12 February 2015.

Singh, A, 'John Cleese marries for the fourth time', *Telegraph* (London, 13 August 2012) available at <http://www.telegraph.co.uk/news/celebritynews/9470746/John-Cleese-marries-for-the-fourth-time.html>, last accessed 12 February 2015.

Websites

American Academy of Matrimonial Lawyers, at <http://www.aaml.org/>

FindLaw, at <http://www.findlaw.com>

LexisOne, at <http://www.lexisone.com>

Other Sources

American Law Institute, *Principles of the Law of Family Dissolution: Analysis and Recommendations* (LexisNexis 2002).

—— Restatement (Second) of Contracts (1981).

Baroness. Deech of Cumnor, 'What's a Woman Worth? The maintenance law' (The Gresham Lectures, 13 October 2009), available at <http://www.gresham.ac.uk/lectures-and-events/what%E2%80%99s-a-woman-worth-the-maintenance- law>, last accessed 12 February 2015.

Cooke, E *et al*, *Community of Property: A regime for England and Wales?* (Nuffield Foundation Report 2006), available at <http://www.reading.ac.uk/web/FILES/law/CommunityofProperty_Version021106.pdf>, last accessed 12 February 2015.

Department for Communities and Local Government, *English Housing Survey 2012–2013: Household Report* (2014).

Halsbury's Laws (5th edn, LexisNexis Butterworths 2010).

Hitchings, E, *Law Commission Report: A study of the views and approaches of family practitioners concerning marital property agreements* (2011).

Judicial Executive Board, Written evidence from the judicial executive board (MSC 84, April 2014), available at <http://data.parliament.uk/writtenevidence/committeeevidence.svc/evidencedocument/justice-committee/impact-of-changes-to-civil-legal-aid-under-laspo/written/9472.html>, last accessed 12 February 2015.

Ministry of Justice, 'News Release: Divorce Myths to be Dispelled' (17 April 2014), available at <http://lawcommission.justice.gov.uk/docs/lc343_matrimonial_property_government_initial_response.pdf>, last accessed 12 February 2015.

Munby, J, 'The Family Justice Reforms' (29 April 2014), available at <http://www.judiciary.gov.uk/wp-content/uploads/2014/05/family-justice-reforms-29042014.pdf> last accessed 12 February 2015.

Office of National Statistics, 'A Century of Home Ownership and Renting in England and Wales' (2013), available at <http://www.ons.gov.uk/ons/rel/census/2011-census-analysis/a-century-of-home-ownership-and-renting-in-england-and-wales/short-story-on-housing.html>, last accessed 12 February 2015.

Office of National Statistics, 'Women in the labour market' (2013) available at <http://www.ons.gov.uk/ons/dcp171776_328352.pdf> last accessed 5 March 2015.

Official Report (HC) 12 June 1969, vol 784, col 2034.

Resolution, *A more certain future—Recognition of premarital agreements in England and Wales* (2005).

Resolution, *Family Agreements—Seeking certainty to reduce disputes: the recognition and enforcement of pre-nuptial and post-nuptial agreements in England and Wales* (2009).

INDEX

www.ingramcontent.com/pod-product-compliance
Lightning Source LLC
LaVergne TN
LVHW052311200926
848481LV00002B/527

* 9 7 8 1 5 0 9 9 1 7 7 4 7 *